JACK KEROUAC:
A BIOGRAPHY

ALSO BY TOM CLARK

FICTION
Who Is Sylvia? (novel)
The Last Gas Station (stories)
Heartbreak Hotel (stories)
The Exile of Céline (novel)

NONFICTION
Champagne and Baloney
Baseball
No Big Deal (with Mark Fidrych)
The World of Damon Runyon
The Great Naropa Poetry Wars
One Last Round for the Shuffler
*Charles Olson: The Allegory of a
    Poet's Life*
*Robert Creeley and the Genius of the
    American Common Place*

POETRY
Stones
Air
John's Heart
At Malibu
Fan Poems
*When Things Get Tough on Easy Street
    (Selected Poems 1963–1978)*
The End of the Line
A Short Guide to the High Plains
Under the Fortune Palms
*Paradise Resisted
    (Selected Poems 1978–1984)*
Easter Sunday
Disordered Ideas
Fractured Karma
Sleepwalker's Fate
*Junkets on a Sad Planet: Scenes from
    the Life of John Keats*

JACK KEROUAC:

A Biography

by Tom Clark

MARLOWE & COMPANY, NEW YORK

Published in the United States by

Marlowe & Company
632 Broadway
New York, NY 10012

The publisher thanks the following for permission to reprint material from sources listed:

Viking Penguin Inc. for selections from *On The Road* by Jack Kerouac,
copyright © 1957 by Jack Kerouac and for portions reprinted from the interview with
Jack Kerouac by Ted Berrigan, from *Writers at Work: The Paris Review Interview*, 4th Series,
edited by George Plimpton. Copyright © 1974, 1976 by the Paris Review, Inc.;

City Lights Books for excerpts from *Book of Dreams* by Jack Kerouac,
copyright © 1961 by Jack Kerouac;

The Sterling Lord Agency, Inc. for excerpts from *Dr. Sax* by Jack Kerouac,
copyright © 1959 by Jack Kerouac; excerpt from *Heaven and Other Poems* by Jack Kerouac,
copyright © 1958 by Jack Kerouac; excerpt from *Visions of Cody* by Jack Kerouac,
copyright © 1960 by Jack Kerouac; and excerpt from "The Origins of the Beat Generation"
by Jack Kerouac, copyright © 1959 by Jack Kerouac;

Farrar, Straus & Giroux, Inc., for excerpts from *Visions of Gerard* by Jack Kerouac,
copyright © 1963 by Jack Kerouac and excerpt from *Big Sur* by Jack Kerouac,
copyright © 1962 by Jack Kerouac;

the unspeakable vision of the individual for excerpts from *The Beat Book—Tuvoti, #4*;
The Beat Diary—Tuvoti #5, The Beat Journal—Tuvoti #8, Tuvoti #10,
Beat Angels—Tuvoti #12, and Dear Carolyn—Tuvoti #13;

Coward, McCann & Geoghegan, Inc., for excerpt from *Vanity of Duluoz* by
Jack Kerouac, copyright © 1968 by Jack Kerouac and excerpt from *Desolation Angels*
by Jack Kerouac, copyright © 1960, 1965 by Jack Kerouac;

High Times Magazine for excerpt from "Kerouac" by William Burroughs,
High Times, No.43 (1979).

Library of Congress Cataloging-in-Publication Data
Clark, Tom, 1941-
Jack Kerouac / by Tom Clark. — 1st ed.
p.   cm.
Reprint. Originally published: San Diego: Harcourt Brace Jovanvich, c1984.
Includes bibliographical references.
ISBN 1-56924-850-8
1. Kerouac, Jack, 1922-1969—Biography.   2. Authors, American—20th century—Biography.
3. Beat generation—Biography.
I. Title.
PS3521.E735Z62   1990
813'.54—dc20   —dc20
[B]   89-48874
CIP

This book is printed on acid-free paper
Manufactured in the United States of America

TO ANGELICA

Kerouac was a writer. That is, he wrote.
Many people who call themselves writers and
have their names on books are not writers
and they can't write—the difference being,
a bullfighter who fights a bull is different
from a bullshitter who makes passes with no
bull there. The writer has been *there* or he
can't write about it. And going *there* he
risks being gored. By that I mean what the
Germans aptly call the Time Ghost—for example,
such a fragile ghost world as Fitzgerald's
Jazz age . . . What are writers, and I will
confine the use of this term to writers of
novels, trying to do? They are trying to
create a universe in which they have lived
or would like to live. To write they must
go there and submit to conditions which they
may not have bargained for. Sometimes, as in
the case of Fitzgerald and Kerouac, the effect
produced by a writer is immediate, as if a
generation were waiting to be written.[1]

—William Burroughs

CONTENTS

ACKNOWLEDGMENTS

The author wishes to acknowledge his personal gratitude to the following people who assisted in this project: Angelica Clark, John Woods, Ilene Shapera, Robert Creeley, Carolyn Cassady, Ted Berrigan, Edward Dorn, Allen Ginsberg, Ed Sanders, Matthew Bruccoli, Gerry McCauley, Richard Aaron, Don Allen, Arthur and Kit Knight, Clarus Backes, Tim Murray (Curator of Manuscripts, Washington University Libraries), George Butterick (Special Collections Librarian, University of Connecticut), Chris Brun (Special Collections Librarian, University of California at Santa Barbara), Ken Lohf (Librarian for Rare Books and Manuscripts, Columbia University), Dianne Levy, Larry Fagin, Barry Gifford, Lewis MacAdams, Bradford Morrow, Jennifer Dorn, Harry Reese, D. R. Wagner, Joy Walsh, David Ossman, Ralph Sipper, Larry Sloman, and Sheera Stern.

Further thanks are owed to those whose scholarship and memoirs on Kerouac were of special help: John Clellon Holmes, Dennis McNally, Ann Charters, Robert J. Milewski, Tim Hunt, Mike McCoy, Gerald Nicosia, Father Armand Morissette, Edie Parker, Jan Kerouac, George Montgomery, and Maurice Poteet.

CHRONOLOGY

1922	Jean-Louis Lebris de Kerouac born, March 12, Lowell, Massachusetts.
1926	Kerouac's brother, Gerard, dies at age nine.
1939	Kerouac graduates from Lowell High School.
1939–40	Attends Horace Mann School for Boys, New York.
1940–41	Attends Columbia College, New York.
1942	Sails to Greenland as merchant seaman on S.S. *Dorchester*. Brief return to Columbia.
1943	Enlists in U.S. Navy; discharged on psychiatric grounds. Sails to Liverpool as merchant seaman on S.S. *George Weems*.

1944   Meets Lucien Carr, William Burroughs, Allen Ginsberg. Jailed as material witness in murder case. Marries Edie Parker; they separate.

1945   Writes collaborative novel with Burroughs, *And the Hippos Were Boiled in Their Tanks* (never published).

1946   Kerouac's father, Leo, dies of cancer of the stomach. Kerouac begins writing *The Town and the City*. Meets Neal Cassady.

1947   Travels to Denver and California.

1948   Meets John Clellon Holmes. Attends New School classes, New York. Completes *The Town and the City*. Begins working at earliest version of *On the Road*.

1949   Travels with Cassady to Louisiana and San Francisco. Moves briefly to Colorado with mother. Visits San Francisco again, returns with Cassady to New York. Attends New School again.

1950   *The Town and the City* published. Travels to Denver, then with Cassady to Mexico. In New York, marries Joan Haverty.

1951   Writes *On the Road*. Separates from Joan Haverty. Hospitalized with thrombophlebitis. After his release, discovers "sketching" (which he later calls "spontaneous writing"); travels to California.

1952   Writes *Visions of Cody* at Cassady home in San Francisco. Writes *Dr. Sax* at Burroughs' apartment in Mexico City. Travels to North Carolina, back to California (where he writes "October in the Railroad Earth"), Mexico again, and finally New York.

1953   Writes *Maggie Cassidy*. Travels to California; works on railroad; takes ship job on S.S. *William Carruth*; leaves *Carruth* in New Orleans. Writes *The Subterraneans* in New York. Prepares major statement of writing principles, "The Essentials of Spontaneous Prose."

1954   Visits Cassadys in San Jose; Buddhist studies in New York and California.

1955   Moves to North Carolina with mother. Travels to Mexico City (where he writes *Mexico City Blues* and begins *Tristessa*), then on to Berkeley. Meets Gary Snyder. Returns to North Carolina.

1956   Writes *Visions of Gerard*. Travels to California; stays in Marin County. Meets Robert Creeley. Writes *The Scripture of the Golden Eternity* and *Old Angel Midnight*. Works as fire lookout in Mt. Baker National Forest, Washington. Travels to San Francisco, then Mexico City, where he completes *Tristessa* and writes Book One of *Desolation Angels*. Returns to New York.

1957   Travels to Tangier, where he types (and titles) Burroughs' *Naked Lunch*, then on to Paris and London. After returning to New York, moves to Berkeley with mother. Visits Mexico City briefly; resides in Orlando, Florida, with mother. Travels to New York for publication of *On the Road*, and again for readings at Village Vanguard. Writes *The Dharma Bums* in Orlando.

1958   Buys home in Northport, Long Island. *The Subterraneans* and *The Dharma Bums* published.

1959   Participates in film *Pull My Daisy*. Begins column for *Escapade*. *Dr. Sax*, *Mexico City Blues*, and *Maggie Cassidy* published. Travels to Los Angeles (for "Steve Allen Show" appearance) and San Francisco.

1960   Travels to California, stays at Bixby Canyon (Big Sur); suffers alcoholic horrors and nervous breakdown. Returns to New York. *Tristessa* and *Lonesome Traveler* published.

1961   *Book of Dreams* published. Moves to Orlando with mother. Travels to Mexico City, where he writes Book Two of *Desolation Angels*. Returns to Florida, writes *Big Sur*.

1962   Moves back to Northport with mother. *Big Sur* published.

1963   *Visions of Gerard* published.

1964   Moves with mother to St. Petersburg, Florida. Kerouac's sister, Caroline, dies.

1965   Kerouac travels to France; writes *Satori in Paris. Desolation Angels* published.

1966   *Satori in Paris* published. Moves to Hyannis, Massachusetts, with mother, who there suffers a stroke. Marries Stella Sampas.

1967   Moves with mother and wife to Lowell; writes *Vanity of Duluoz.*

1968   Cassady dies in Mexico. *Vanity of Duluoz* published. Kerouac travels to Europe with Lowell friends. Appears on "Firing Line" TV show. Moves with mother and wife to St. Petersburg.

1969   Dies in St. Petersburg, October 21, of abdominal hemorrhage.

1971   *Pic* published.

1972   *Visions of Cody* published.

INTRODUCTION

John Ford said, "Between fact and legend, one should always prime for the legend." This has been largely the case with Jack Kerouac. There have been four major biographies and dozens of minor ones, some of which continue to promote the legend, albeit unwittingly, since even some facts in all the biographies fall victim to the legend.

Perhaps this is not too surprising in that Kerouac had a most enigmatic character; he lived dichotomies. The one trait that remained consistent—other than his consistent inconsistency—was WRITER. This drive took precedence over every other.

And that is the focus in this biography. Jack Kerouac, the writer. Here episodes in his life are succinctly revealed without a mountain of incidentals and gossip, so the intimacy is preserved. We are given Kerouac's view of his characters through his *writing,* and we have Kerouac's own words for most of the history, not so much the recollections or interpretations of those of us who knew him and whose memories can be unconsciously selective or biased.

Although Kerouac romanticized his experiences, sometimes this in itself tells us more about him. Often he put his own thoughts into the mouths of his characters and mirrored his own desires in their actions. The trick is to discern fact from fiction. Clark draws us into Kerouac's life, not with a rush of data but in the same manner as Jack would tell the story, with emotional pegs and poetic prose. We feel his feelings as the events unfold, so that by page twenty we have found the seedlings that will grow within the mind and heart of the man and writer who became Jack Kerouac.

The "legend" of Jack Kerouac distorts his life as it is viewed through the eyes of each successive generation in relation to their own present norms. Rarely do they relate him to his own time. I recently heard Doris Lessing emphasize, "We are all prisoners of our time," and I agree. When referring to events or persons in previous centuries, or even as near a decade as the 1920s, immediately one imagines the dress, the architecture and arts, and the social influences that helped mold them. This became more difficult when points of view changed more rapidly within a decade. In the late twentieth century, expressions of rebellion flashed in quick succession with little lasting effect other than an accumulative one. After Ginsberg's *Howl* and Kerouac's *On The Road,* a definite change occurred in literary tastes and social behavior, whether intended or not. Jack may have shocked his more staid contemporaries by his unconventional frankness, but many of them were themselves hypocritically practicing amoral behavior in secret. Why else did they feel so threatened by Jack and denounce him so viciously?

Lawrence Ferlinghetti has said that Jack wanted to "glorify middle American middle-class values." This is not the impression the legend gives, yet there is more truth in that opinion than is realized by the sycophants. I am periodically subjected to attempts to dramatize the lives of Kerouac and Cassady by playwrights and filmmakers who have so far ignored these influences and portray their characters in present time. This results in the persons depicted appearing to be no more than hedonistic airheads or juvenile delinquents, or both—really boring people who couldn't possibly have changed the history of society and literature. One even wonders what attracted them to one another.

On the contrary, in Kerouac's novels there is an underlying stream of Victorian standards running beneath his nonconformist observations, and when these are ignored the final view of him is false. . . . Adrian Noble set his London production of *Measure for Measure* in the thirties, "when fingers of Victorianism still penetrated . . . a decade when the audience believed morality could be a matter of life and death."

Throughout his life, Jack shared a common inherited cultural dream of our times—that of home and family—a solid expectation often referred to in his books. By the time I met him he had abandoned his earlier attempts at self-analysis, so this dichotomy seemed not to have occurred to him until near the end of his life. In *Maggie Cassady* I was amused to find his confession of not touching Maggie in the "focal points," since I never heard of a man before the sixties who had any idea what those were. As far as I know Jack was unable to "seduce"—that was one of the talents he greatly admired and envied in Neal. (An irresistible aside. Jack's wonderful says-it-all description of his falling in love: "I accepted everything." Think about *that*.)

Readers today aren't aware of how ignorant we all were about sex and its ramifications, any more than society now is guided by "old-fashioned" ideas of morals, honesty, honor, integrity, vows, or commitment as we once were, at least publicly. Even if we didn't always live up to these ideals, they were strong forces in our consciousness.

Jack was not only conditioned by his cultural heritage but also by his early indoctrination into Catholicism. Both he and Cassady shared an ingrained belief in their unworthiness and guilt, which they never could overcome, no matter how clearly they saw Church dogma as counterproductive.

The Catholic rituals and dogma are rich in emotional images, and Jack took them in through the pores. For him it was easy to respond to the "bleeding heart" of Jesus and later to Buddha's "all life is suffering." He was unusually sensitive to criticism, and this only made the suffering and guilt more intense. He was never as *good* as brother Gerard, he couldn't live up to his father's aspirations, and his choice of college put Leo out of work. He didn't support his mother and was frequently chastised for it by his sister. He was "inferior" to the rich boys at Horace Mann, etc., etc. All these he took "to heart." Perhaps it contributes to his haunting search for his antecedents in order to "establish" himself. They had to be aristocratic on the one hand and "fellaheen" on the other.

Even with his conditioning, Jack's intuition tapped a high level in knowing right and wrong, good and evil, yet somehow the will to experience all of life and not judge it only increased his need to escape it, while adding more guilt and moral confusion. In both of his religions he chose to revere the bits that offered comfort, beauty, serenity, peace and love, and the acceptance of suffering. The instilled Catholic obsession with "death" created a growing cancer of fear within him, and he looked at life often as just a shortcut to this horrible ending of all that he so warmly celebrated.

In a review of the film *La Reina de la Noche*, Rose Bosch wrote: "These are pieces in the emotional life of a fiercely independent woman for whom life never went right and eventually managed, along with alcohol, to drive her to suicide. But it also stands for the *freedom of spirit and lust for life which characterized those times and which would be very welcomed in the nineties.*" (Italics mine.) I was struck by the resemblance to Kerouac and his times. (And incidentally, Jack told Fran Landesman privately that he *intended* to drink himself to death.) His Catholic conditioning prevented his acting deliberately or acknowledging that desire in public, but certainly his last years corroborate it.

Kerouac had what Aristotle called *"nous"*—apperceptive intelligence, and along with his emotions, intuition of this sort ruled his mind. He seemed to get a feeling and then have to rationalize it into his intellect—or as one of his idols, George Shearing, put it, "our instincts have to filter into our mind." His emotions and instincts responded first to incidents and other people. Generally, our thought creates a feeling. We can change our feelings by changing our thoughts (except, perhaps, in emergencies, when a feeling comes first and the mind must quickly pick up the emotional pieces). Jack seemed to reverse this process most of the time. He was cocooned within his own mind and heart, giving his attention to others more often for his own sake than theirs. That wasn't always true, of course, and his hearty approval of Neal enhanced them both. In contrast, Neal, whose Catholic origins had convinced him of his own utter unworthiness, felt his only redemption lay in giving all he could of himself to others. He is usually depicted as [nothing so much as] a great super-con man, but that presumes selfishness and/or a desire to humiliate and have power over others, which was not the case. A large part of Jack's attraction to Neal was this shared compassion combined with the image of Real Man.

Jack was intensely curious and hungry to know and experience, yet he seems to have looked at life through a veil of romance and fantasy. Every man he liked became a "hero," every woman either a madonna or a whore—but both *important*. When reality became too demanding, he would run off to "sail the seas" or "ride the rails" with large romantic adventures in view, only to run into very real brutal bosuns or critical conductors to spoil his vision.

Jack's self-absorption in observation sometimes put a barrier, a certain objectivity between himself and the person or thing observed, so that when called upon for a response his mind and emotions became entangled, and he often blurted out a first thought-emotion, which was perhaps unconsciously censored, guarded, or just confused. He didn't learn to play polite society games which offer practice in acceptable poised reactions. To this extreme shyness-guilt add a rebellion against such social superficialities, and you get a gauche, bumbling, often silly man. Unable to face this in himself he would turn his back, retreat more deeply into himself, run away impulsively into some new unknown or drink to counteract it. He opened up unselfconsciously only when a trusted person was willing to listen and give their attention solely to him or with whom he felt total approval—why, I think, his mother meant so much to him.

Some have said it was Jack's "great misfortune" that led him to Buddhism. As far as I can see he had no such great misfortune but brought most of his acute suffering upon himself by this inability to acknowledge the nitty-gritty of the real world. Everyone is the author of his own pain, and Jack acted primarily from his dream world or wishful thinking. Daily he outlined specific detailed plans for the near future that would lead to an idealized far future, yet not one of these ever materialized. This in no way discouraged him from continuing the process. This constant irrational fantasizing was also illustrated by his frequently aborted sea journeys and his ivory-tower attempts to be alone in a "wilderness." He was truly his own worst enemy.

After World War II he sought a "new vision," but he had no orderly idea of life's purpose and meaning and these forays into wonderland may have represented efforts toward finding such a sustaining philosophy to guide him. Chaos was the rule until Buddhism came along and supplied the answers he sought—or so he believed. The tenets of Buddhism became a balm to his emotional and spiritual aspirations and fit his own psyche, but they related very little to the demands of daily life nor did they provide practical help. He ignored the rule against alcohol, for it, too, provided escape from reality. Now, however, when life became confusing or painful he had found an accepted means to avoid dealing with it face-to-face [by opting out for] "everything is illusion." He must have had some inkling that this means only ideas are permanent; their manifestation in matter transitory, but he preferred to think simply, "It doesn't matter; it isn't real; it will go away." This he found comforting, and with it came temporary peace, but he kept finding the damn thing, person, or situation had to be dealt with all the same on this earthly plane.

Ginsberg and other writers in the Beat genre mention "spiritual" and "spirituality" a good deal, and there are probably as many definitions as there are writers. Organized religions and the ruling scientists remain firmly entrenched in earthly knowledge gained through our five senses only. Yet all of us have easily accepted living with the invisible higher dimensions in which those senses play no part—radio, TV, telephone, sound waves, radiation, space travel and all it involves, etc. Still, the idea that the immense power that permeates everything and everybody is likewise invisible and operates on all dimensions causes great concern and/or horror. We keep forgetting pioneers like Galileo and the Wright brothers.

Neither Neal nor Jack were entirely at ease in the material world, even though they reveled in its sensory delights. They were, so to speak, *in* the world but not *of* it. Neither man was practical. Money was a nuisance. Neal was passionate about cars, but only because they were a means to move through space and defy the earthly law of gravity. He was hopeless or utterly frustrated with any attempt to use tools. I do think Jack perceived intuitively this Universal Force and tried to consciously tap it through meditation. This awareness also must have been behind his sporadic attempts at disciplining his physical desires by periods of celibacy or abstinence from alcohol, but he was never able to gain a clear enough understanding to prove it practical and sustained.

Neal, on the other hand, whose mind was logical and skeptical, ready to analyze all ideas intellectually, agreed with Emerson whose definition of life was "A perpetual instruction in cause and effect." Neal studied ancient texts and religious origins of all kinds and came to believe wholeheartedly in this supreme power. He even managed to prove it several times in his own experience, which overwhelmed him with joy. Nevertheless, his early conditioning in worthlessness and his abnormal physical desires were too strong for him to overcome. By the time he found *his* answers drugs had destroyed his power to choose. He could not set the example he yearned for, and neither Allen nor Jack were able to listen to or "hear" him. Most of his peers weren't as highly developed as he and wouldn't understand him either, so that which was at the core of his being has been avoided and ignored ever since. One day his beliefs may be seen to be the same as those which underlie Buddha's.

Other escape routes were offered Jack in the form of material chemical substances that were said to provide instant Nirvana and satori—increased mental and spiritual powers. Jack rejected the psychedelics—perhaps his mind already had enough of that sort of stimulation—but did often indulge in marijuana and Benzedrine for particular purposes. Neal used them more to enhance life-forms. He eventually learned there are no shortcuts to spiritual attainment, but was too undisciplined to act on that knowledge. One teacher he often quoted said that the three dimensions on this planet could be thought of as "Time, Space, and *Patience*—we must use our will to *consciously* overcome our errors, *step by step.*" The rub is that once those abilities are extended artificially, it becomes far, far more difficult to slow down to the "one step at a time" method. Hence, both men found the drugs a handcap in the end; in fact in one form or another, they were killed by them. They have both demonstrated that the use—or abuse—of these substances did nothing to bring them any closer to lasting peace and fulfillment. How much they contributed to Kerouac's writing no one can tell.

I see his life in one way as a constant tug-of-war between a desire for a serene and orderly life, writing by the fireside with his cats, kids, and wifey nearby but not intrusive. Periodically he could allow himself to explore all the marvels of the world, the people and places as he envisioned them, and return "home" to write about them from his jottings along the way. On the other side was the pull of the flesh which he condemned; his weak self-discipline, self-doubt, self-absorption, guilt. There's a fine line between his "I can do anything I want" in the sense of achieving goals through an awareness of inner strength, and the "I can do anything I want" of a spoiled child. Falling more and more into the latter frame served to undermine further the former confidence, and the "illusions" failed to disappear.

Restlessness increased with age. Running away began to supersede running to, until he at last stopped running and finished his life seated and sated with the real illusions of television and alcohol.

Tom Clark's concise and moving telling leaves the reader almost overwhelmed with compassion for the man who himself was known as the "Heart."

Carolyn Cassady

PART ONE

VISIONS IN THE
LOWELL NIGHT

．　．　．

JACK KEROUAC, who wrote American English with an almost physical love for the rough, rangy complexity of the language, didn't speak it at all until his fifth year. He is arguably the most important writer since Conrad to adopt English as a second language. His first tongue was the Franco-American *joual*.

Joual, a term coined in the 1950s, comes from the French-Canadian local pronunciation of *cheval*, the French word for horse. It refers generically to that Anglicized, abbreviated, and musical form of French spoken by the Quebecois of the St. Lawrence Valley and by the waves of their descendants who came down to New England mill towns and built a separate culture. But Kerouac's form of *joual*, a sublingo of a sublingo, was particular not only to New England and Lowell but also to his own family; since *joual* is a spoken language, not a written one, it has infinite varieties. Kerouac's *joual* could not pass as "proper" in Paris *or* Montreal.

The *joual* was the language of Jack's heart, which he identified with childhood and suffering (his father's dying plaints); it was the language he

3

spoke with his mother throughout his adult life and in which he could tell only the truth, like a small child.

Kerouac regarded the external manifestations of his non-English-speaking working-class background in much the same instinctive fashion as do most people who come from such backgrounds—that is, with an alternation of pride and embarrassment. But in Kerouac the sense of foreignness is never completely sublimated, never fully Americanized. The ambivalence of his feelings about nationality is honestly represented in the *Book of Dreams*, a literal record of his dream life during the 1950s. In one dream Kerouac's mother follows him to work on the Southern Pacific; her French-Canadian pronunciations of brakeman's jargon "tear [his] heart out" (". . . that French-Canadian way of using English to express its humility-meanings").[1] A few nights later, an abashed Jack finds himself with his mother and sister in an embarrassment dream. In it the Kerouacs are dé-classé Canucks at a glamorous Hollywood party thrown by either Dinah Shore or Olivia de Haviland—"my sister sees that I am botching everything so she steps in and in an even more beat awful gauche way begins trying to impress Dinah with a kind of halting Canuck-English speech (attempts at 'social smartness') (and really painful to hear)."[2]

KEROUAC believed himself to be the scion of an ancient and significant Celtic strain, descendant of Cornishmen who had traveled to Brittany and become "the most independent group of noblemen in Europe." Musings over his ancestry occupied his mind with increasing power in the last decade of his life, at times to the point of obsession. Writing to Raman Singh in 1965, he explained that his family had come from Ireland ("the Tristan-and-Isolde court of King Arthur") to Cornwall—"(not Anglo-Saxon of course, but Celts)"—and from there to Brittany in France. "Ker," he told Singh, meant "house," and "ouac" meant "in-the-field."[3] But two years later, in an interview, he revised this etymology entirely, suggesting that "Ker" meant "water," and "ouac" meant "language of"—and proposed that "Kerouac" was a variant of the "old Irish name Kerwick."[4]

In his boyhood Kerouac heard many tales about his ancestry from his parents, aunts, and uncles. From them he learned that his first North American ancestor was a Breton baron from Cornwall named "Louis Alexandre Lebris de Kérouac," who—in the family's version of the story—came across the ocean in "1750 or so,"[5] fought with Montcalm's army, and after the hostilities against the English was granted land along the Rivière du Loup in Quebec. But when Kerouac went to Paris in 1965 to try to find records that would prove his ancestor to have been an officer under Montcalm, he was unsuccessful. Subsequently, scholarship has traced the family back to a certain Maurice-Louis-Alexandre Le Brice De Kerouack, though this antecedent was, in fact, neither baron nor soldier but a bourgeois merchant from France, who married a Louise Bernier ("related to the explorer Bernier,"[6] was Jack's claim for this particular trace in his blood) at St. Ignace, Quebec, in 1732, and died on March 6, 1736.

Quebec provincial archives indicate that Louis-Alexandre's three sons married French-Canadian women. Kerouac believed his bloodline to have been mingled at various points with those of Indian tribes, and in 1960 he wrote that Louis-Alexandre's descendants married members of the Mohawk and Caughnawaga tribes. Five years later, however, in sway of a con man's story about the survival of certain ancient Kerouac sachems near the North Pole (which his mother held to be "a lot of bunk"),[7] he had become convinced these Indian ancestors of his were Iroquois. Near the end of his life, he told an interviewer he had been jotting down "silly Indian poems" in his notebook, and when asked "what kind of Indian," he replied, "Iroquois, as you know from looking at me."[8]

After acquainting himself in the mid-forties with the racial theories of Oswald Spengler, and later visiting Mexico repeatedly, Kerouac grew increasingly convinced of the authenticity of his connection with the worldwide population of primitive and "fellaheen" peoples—who were, as he felt himself to be, instinctive beings, guided by mother wit, tuned in with the cosmic beat, and totally devoid of the modern sense of nationhood. This feeling of instant identification with the spirit of "the Indian" was something Kerouac was sure he had to be receiving from his genes.

His family's motto, Kerouac often said, was *"Aimer, Travailler, et Souffrir"* (Love, Work, and Suffer).[9] A disposition to bewail their harsh fate was ingrained in the Kerouacs. Jack's mother, in his father's sad later days, constantly sighed over this manifestation of the family malady: *"Un vrai Duluoz, ils font ainque braillez pi's lamentez.* (A real Duluoz, all they do is cry and lament.)"[10] Jack's preoccupation with suffering placed him solidly in the family line. In middle life he plunged into prolonged studies of Eastern religions, spurred by his discovery of Buddhism's First Noble Truth: *existence is suffering.* It might be argued that not some putative "family malady" but real misfortune drove Kerouac to seek consolation in that tenet of Buddhist philosophy. But Kerouac's friend Allen Ginsberg says no, the interest in suffering was just something that was there in Jack's nature. "Kerouac was *fascinated* by suffering,"[11] Ginsberg proposes.

LOUIS-ALEXANDRE'S sons were potato farmers in Quebec. Some of their sons learned trades. The first Kerouac to emigrate to the United States was Jack's grandfather, Jean-Baptiste, a carpenter, who came to Nashua, New Hampshire, sometime after 1889. In that year Jean-Baptiste's wife gave birth to Jack's father, Leo, in St. Hubert, Temiscouata County, upriver on the St. Lawrence, Quebec.

Jack invoked his Canadian grandfather—who appears to have epitomized the independent unreconstructed cast of *les hommes Kerouac*—in his 1958 speech at Hunter College, on "The Origins of the Beat Generation." Referring in that talk to the "wild eager picture" of himself on the jacket of his novel *On the Road* (then a best seller), Kerouac attributed his crazy look in the photo, and "all this Beat guts"[12] as well, to his ancestry—particularly to Jean-Baptiste.

Jean-Baptiste's infant son Leo was baptized in St. Hubert before the family's emigration to the south. The baptism was pictured by Jack in *Visions of Gerard* as taking place in "some wind whipped country crossing Catholic Church . . . forlorn, the plains of Abraham"—a site evoking in Kerouac's imagination "the utterly hopeless place to which the French came when they came to the New World."[13]

From that bleak northern place, with its barren potato farms, Jean-Baptiste, like thousands of other Quebecois, came down to the mills and factories of New England towns like Nashua, where they found what Jack described as an "early Americana New Hampshire of pink suspenders, strawberry blondes, barber shop quartets."[14] Jean-Baptiste, an "old gaffer carpenter," built his own house in the French-Canadian section of Nashua.

Jean-Baptiste's son Leo went to work for a local French newspaper as reporter and typesetter. Sometime around 1914, when he was twenty-five, Leo met and courted a "neat French Canadian"[15] girl from Nashua named Gabrielle L'Evesque. Gabrielle, born in St. Pacome, Quebec, came from Norman stock. She was the daughter of a Nashua mill worker who rose to the status of tavern keeper but then died in 1909 at the age of thirty eight, leaving the fourteen-year-old Gabrielle (whose mother had died earlier) an orphan. The girl went to work in a shoe shop; that was her job at the time Leo married her.

From Gabrielle's ancestry came Jack's legal Christian names, Jean-

Louis. Her half-Indian grandmother, from a family called Jean, had married a L'Evesque, and they had produced a son named Louis (who, like Jack, had the dark hair and high cheekbones of an Indian).

Shortly after their marriage Leo and Gabrielle moved fourteen miles down the Merrimack River to the textile and tenement town of Lowell, Massachusetts. There Leo first sold insurance, then went into the printing business. With his own shop ("Pop's pure hope shop,"[16] Jack later called it) in a rented, run-down colonial building along Lowell's downtown canal, Leo became a visible part of the town's commercial life. Gabrielle, meanwhile, gave birth to three children—Gerard, in 1917; Caroline, three years later; and Jean (full name Jean-Louis Lebris de Kerouac) on March 12, 1922.

This last event took place in an upstairs bedroom of the frame house on Lupine Road where the Kerouacs were living at the time. It was five o'clock in the afternoon, and the rosy, late winter sundown suffused the natal chamber with a pink glow that Jack later claimed to recall. "I remember that afternoon," he wrote in 1952, "I perceived it through beads hanging in a door and through lace curtains and glass of a universal sad lost redness of mortal damnation . . . the snow was melting."[17] In Kerouac's adult work, dream and half-waking images frequently evoke this "sad lost redness" of his nativity, associating birth with violence and the pain or "damnation" of consciousness.

EXACTLY a week after the birth of their second son, Leo and Gabrielle bundled him up and took him out into the greater world beyond the upstairs bedroom on Lupine Road for the first time. Jack was accepted into the faith of his French-Canadian ancestors on March 19, 1922, the feast of St. Joseph (that "humble self-admitting truthful saint"[18] who was to be Jack's favorite). Holy water from the baptismal font at the cellarlike basement church of St. Louis de France (at Boisvert and West Sixth in the Centralville part of Lowell) was sprinkled on the infant's head by a parish priest, who entered him into the church rolls under the name "Jean Louis Kirouac (Keroack), son of Leo Keroack and Gabrielle Levesque."

At the time of this event, the Roman Catholic parishes of the northeastern industrial towns held over the lives of their Franco-American parishioners a power that was secular as well as spiritual. The church encouraged the perpetuation of traditional practices that had prevailed in Canada, particularly the use of the French-Canadian language, which at the time of Jack's birth was still taught in all the parochial schools of the diocese of Providence. This pervasive Quebecois influence in the lives of parishioners was to come under challenge during Kerouac's later childhood; but during his early youth the religiosity of the French-Canadian immigrant home, a flame guarded chiefly by the mother, still remained unbanked. Its principal symbols were, in order, Christ, especially in diminutive form, and the Virgin, who figured as intercessor to and protector of the beloved Baby Jesus. Beyond this pair, the figure most revered by the Franco-Americans—and especially by the devout Gabrielle Kerouac —was Ste. Thérèse de Lisieux, beatified by Rome in 1923 (and later called "the greatest saint of modern times" by Pius X).

Before Thérèse Martin died in 1897, in her twenties, of the condition all northern factory workers dreaded—a consumptive affliction of the lungs —she had promised that after she passed into the higher world she would let fall a shower of roses. The "Little Way" of Thérèse spread in influence after her beatification. Her message of seeking good with childlike simplicity was a teaching Gabrielle Kerouac transmitted to Jean-Louis, largely through his "saintly" invalid brother Gerard.

Gabrielle filled the Kerouac house with holy cards and pictures of Ste. Thérèse and taught the children to say little prayers to her, asking for showers of roses. The efficacy of these prayers was accepted as a matter of course by the children—an impression that lingered indelibly in Jean. Later this sentimental image of Ste. Thérèse always touched the gentle side of Kerouac's nature, even in his bottom-depth days as a Dharma wanderer. When, at the age of thirty-four, after much study of Eastern philosophy, he sat down like a Chinese monk in a Marin County hillside garden finally to compose his own Buddhist sutras—"The Scripture of Golden Eternity"—he wound up writing about the Little Way: " 'Love is all in all,' said Sainte Thérèse, choosing love for her vocation and pouring out her happiness, from her garden by the gate, with a gentle smile, pouring roses on the earth. . . ."[19]

WHEN Ti Jean (Petit Jean)—as the younger son was called at home—was two years old, the Kerouac family moved from 9 Lupine Road to a rented cottage at 35 Burnaby Street. The only thing Jack later recalled about Burnaby Street was a hungry urchin Gerard brought home one day to share Gabrielle's bread-and-butter sandwiches. The boy's name was Plourdes, a word Kerouac never forgot because it contained for him "all the despair, raw gricky hopelessness, cold and chapped sorrow of Lowell—Like the abandoned howl of a dog no one to open the door."[20]

The next year they moved to another house in Centralville at 34 Beaulieu Street, a dirt thoroughfare that was to take on exaggerated importance in the "legend" Kerouac wove of his life. It became "the little street that bears the great weight of Gerard's dying."[21]

The Beaulieu Street house, in Jack's adult memory of it, was "sadly brown,"[22] associated with earth, time, and graves. The house, he said, had been built over an "ancient cemetery."[23] Ti Jean, at the ages of three and four, heard elaborate ghost stories about the house from his brother, Gerard. The house sometimes rattled, knocking his sister Nin's dolls and Gabrielle's crockery off their shelves. Nine-year-old Gerard ascribed this phenomenon to the activity of the ghosts of the dead people under the house.

Ti Jean looked up to his invalid brother with a reverence that bordered on adoration and so believed implicitly in the remarkable sanctity of Gerard—which was attested to not only by their parents but also by neighbors and other relatives (who swore that, like St. Francis, Gerard had birds that "did know him personally" and "came to his windowsill in the time of his long illnesses")[24] and by the nuns of St. Louis de France, who had "heard his astonishing revelations of heaven delivered in catechism class on no more encouragement than that it was his turn to speak."[25]

By the end of 1925, Gerard's malady, a rheumatic condition affecting the heart, had become grave. Jack later claimed to remember "sad red Sunday afternoons" with Leo (the "big scowling father") reading the funnies in his shirtsleeves, "in the corner by the potted plant of time and home—patting his poor sickly little Gerard on the head, '*Mon pauvre ti Loup*, my poor lil Wolf, you were born to suffer. . . .' "[26] In the cruel decline of Gerard, the older Kerouacs recognized what the innocent eyes of Ti Jean missed, a characteristic outcropping of meaningless suffering of a kind the family seemed destined by fate to bear (*Aimer, Travailler, Souffrir*).

On July 8, 1926, in the wake of a bedside visit from the nuns of St. Louis de France, who took down his last words about heaven and then left in a swirl of black habits, the serious, pale, blue-eyed first son of Leo Kerouac died. The relatives wailed in the kitchen, but Ti Jean was too young to understand. After dutifully sitting through an unintelligible funeral service among glum adults in overshoes at the damp basement church of St. Louis de France, he rode in the rain with his parents to

Nashua—Nashué was how they said it—and, while his Ma and Ti Nin sobbed in the back of the black car, watched with "questioning eyes"[27] as the saintly Gerard was planted in the wet, cold sod of the family plot.

HOME was a principality ruled over by Gabrielle and the values of the Little Way, with Leo on the scene as the sometimes uneasy cigar-smoking male-in-residence. Gabrielle's seat of power was the kitchen. Leo's was the world, of which Ti Jean had still seen little. His trips into it with his father, beginning around the time of Gerard's death, left him agog. At home there was a poetry in the brown gloom, but in Leo's greater world of downtown Lowell there was a rugged, alluring prose of real life.

One of the first things Jean learned on his strolls around town with the "frowning, serious, Bretonsquat"[28] Leo was a smattering of English, the language you had to use when non-French people were around. (Leo spoke passable English, but Gabrielle did not, so English wasn't spoken in the Kerouac home.) Jean sensed immediately that the language difference was a chasm between people and that English, the designated bridge, was an undependable structure. It couldn't be counted on to get you across. Even his father, that worldly and proud figure, seemed to relax back into more comfortable words and thoughts in the company of fellow Canucks.

On the way to the print shop with Jean in tow, Leo stopped off at the "raucous tenement"[29] where his shop assistant lived. A domestic dispute was underway. Jean had never heard anything like it. To the silent, wide-eyed boy, the tenement visit was like a plunge into the Francophonic verbal ocean of Lowell. Here was the huge animal presence of *la langue* as Kerouac would again experience it later in his prose composition. "It swims in thru all windows and revolves around the rumors and runs like a river, voices, language, gossip, crashes, jingles and jangles—'There's no end to it!'— Whole rant-sentences can be heard in rising and falling snatches of vigorous Canuckois,"[30] he wrote, recalling the visit in *Visions of Gerard*.

Down the alley past the Royal Theatre, where in a few years he would learn more English from the first talking pictures, Jean followed Leo to the dark back-street printing shop. There he watched the men work feeding sheets into the press, yawning over inkpans and types, grinding out handbills, wedding announcements, and advertising circulars.

When the Irish shop workers went home, Jean noted that Leo and his assistant, who had been forced to speak English on the job, suddenly reverted "to French slang"—the *joual*—"since nobody's there to hear them anyway, just as you might expect the Greeks that you could see across the way through the great dirty windows, breaking from their usual Greek to talk some English for the benefit of business there 'ska pa la pa ta wa ya' here we go again, the great raving *patois* of Lowell on all sides, Polocks on Lakeview Avenue and Back Central, and practically pure Gaelic or at least lilting Gaelic English on the Highlands and downtown—Syrians to boot, up the canal somewhere—and your New England Yankees eating Indian Pudding for dessert in old stately houses and lawns . . . with . . . thin noses and thin lips."[31]

Lowell was a multilingual soup of speech out of which a boy like Jean, thirsty for knowledge and with alert ears, could pick up the kind of balanced verbal nutrition that later makes the best writer's vocabulary. Jack eventually sought to emulate the linguistic generosity of Shakespeare and James Joyce, but his taste for words was first whetted on this protoliterate stew that overflowed from every door and window in his hometown.

GERARD'S death propelled Jean farther into his already active imagination. He was told that his brother was now with Jesus. Was this true? The whole thing was a mystery, which grew with each passing day that Gerard failed to return from the cemetery in Nashua.

In Jean's inner life, the powerful presence of his brother, who had been his faithful companion and kindly teacher, was replaced in two ways. First, as death always shocks the child into self-awareness, Jean began to explore his own physical individuality and, under the tutelage of some twins who were his neighborhood playmates, started to masturbate. (It made him dream of "shrouds.")[32] Around the same time, he also attempted to replace his lost brother by making up little "silent movies" in the family parlor.

These were pantomimes with complicated action and many imaginary characters, all played by Ti Jean himself. Thirty years later Jack's memory of these first little wordless plays was dim ("now I write them,"[33] he said), but his mother and sister remembered, and they related to him the way, in the days after Gerard's death, he "began to sit motionlessly in the parlor, pale and thin, and after a few weeks of sorrow began to play the old Victrola and act out movies to the music . . . Some of these movies developed into long serial sagas, 'continued next week,' leading sometimes to the point where I tied myself with a rope in the grass and kids coming home from school thought I was crazy."[34]

Kerouac birthplace, Lupine Road, Lowell (photo by Joy Walsh)

Kerouac as a child: " 'I tied myself with a rope in the grass and kids coming home from school thought I was crazy.' "

Jack's principal adult recollection of these parlor "silent movies" was that they had been "Chaplinesque."[35] But Ti Jean had not yet seen Charlie Chaplin. In fact, he did not see a "real" movie until about six months after Gerard's death.

The first picture he saw was a Tom Mix western. Mix, galloping across the amazing "muddy movie screen california" in a white hat so "snowy" it made him look like a "glowworm," finally leaped "across rainy shacks . . . landing on maniacs in the dark," so horrifying Jean that later he "was afraid to stick my hand out in the dark until I was twenty-nine years old."[36]

Jack saw this memorable movie at the Royal Theatre, just up the alley from Leo's shop. Nin and Jean enjoyed that childhood dream, free passes to the movies, because their father printed the Royal's programs. From the time Jean was five, they went every Saturday, arriving at 12:30 for the 1:15 show, dangling their feet over the balcony seats high out of sight of the raspy-voiced usher and studying the gilt Moorish angels on the theater ceiling until the lights went down and Tim McCoy or Hoot Gibson galloped onto the screen.

The movies, even the westerns—or *especially* the westerns, which were his favorites—encouraged the already flourishing Gothic element in Jean's imagination. To him these moving images were strange and chilling texts, food for endless speculation. Were Tom Mix's maniacal victims now off in heaven with Jesus and Gerard?

T H E year after Gerard's death, Gabrielle once again took up work in a shoe shop and the Kerouacs moved again to another in a long series of rented frame houses and tenement flats, this one in a low, blockish Kellostone house at 320 Hildreth Street, Centralville. Across the street was a "haunted Pine ground with deserted Castle-manse,"[37] which was to figure later in Kerouac's Gothic vision of Dr. Sax.

The house itself was a cabinet of secret horrors for Jean. Open closet doors made him shudder, a coat on a hook on a white door in the dark sunk his heart into panic fright. A black-lacquered phosphorescent cross his mother had bought from a traveling salesman hung on the wall and "glowed Jesus in the Dark, I gulped for fear every time I passed it the moment the sun went down." This was not the sweet Baby Jesus of Gerard's pious musings about heaven, but a "Jesus Christ of passion plays in his shrouds and vestments of saddest doom."[38]

The death of his brother had acted on Jean's imagination like a fine tuning. He was sympathetic to the slightest resonances of threat—of death —looming everywhere in familiar things. The loss of Gerard was now completely internalized, the world fear of the child grown enormous, yet unnoticed by the surrounding adults. (Jean was a blank wall—"I pouted in my childhood";[39] these secret frights could not be betrayed.) All of this speeded up the process of his individuation, the growth of his belief in his own *difference*. "I was the strangest creature of them all," he later wrote in a poem describing himself at six. In the poem he recalls playing with toy soldiers and wondering " 'What is this?—mystery of little people./Is each one as frightened as me? Is each one afraid as me?' "[40]

After twenty-five years he was still having nightmares in which "the red living room rattle furniture" of the flat in which he had lived from the ages of five to seven became again "responsible for the horror, the hanging, the guilt, the old Victrola's just a TV now, is all—the coffin that's never been moved from the parlor of the Kerouacs—le mort dans salle des Kerouac."[41]

LEO'S two sisters, Marie and Louise, often visited from Nashua. (Jack later remembered taking "long walks under old trees of New England at night with my mother and aunt," listening "to their gossip extensively."[42]) One morning in September 1928, when both Leo and Gabrielle were busy getting ready to go off to their respective jobs in the cold, crisp Lowell dawn, it was Tante Louise who took Ti Jean "par la main" and walked him to his first day at the parish school of St. Louis de France. Jean was dressed in "little black stockings and pants."[43]

The parish school provided another trial for Jean's already sensitive imagination. To start with, it was presided over by the Sisters of the Assumption of the Blessed Virgin Mary. Jean had seen them before; these were the "dark nuns of St. Louis" who had swooped in to transcribe Gerard's heavenly visions, and then returned for the "hoary black funeral in a gloomy file (in rain)."[44]

The parochial school, like the church, was in a basement, "dungeon-like,"[45] as Jack later recalled it. He remembered the school's "ghost yards" with their "crunchly" gravels, the "banana smells in lockers"—but mostly the "vast and dark" underground halls of the school, where the nuns combed the students' hair with water from the drip-pipes of the pissoir in an atmosphere of "dank dark gloom." The school had "darkness in niches."[46]

The discipline at St. Louis de France was as stringent as Jean had expected. One day his little friend Joe Fortier—son of a pal of Leo's—committed a *péché* and was beaten on the behind by the Mother Superior, using a iron-rimmed ruler. Jean was careful to avoid a similar fate.

Another day the children were filed into the school auditorium and shown "an antique Catholic twenties film"[47] that made a stronger impression on Jean than anything else he was taught at St. Louis. The film employed a trick effect that seemed to make a stone statue of Ste. Thérèse slowly turn its head. The mechanical effect had been conceived out of a spirit of naive proselytism, but to Jean it contained mystical revelations that immediately extended the realm of his secret fears to include the possibility that religious emblems and symbols were actually *alive*.

In the spring of 1929, he reached the church's prescribed "age of reason" and became eligible to receive the adult sacraments. This meant, above all, a first tentative Friday afternoon visit to the dark booth of the confessional. A parish priest, who was only a blurry shadow across a wire screen, made things no easier for Jean by posing the traditional question. "And you played with your little gidigne (dingdong)?' 'Yes *mon père.*' 'Well therefore . . . say a whole rosary . . . ten *Notre Pères* and ten *Salut Maries.*' "[48] Then, on Sunday, dressed in his best clothes, and in front of his adoring mother, Jean knelt obediently at the altar rail in the basement church, stuck out his tongue, and tasted for the first time what the catechism had told him was the "body and blood" of Christ.

Later that year his family moved down the block to 240 Hildreth. Jean—or Jacky, as he was beginning to be called by playmates—had retained his solitary kingdom in the pine woods across the road, where breathtaking games of the imagination took place. The woods were exciting by day, terrifying by night. Jean had the run of them all summer and only unwillingly returned to school in the fall. On Armistice Day he stood in the "cold red morning" watching the annual parade from his third story wood porch, crying because he "wanted to go back in the woods of all that summer."[49]

In 1930 the family moved again in Centralville, this time to a cottage at 66 West Street. (It reappears as the "little cottage" of the "trellised rose sadness"[50] in *Book of Dreams.*) To Jean the most memorable feature of this house was its big, gloomy living room, which was "dark, like black water." It contained "leather-thickwood furniture"[51] and a large mahogany radio, the family's first. There was also in the house a statue of Ste. Thérèse, which had been acquired by Gabrielle. The statue reminded Jean of the one in the "antique Catholic film" he had seen at school. One night, passing by in the dark, Jean couldn't keep himself from glancing at it. The statue seemed to turn its head, just as the one in the religious educational film had done. Jean's hair stood on end.

By 1930 Jean's little plays and pantomimes had progressed in complexity to a point where the parlor "silent movies" could not contain all their details. He began to put them on paper. Earlier Gerard had coached him in drawing. Now he started to produce his own comic strips. "Kuku and Koko at the Earth's Core" was the first. It was "crudely drawn," Jack said later, but before long he was sketching out entire "highly developed sagas like 'The Eighth Sea.' "[52]

IN the fall of the family's first year in the West Street house, Leo Kerouac, an avid fight fan, began operating a small training gym for boxers in Centralville. Not long after he opened his gym, somebody told him there was more money in wrestling; the boxing game was taking a beating because everybody knew the fights were fixed. Leo converted his string of boxers into wrestlers and the training gym into a wrestling club.

The young boxer-wrestler Jacky admired most was Armand Gauthier, an amiable epileptic who was also an employee in Leo's print shop. When Leo bought his first automobile, a model A Ford, he found that he had a hard time driving it; his legs were too short to reach the pedals comfortably, and worse, he couldn't cure himself of the dangerous habit of talking to people in the back seat while at the wheel. So Armand, who was an able driver, became the official chauffeur on Kerouac family outings—including Jacky's first trip to the province of his ancestors, Quebec, on the Fourth of July 1931. Gauthier was also invited to the Kerouac home for holiday suppers, important occasions for Jacky because they permitted him to examine the athlete's bulging muscles up close. Armand "always obliged," Jack wrote in a 1968 magazine article, "and I hung from one biceps and Nin from the other." Imitating Leo, Armand called him by the affectionate name "Ti Pousse" (Little Thumb).[53]

NINETEEN thirty-two was not a good year for most Canucks in Lowell. Hard times had hit the mills; workers were laid off and many suffered. Leo had had to borrow several thousand dollars to relocate his shop. In 1932 he moved the family again, this time out of the ethnically mixed working-class district called Centralville to the Franco-American neighborhood known as Pawtucketville.

The democratic outwardness of Pawtucketville immediately delighted Jacky. The neighborhood had an active street life; there were many boys his age. At this time he yearned to enter a world of societies and sports and school interests, if only to shed or transcend the fears that had made life in Centralville a constant trial. "I had learned to stop crying in Centralville and I was determined not to start crying in Pawtucketville."[54]

The third evening after the Kerouac family moved into the rented house at 16 Phebe Avenue, he took up a watchful post on the green-painted front porch. Before long a boy came along and struck up a conversation. The boy's name was Zap Plouffe. Soon Jacky was swept away on a tide of "screams in the nightfall street of play."[55]

Zap Plouffe proved to be an ill-fated child, who, not long afterward, died from an injury sustained when a milk wagon ran over him. When this happened Jacky couldn't help wondering if Zap's tragedy was associated with his own darknesses of the Centralville period. Walking at night across the little park that separated his home from the neighborhood candy store, he "began to see the ghost of Zap Plouffe mixed with other shrouds."[56] It took a conscious effort to dispel such thoughts, to make them retreat into the safe distance of an infantile past where they could be, if not completely forgotten, at least harmlessly stored.

There were to be other and closer Pawtucketville pals. Almost all of them were Canucks like Jacky, but—now that he spoke a halting demotic English that extended his social qualifications enormously—there were also a few Greeks and even an Anglo lad named Billy Chandler, Jacky's first and "greatest English chum."[57] In *Dr. Sax*, Kerouac's ode to his early adolescence, it is Billy Chandler ("Dicky Hampshire") whose bathing trunks Jacky steals, in his role as sinister neighborhood "Black Thief," causing the exasperated Gabrielle to vow, "I'm going to stop you from reading them damned Thrilling Magazines if it's the last thing I do."[58]

In the fall of 1932, Jacky enrolled for the fifth grade at a new school, St. Joseph's parochial, taught by French-Canadian Jesuit Brothers.

Jacky's first day at St. Joseph's included the ordeal of crossing the Merrimack River, which separated Pawtucketville from the rest of Lowell. This meant negotiating the Moody Street Bridge, a perilous-looking iron and wood structure through whose grillwork anyone courageous enough to look down could see the "100-foot drop to the roaring foams of the rocks in their grisly eternity."[59] Jacky was lucky his first morning: a schoolmate walked him across the bridge while he tremulously clutched the iron railing. But that afternoon, after taking a deep breath and crossing it solo, he was ambushed at the other side by a malicious boy he later named Fish, who for no apparent reason punched him in the face.

Jacky became a better student under the Jesuit Brothers, whom he later credited with giving him the "good early education" that made it possible for him to start writing novels ("When I got to public schools and colleges I was already so far advanced I set records cutting classes to go to the library and read all day, or stay in my room . . . and write plays").[60]

The brothers saw in Jean Kerouac a quiet, undemonstrative boy with serious blue eyes that suggested a soul of unusual depth. Before his year at St. Joseph's was over, they had taught him to perform as an altar boy (he served Mass on the prestigious main altar of St. Jean Baptiste) and also to invite into his heart that beam from God that would indicate he had a "vocation" for the priesthood.

The brothers' designs for him might have been achieved had not their scholastic instruction been so efficient. But Jacky's rapid progress in the fifth grade at St. Joseph's made him eligible the following year to pass directly into the seventh grade at a public junior high school; and so the Jesuits lost their man. (Perhaps the loss was only temporary; late in life Kerouac often claimed, with a sly look, that he had remained a closet Jesuit and was indeed a secret "general" of the order, named "Everhard Mercurian.")[61]

The spiritual vibrations stirred up by the brothers reawakened Jacky's interest in the mystery of death. This was the most important of mysteries, since it separated him from his lost brother. Then and later Kerouac actively struggled to bring Gerard back to life, either by remembering him— which was getting harder as the years went by—or by "seeing him" in living individuals. Several of his closest friends in life first attracted Kerouac because of their physiognomic or spiritual resemblance to the "angelic" Gerard. The first in this series of false-sibling crushes was a boy in the fifth grade at St. Joseph's, Arthur Eno, referred to in *Dr. Sax* as "Ernie Malo." "I'd pray at the crucifix for the love of my Ernie Malo," Kerouac later wrote, "who because he was like my brother Gerard I loved with as sublime a love."[62] When they stood in line in the schoolyard, Jacky's eyes were fixed adoringly on Arthur Eno.

Leo's ailing older brother Joe lived in Pawtucketville. Once Leo's family moved into the neighborhood, Joe's wife and daughter often came on summer evenings to visit with Gabrielle. She and Jacky would walk them home. The walk took them past a site called "the Grotto," on the grounds of an orphanage, where under large arching trees were placed a dozen kiosklike altars, each containing the imagery of one of the twelve stations of the cross—mementos of the agony of Jesus. One night after reading a pulp detective magazine called *The Shadow*, Jacky thought he saw some kind of shade "flit from station to station"[63] in the Grotto. This shade, distilled in his imagination, became "Dr. Sax," the shadowy protagonist of many later reveries and tales.

The trips to Uncle Joe's, as Jack later recalled them, always seemed to take place (appropriately enough) on "a baneful black night." Joe lived just off Pawtucket Street in a dreadful "drear brown house," where he had been "dying these past five, ten, fifteen years, worse." Next door was a large barnlike "garage for hearses leased by one of the undertakers around the corner on funereal Pawtucket Street," which had a "storage room for coffins" that often featured in Jacky's subsequent "dreams rickety and strange."[64]

Uncle Joe smoked his asthma cigarettes, the odor of which Jacky hated (though years later he changed his mind after hearing that his beloved Proust also had smoked them, and decided they smelled like marijuana), and gave the boy long, wailing lectures in *joual* about the horrors of having been born a Kerouac. "You are destined to be a man of big sadness and talent," Uncle Joe told Ti Jean, "it'll never help to live or die, you'll suffer like the others, *more*."[65]

One evening in July 1934, Jacky and his mother escorted his cousin back to Uncle Joe's and then, returning home across the Moody Street Bridge, saw a man collapse in a heap on the bridge planks. The man was carrying a watermelon. Gabrielle saw that the man had stained his pants and told Jacky, "*Il meurt*, he's dying."[66] After years of brooding on death, this was the first time Jacky had ever witnessed the event that was the source of so much mystery.

Back home his hair stood on end, his soul awash with "gloomy music." He remembered the sinister turning head of the Ste. Thérèse statue; he feared that his parents too might die. That night he developed a fever. Gabrielle took him into her bed:

" 'The Grotto'. . . where under large arching trees were placed a dozen kiosk-like altars" (courtesy Marshall Clements)

The Moody Street Bridge, Lowell (courtesy Marshall Clements)

[He] lay huddled against the great warm back of my mother . . . this whole night could only take me if it took her with me & she wasnt afraid of any shade . . . Luckily after that, and by unconscious arrangement, my mother and I were semiquarantined in bed for a week where (mostly it rained) I lay reading *The Shadow Magazine*, or feebly listening to the radio downstairs in my bathrobe, or blissfully sleeping with one leg thrown over my mother in the night—so secure did I become that death vanished into fantasies of life . . .[67]

IN the fall of 1933, Jacky entered the seventh grade at Bartlett Junior High School, where instruction was entirely in English. This was the "Harsh Northern School" revisited in Jack's dreams of the 1950s. In those dreams Kerouac returns to a mechanical drawing class in an outbuilding at Bartlett; Jacky is the gauche Canuck, and the teacher is a "freckled red-haired scotchman," who "acts a little contemptuous of the Frenchies."[68]

Outside public school Jacky's French-Canadian friends sometimes accused him of arrogance, calling him a "big punk"; in the classroom, though, he clammed up completely. One fellow student of the time later said that though they took the same courses, he did not remember Kerouac ever saying a single word in class. "He was like a tomb—all closed-in."[69] Indeed, Jacky had no chance to say much in class; he was too busy simply keeping up with the English language.

In French the boy had never read beyond the catechism, passages of the Bible, religious texts for children. Now, at the public school, he began to devour every printed work in English he could put his hands on. In a few years he progressed from the Bobbsey twins, *Rebecca of Sunny Brook Farm*, and James Boyd's *Roll River* to *Tim Tyler's Flying Luck*, *Huckleberry Finn*, and *The Last of the Mohicans*. He read Lowell's morning and afternoon papers and Hearst's *Boston American*, flying over the news sections, slowly digesting the more graphic prose of the sports pages. But the principal sustenance for his imagination came from pulp mystery thrillers—*Phantom Detective*, *The Shadow* magazine, and *Operator 5*—which he consumed from cover to cover within twenty-four hours of their appearance on the candystore shelves. On days when there were no new pulps, he contented himself with *Liberty*. Before long he was at work on his own "imitations" of everything.

The earliest of these imitations date from late 1933 and early 1934 (his first months at Bartlett Junior High School), when he began making little home magazines and newspapers, printed laboriously by hand in pencil and illustrated with drawings. These miniature self-publications evolved over the next few years into a sort of historical record of Jacky's "fantasies of life"—in which, like the autobiographical character Micky Martin in *The Town and the City*, he "conducted a whole, perfectly ordered, imaginary 'world' of his own which was exhaustively set into motion and recorded each day in his own 'newspaper.' "[70] These first little newspapers were the ancestors of all the extensive diaries, journals, and notebooks he was to keep faithfully for the rest of his life.

Around the same time that he began to historicize his fantasy life in the first relatively primitive editions of his home newspaper, Jacky was also at work on his first "novel." He had read and been much impressed by *Huckleberry Finn*, and he now decided to sit down at his "first brown desk" in the dining room of the Phebe Avenue house and make his own imitation novel. It would be about "an orphan boy running away, floating down a river on a boat."[71] The river, naturally, was the Merrimack, which bisects Lowell. He hand printed the whole novel carefully in a five-cent pocket notebook. It was called "Jack Kerouac Explores the Merrimack."

This "first novel," now lost, is described in *The Town and the City* as a "carefully wrought-out epic"[72] done in deliberate and fairly strict imitation of the Twain classic. In *Visions of Cody*, a book that delves deeper into memory and salvages more, Kerouac attempts to show what the little "Merrimack" novel was really like. This 1952 paraphrase-from-memory may have been affected by his adult discovery of Rimbaud and the "Drunken Boat" of postsurrealist mythology, but it also gives a good picture of the drift of his own imagination in 1933–1934. The compulsive attraction of an outer world that promises an unraveling of fantastic adventures —his first theme as a practicing eleven-year-old novelist—was one that would continue to engage and sustain him into his early years of maturity as a writer.

In *Visions of Cody* Kerouac says that his autobiographical protagonist started out "in the swamp of the Merrimack somewhere," then went "floating down that little Indiana, river, further and further down into lighter, stranger, greener ever expanding adventures that must and do ultimately take you to a flat marsh by the sea, great ears of corn along a waving grass veldt, scents of something, smoke of a city, something mad and wild and far far gone from the tangled viney place where you started when the dream began . . ."[73]

The same basic story of a tantalizing power that removes one from humdrum existence and takes one on a remarkable voyage can be found underlying almost everything Kerouac wrote for the next eighteen years, up to and including the best known of all these fantasies of life, *On the Road.*

A N D so by 1934, when he was twelve, the relation between written words in English and his most hopeful fantasies of life was at least a glimmering perception in Kerouac's mind. He later marked this period in his life as a kind of second birth. "Way back in the beginning, the dismal rainy 1934's when I used to keep history of myself—started that long before Scotty and I kept baseball histories of our souls . . ."[74]

The "Scotty Boldieu" of Kerouac's novels was a boy named Joseph Beaulieu, one of Jacky's new Pawtucketville friends. On a crisp October morning at the ballfield of Lowell Textile Institute, Beaulieu turned in a "great pitching performance"[75] that made him an instant hero in Jacky's private sports mythology, which he chronicled each night at home. A year or two later, Jack and Scotty were keeping the "baseball histories of our souls," with Jack as statistician, recording their batting and fielding averages in red ink after games played by the neighborhood team. Jack became Beaulieu's catcher. Other players included their pals Roland Salvas ("Albert Lauzon" or "Lousy" in Kerouac's books) and George Apostolos ("G. J."). This group remained steady companions for the next several years. They had a sandlot football team, the Dracut Tigers. They also held track meets at the Textile Institute field, arranged and timed by "big punk" Jacky, who had invented his own "timing clock"[76] out of the turntable of a disused Victrola.

The boys in Jacky's gang whipped themselves up to a frenzy of play, expressing preadolescent sexual tension in ways that went beyond the implicit. Occasionally, they achieved a transferred culmination by goading a local "madboy" ("Zaza" as he is called in *Doctor Sax*) to masturbate repeatedly, while they watched. And once, at play in the Textile field, Jacky saw a boy go off to one side and unexpectedly begin masturbating into a bottle. The tension and the exultation of sexual release in play were creative—at least for Jacky—disclosing "something secretively wild and baleful in the glares of the child soul, the masturbatory surging triumph of the knowledge of reality."[77]

The closest Jacky came to "knowledge of reality," he felt, was when he was being swept away by imagination—consumed in the growing heat of his fantasies of life, those imaginary narratives that now took place in an aura not of mystical gloom but of heroic romance. His real experiences at games became nourishment for a greater "self" that emerged only in the amplification of the secret written chronicles, the "histories of my soul." These were perfect scenarios—complete with sets and sound tracks—for Jacky's complex, self-enlarging fantasies.

Although the fantasies often ended prosaically in the act of masturbation, the way they got there was sometimes sheer poetry. Jacky inaugurated, for example, his "summer league." This was a baseball game intended to fill long, idle, warm-weather afternoons and evenings. Jacky named the players and teams and kept the records on cards. When the Kerouacs moved from Phebe Avenue to Sarah Avenue in 1935, he began acting out games in his summer league by hitting an iron ball bearing with a nail under an apple tree in his back yard. The game could also be played with playing cards.

The original summer league—as described later in *Visions of Cody*—was an involved network of fantasies that engaged not only Jacky's naive sexual yearnings but also his first suppressed social aspirations. The imaginary league had a daydreamy "Latinness even . . . as it were a tennis-and-knickers-Barnstable Cape Cod league coolness . . . the names of the teams in the summer league were Tydol, Gulf, Texaco. . . ." On an ideal summer day, the league "transpired in the afternoon," when it "had a life of its own," occupying him "with the seriousness of the angels." At night in bed there was the review of the day's games. Then the names of the teams became "so soft and orange and yielding to my touch, to my kicks, I lay there, twelve, high on the colors of the imaginary uniforms of imaginary baseball teams on cards. . . ." Jacky had no doubt, as he lay there, that players like his star Latin first baseman Art Rodrigue and "other ball players throughout the league, imaginary as it was, went out and spent evenings with naked and willing women; I could even see Art Rodrigue sitting facing a naked Armenian girl sitting on a Cape Cod settee with a book and great perfect breasts regardant and soft. . . ."[78]

Even the summer league, however, fell short of the furious associative complexity of Jacky's most evolved fantasy universe, the one that surrounded his "Turf." This was a horseracing newspaper, begun in the "gray and hoary" days of late 1934 on his new little green "editorial desk" in his upstairs bedroom at Phebe Avenue. At age twelve Jacky had seen a movie about "a young kid—I think it was Frankie Darro—who became a jockey and won great fame and fortune." He now "lived and breathed the ambition of becoming a jockey"[79] and conducted his own imaginary races by rolling randomly chipped ("handicapped") glossy marbles down a parcheesi board propped against his bed and along the floor of his room to the tune of records played on his Victrola. Afterward he wrote up the "results" in a mixture of statistics and prose that imitated, but in bulk of detail went far beyond, the conventional format of the horseracing newspapers Leo brought home.

In the world of the "Turf," Jacky became "Jack Lewis," who not only edited the "Turf" but also served as racing commissioner, track handicapper, and horse owner, as well as jockey. Jack Lewis had his own stable, colors cream and cerise, to rank among the colors "of the great silks of great proud socialite stables." At night these elegant colors always figured somehow in the romantic off-track escapades of Jack Lewis (or Jean-Louis)— silent, sheet-twisting, presleep episodes that usually took place to the mentally recreated background music of "oldish and sentimental . . . racetrack cool"[80] records Jacky had heard played between races at the track.

Whenever Leo Kerouac had a few extra dollars in his pocket, and was not bothered too much by the nagging rheumatism that now sometimes forced him to bed for days at a time, he covered the local race tracks like a blanket. In the fall of 1934, he took Jacky along for the first time—to Rockingham Park in New Hampshire. Before they left Lowell, father permitted son to "handicap" the races on the typewriter at the printing shop, an indulgence that became a ritual on their race days together. Sometimes Leo even let Jacky typeset his one-page race day newspapers and print them on a hand press. (Jacky called these his *Racetrack News*.) Leo also took Jacky to races at Suffolk Downs in East Boston and Narragansett Park in Pawtucket, Rhode Island. Jacky's first visit to Narragansett in November 1934 was a big event, the inaugural of a major stake race, the Narragansett Special. Jacky later remembered the trip to Pawtucket as a "grim voyage south in the rain . . . through exciting cities of great neons, Providence, the mist at the dim walls of great hotels. . . ."[81]

AFTER several years of absorption in his self-enlarging fantasies of life, Jacky discovered another route to the tantalizing outside world of "neon cities" and "great hotels," one that led down an avenue of real life. The discovery came in 1935. The avenue was the game of football.

Jacky was a strong, stocky boy, built like his father—and fortified by his mother's abundant home cooking. In the sandlot football season of 1935, he found out that this was the one game he could play better than other boys. It was a discovery that he later nominated as the beginning of his "vanities"—his struggle to make good in life.

Kerouac's career in organized sports dates from a letter of challenge he sent to the *Lowell Sun* in October 1935. Drafted by Scotty Beaulieu, edited and hand printed by Jacky, the letter invited local football teams in the thirteen-to-fifteen-year-old age range to a Saturday game against their team, the Dracut Tigers, on their home field in an empty lot among the pine woods north of Lowell. A team called the Rosemont Tigers accepted. In this duel of Tigers, played before an audience of relatives and friends, the strong-legged Jacky Kerouac was both the youngest and most powerful player on the field. He ran at will through the tamer opposing Tigers for nine touchdowns and a 60–0 victory, then rushed home to his bedroom to hand print a headline and game account of his own heroics that for once contained more truth than fantasy.

The word that Leo Kerouac's boy had scored nine touchdowns in a sandlot game caused a certain flurry at the Pawtucketville Social Club, a politically sponsored pool hall and bowling alley for the young men of the district. Leo was managing the Social Club, a part-time job he had taken on because business was off at the print shop. When some Canuck young bloods ran up tabs at the Social Club, Leo cut off their pool and bowling privileges. These youths banded together for a revenge game against Leo's son's team. During the first pileup, thirteen-year-old Jacky was punched in the face by a seventeen-year-old, who then exhorted the other bloods to "Get that little Christ of a Kerouac!"[82] As his cigar-chomping, red-faced father looked on angrily from the sidelines, Jacky retaliated with a clean, hard tackle, putting the seventeen-year-old out of the game.

In subsequent weeks the Dracut Tigers were invited to perform not only on cow fields and lots but also in the junior high school stadium and on Lowell's North Common. Their opponents were usually tough local Greeks. Kerouac later remembered these as "awful blood-flying games, . . . Homeric" battles spiced with ethnic antagonism. A few years later, the same Greeks would be Jack's teammates on the Lowell High School eleven, but for now he was almost "afraid to get up on Saturday mornings and show up."[83]

AFTER reading Spengler ten years later, Kerouac decided Lowell's "unaccomplished mud-heap civilization" had been caught "with its pants down"[84] by the great flood which took place in March 1936. The product of an early thaw releasing the long winter's mass of ice and snow, flood-waters rolled down on Lowell from the mountains of New Hampshire, inundating the canals and mills and everything else on the banks of the Merrimack—including Leo Kerouac's printing plant, which was submerged in six feet of water, causing extensive damage to the presses and other essential equipment.

The flood dealt Leo, the independent businessman, a lethal blow. For Jacky, though, it created a week-long festival of interesting activity. School was canceled; the bridges were threatened. Jacky practiced his open-field running over sandbagged, nearly bursting banks. He and his friends told each other they wished the banks would be washed away. "We wanted the flood to pierce thru and drown the world, the horrible adult routine world."[85] Jacky sang ecstatically to himself, *I got a nose, you got a nose*— "crazy" lyrics he thought he had heard on Tommy Dorsey's new radio hit, "I Got a Note."[86]

By the end of the week, Saturday, the climax was past. The river shrank, disaster was averted. The sun came out; Jacky and sister Nin walked under skies "piercingly heartbreakingly blue" across the Moody Street Bridge to the public library. The library was Jacky's Saturday morning home-away-from-home. He lost himself in the "rows of glazed brown books" in the basement children's section. After a night of dreaming about which books to choose, he gave up all thoughts of selection, reached out and opened the nearest volume, electrified by the touch of its "soft used meaty pages covered with avidities of reading."[87]

IN the spring of 1936, Jacky graduated from Bartlett Junior High, a semi-accomplished English scholar. That summer he spotted pins for his father at the Pawtucketville Social Club and spent his spare time running the summer league and the Turf or else hanging around with his usual sporting pals—Roland, G. J., Scotty. The gang now had a new member, Vinny Bergerac, at whose apartment in a tenement "across the river, on Moody Street, in the slums,"[88] the boys gathered regularly; Vinny's mother was off working in the mills. These were the French-Canadian mill workers' lower depths—a neighborhood Jack associated with raucous, screaming poverty. (In *Dr. Sax* he refers to Vinny's "screeching tenement.")[89] The two-story wood building was across the street from the Social Club. Jacky could pick up a dollar spotting pins, then cut across Moody and be with his friends.

At Vinny's they wrestled in the dark parlor, played games of whist for Wings cigarettes, competed at identifying jazz and blues songs on the radio —Jacky would sing along, at the top of his voice, to drown out the background volume of the tenement. Jacky acted big-punky and directed the other boys in plays he made up on the spot. These were not romantic fantasies involving socialites and the sporting world, like the self-dramas in his private newspapers, but crazy comedies based on Frankenstein or Dracula, or depraved westerns. His pals called him "Zagg" or "Memory Babe."

In the fall Jacky matriculated at Lowell High School, entering for the tenth grade. To his surprise and disappointment, he failed to make the varsity football squad. A single practice left him so exhausted he missed his bus home and was unable to eat dinner. He explained to Leo, when he regained his strength, that the high school players were much taller and heavier than he was. Leo exploded Francophonic oaths against the coaches, convinced the "fix was on."

By the middle 1930s, Leo had come to suspect there was some kind of "fix"—commercial hanky-panky, political payoff, or bureaucratic back scratching—behind just about everything that happened in Lowell (which he had taken to calling "Stinktown on the Merrimack").[90] He said so emphatically in private and almost as openly in public, through the political articles he published both in the local Franco-American newspaper and in a maverick paper of his own. The latter he named the *Lowell Spotlight*. The *Spotlight*, Jack later maintained, was designed to "expose graft"[91] in Lowell; one reader of the period remembers it as "mainly a political sheet that criticized everybody." Leo was well known in Lowell political circles as either a "fierce fighter"[92] (to quote a local priest) or a fierce pain-in-the-rear, depending on one's viewpoint. By the time his son entered high school, Leo had more enemies than he had long shots.

Leo's side interests in politics and gambling were hurting business at the print shop. He owed money all over town and had political opponents who, he believed, wanted to see him out of business. The cost of replacing equipment lost in the Great Flood had been sizable. By the middle of 1937, several thousand dollars in debt, he could no longer pay his employees. Spotlight Print, as the business was called, was sold to one of his former customers.

For months Leo sat idle at home, scowling and complaining about the "liberals" and "crooks" he blamed for his decline. At length he found work with a printing company in Andover, New Hamsphire, to which he rode off "downtrodden" on "sooty old trains."[93] On weekends, when he came home from Andover, the family could see that his dreams of independence had been washed away by an encompassing bitterness.

The Kerouacs moved out of the Sarah Avenue house, where the rent could not be met, and into a square, whitewashed wooden tenement building at 736 Moody Street, on the corner of Moody and Riverside, in the heart of the Canuck mill workers' slums.

From the apple-blossom back yard on Sarah to the frightening Moody Street flat—for Jacky, this was the first dramatic sign of how the family had fallen. The fourth-story apartment above a lunch counter (Textile Lunch, "scene of greasy midnight hamburgs") with its "loose-plastered, . . . dim, dusty, strange"[94] back stairs, dark interior corridors, and precarious exterior porches, later became the stage set of many of Kerouac's recurrent nightmares as an adult. These "rueful dreams of rust and loss"[95] often end with Kerouac being followed by a "Shrouded Traveler . . . in wooden tenement hall."[96] The shrouded traveler in such dreams is clearly Leo. The dreams reflect Kerouac's adolescent horror vision of the collapsing of the family dignity, concomitant with Leo's reverberating declension into ghostly impotence and failure.

Gabrielle kept her balance better than the Kerouac men and at this point began to assert a new power in the family. Formerly a quiet adjunct to Leo, she now became the decision maker. While Leo sat nursing a cigar, grumbling and frowning over his fate, Gabrielle not only looked after the family but now also worked daily at a shoe factory, holding strips of leather against a moving steel blade, to pay the rent. At home she calmly placed her favorite chair at the edge of the most perilous porch. Every evening, after her factory shift, she sat out with "one foot inside the house in case the peaked inside porch on top of things and wires with its frail aerial birdlike supports should fall."[97] Jacky, himself terrified of the porches, was amazed at his mother's fearlessness. She was a strong-willed, dogged woman.

JACKY went out for football again in the fall of 1937. When the season began, he was demoted to the junior varsity and never got into a game. The coach told him that, at fifteen, he was too young to play. Leo fumed about "Stinktown" and suggested that "somebody was being paid."[98]

That winter Jacky continued to haunt the Lowell Public Library, sometimes cutting classes to sit in the adult section and read. In the spring he met a Greek boy named Sebastian Sampas ("Sammy"), who was a fel-

Sarah Avenue, Lowell, Kerouac house third from right: "He began acting out games in his 'summer league'... under an apple tree in his backyard." (courtesy Marshall Clements)

1936, graduation from Bartlett Junior High (courtesy David Stivender)

ABOVE: *Lowell High School*
(courtesy Marshall Clements)

TOP RIGHT: *Rear of 736 Moody
Street, Kerouac apartment top
floor left: "Precarious exterior
porches"* (courtesy Marshall
Clements)

RIGHT: *736 Moody Street
fourth-story apartment above
Textile Lunch: " 'Scene of
greasy midnight hamburgs' "*
(courtesy Marshall Clements)

low student at Lowell High and a self-styled poet. Sampas declaimed his own verse for Jacky and encouraged him to read Thomas Wolfe and to cultivate a "Byronic," poetic life style. Jacky recognized in this passionate, sweet-natured Greek boy "the definite mortal idealism which had been imparted me by my holy brother."[99]

Around the time of his meeting with Sammy, and under the influence of their heart-to-heart talks about books and shared reading, Jacky's concept of writing expanded dramatically. His previous literary conception—from what he has recorded of his earliest stories—seems to have involved a mingling of his own fantasy life with the movie heroics of dashing leading men like Cary Grant and Richard Arlen ("I saw enough Richard Arlen movies at the Rialto Theatre till I began thinking that I was Richard Arlen"). In his first "serious" stories from 1936–1937, Jacky appeared in Arlenesque roles like that of "a great mining engineer"[100] in a cabin in the Rocky Mountains, tramping open spaces in jodhpurs by day and drinking the best Scotch with beautiful women by night. The prose style he employed in these cinematically inspired stories was derived from the heroic period in American sports writing, examples of which he studied daily in the newspapers. After entering into literary companionship with Sebastian Sampas, however, Jacky began to take his tone and approach in writing less from movies and newspapers than from books.

From around this time dates the birth of Kerouac's resolve to become a writer. Leo, who had failed in his own independent business venture, was hardly in a mood to encourage his son to strike out on such a risky course. Jack took the matter to a parish priest, Father "Spike" Morissette. "I told him that he should eventually go to New York if he really wanted to be a writer," the priest recalls. "Of course he was too poor. I suggested he should try for a scholarship of some kind; I suppose other people gave him the same idea."[101]

Jack was a good student, but not good enough to qualify for a scholarship on grades alone. He had no "connections," his family exiled to a tenement in a slum. His only hope for escape was football. Earlier, coaches had called him too small or too young. But in 1938 he turned sixteen, and over that summer, while he spotted pins for Leo at the Social Club as usual, his body filled out, with prominent hard knots of muscle in the arms and legs. He began to shave and to comb his black hair in a wave. In photos of the period, his eyes show a look of serious aspiration that had not been there previously. Physically, he had become a man. On the gridiron he would no longer be denied.

Kerouac made the varsity football squad and started the first game of the 1938 football season, substituting as halfback for an injured regular. Back on the bench in the following game, he got into action only for the last two minutes but made two fine runs. In the third game, he ran back a punt for a touchdown, scored two other touchdowns, and gained 182 yards. But in the fourth game, a big test against Manchester, he did not play and the game ended with disappointed Lowell rooters chanting "We Want Kerouac." Coach Frank Leahy of Boston College was said to be scouting Jack Kerouac, but the boy couldn't even get into a game, reported the *Boston American*. Leo ranted about political favoritism. At least one local sports writer agreed with him, hinting in print that "figures don't lie."[102]

In mid-November, however, Jack played brilliantly in a game against Nashua—and then on a freezing Thanksgiving Day, in the annual grudge match against Lawrence, he caught a pass and ran it in for the day's only touchdown. Suddenly, he was a hero in Lowell—and even beyond. Within weeks of the Lawrence game, representatives of both the Boston College coach and Columbia University coach Lou Little were climbing the rickety stairs at 736 Moody to talk to the Kerouacs about their son's future.

Columbia appealed to Gabrielle. In New York, she believed, Ti Jean could become "a big executive in insurance companies." But Leo had strong reasons for favoring Boston College. After being laid off in Andover, he had finally found work in Lowell as a linotypist at a printing firm owned by an Irish family. The firm did all Boston College's printing; indeed, the school was its principal account. There were hints that Leo could lose his job if Jack did not attend Boston College. (His Irish boss had received a postcard from Frank Leahy: "Get Kerouac to Boston College at all costs.") Nevertheless, Gabrielle was adamant. Jean would do better in New York; she didn't care what any Irishman said. There ensued months of "big arguments in the kitchen."[103] Boston College did not get Jack Kerouac.

It was not merely Gabrielle's influence. One of Jack's idols of this period was Damon Runyon, whose widely syndicated column he followed in Hearst's *Boston American*. Jack could see himself preparing for a Runyonesque career at Columbia. "I wanted to dig New York and become a big journalist in the big city beat."[104] His vision of himself as a sort of experienced writer-about-town in the Runyon tradition (race tracks, night clubs,

1938 football season, Kerouac and teammate (courtesy the unspeakable visions of the individual)

Kerouac carries the ball for Lowell High School.

show girls) made it easy to go along with his mother's choice. Besides, Boston College was a Jesuit school. Jack at this point wanted no more of the Jesuits, whose idea of "liberal" education was laced a little too strongly with discipline to suit him.

Jack's choice put his father out of work. The Boston Irish printing family decided Leo lacked loyalty. He was humiliatingly fired. He had been laid off before but never fired; the event did serious damage to what remained of his self-esteem.

F O R the rest of his senior year, Jack attended only as many classes as were required to keep up his B average and spent the rest of his time elsewhere— at the public library, the Rialto Theatre, or in "suicide hookies" with his old gang ("wild parties all day screaming").[105]

That winter he fell in love for the first time, with a seventeen-year-old Irish girl he met on New Year's Eve at a dance at the Rex Ballroom in Lowell. Her name was Mary Carney. Kerouac later described it as love at first sight: at the dance "she descended to me from the upper dark . . . I accepted everything."[106]

At Lowell High, Jack sat by an open home-room window and took part in the furtive flirtations of the senior class. Like the other boys and girls, he passed gossipy notes about romance, "like Date-with-Judies self-communing monologues." Every time he linked eyes briefly with one of the pretty girls in class, however, he was surprised by a new kind of experience. Instead of turning away, the girls were now "looking into my blue windows for romance."[107]

For a while one of these girls, Peggy Coffey, would meet Jack after classes under the big clock outside the low-roofed gymnasium across from the high school and sweet-talk with him there until it was time for him to go inside and suit up for track practice. That was in December. But by January, heart-torn in love and saving himself for Mary Carney, he had given up flirting with Peggy under the clock and had begun to kill the time before track practice by walking the two miles to his home and back. There in the quiet gloom—everybody else in the family was usually off working, even sister Nin now had a job as a bookbinder—he took his "rest hour," eating Ritz crackers and peanut butter over a library chess book at the kitchen table.

After track practice, Jack, the team's best dash man, walked home again, this time with legs aching from the last grueling sprint on the 300-

relays (in that event Lowell was state champ). As soon as supper was over, he escaped to the telephone—and Mary's voice.

It was an exciting but frustrating romance, on both sides. As much as Mary inflamed Jack's emotions, her tentative expressions of desire only confused him and left him in a tangle of guilt, embarrassment, and mistimed passion. His bus trips across Lowell to visit her (she lived in South Lowell, along the Concord) ended abortively. Despite torrents of kissing, Jack "never touched her in the prime focal points . . . I avoided it to please her."[108] On the long, rueful bus ride back to Pawtucketville, he tried to imagine a life in a little house by the railroad tracks, working on the Boston & Maine and having babies with Mary.

As spring approached, Jack and Mary's romance foundered on the boy's ineptness. In love, as in spring baseball practice, Jack was destined to remain "all unknown" because he "kept missing those curve balls." Finally, Mary tired of his balky courtship, consisting mainly of walks and talks by the river near her house, and one night broke a date with him to wander off with another boy in the "sexy sand."[109]

Jack went around for weeks with his "love" and "sick sense" of Mary Carney roaring in his "noisy head" like a "tumultuous sorrow." In a climactic track meet against St. John Prep, he dropped the baton in the 300-relays. He blamed it on his mooning over Mary. He wasn't seeing her any more, but in his mind's eye he still couldn't keep from conjuring up their "little red window house by the railroad tracks."[110]

His destiny, now taking the form of graduation from Lowell High School and a visit with his mother to Coach Lou Little at Columbia, finally rescued the seventeen-year-old Kerouac from these romantic agonies.

COLUMBIA informed the Kerouacs that because Jack had to make up credits in mathematics and French (and because the football coaches wanted him to put on weight), he would spend one year on a football scholarship at Horace Mann School for Boys, an exclusive academy in the Bronx, before moving on to college.

Delighted by the mere prospect of such elevated circumstances, Gabrielle bought her son "big sports jackets and ties and shirts out of her pitiful shoe shop savings that she kept in her corset"[111] and arranged for Jack to board with her stepmother in Brooklyn.

Before his first day at Horace Mann, in the house of Gabrielle's stepmother, Jack spent a wakeful night looking out through the "vast . . . Thomas Wolfe windows" above his "scared bed," trying to convince himself that he was seeing "exactly what Wolfe always saw." That night he self-consciously started a new journal of serious reflections, designed to mark the "completely formal beginning of my search for success."[112]

But "Ti Ma's" in Brooklyn was a two-and-a-half hour subway ride each way from the school at 246th Street in the Bronx. After a few days of the subway-classroom-football grind, Jack was too tired when he got back to Brooklyn at night to do more than eat his supper and climb into bed. His formal success journal was forgotten.

Horace Mann, with its "English"-style hilltop campus, was simply another world. Jack's first expansive vision of the school—involving "Jews and Italians of a new heroism of another sort of Kingdom Lowell"—quickly ran up against the hard facts: "it was a rich school for young Jews,"[113] and he was a déclassé Canuck. "I was just an innocent New England athlete boy thrown into what amounted to an Academy of incunabular Milton Berles,"[114] Kerouac later joked.

His inferior social level was no small part of what Jack learned in his year at Horace Mann. Unlike his classmates he had no comfortable allowance from home. To get spending money he wrote about a half-dozen $2 term papers "for wealthy Jewish kids." At noon he ate his "humble awful lunch among fragrant turkey sandwiches." Occasionally, an overfed "rich kid" would notice and slip him "a delicious fresh chicken sandwich, ah wow."[115]

One "rich kid" started a relationship with Jack by the chicken sandwich method and later took him home to a plush West End Avenue apartment. Subsequently, the same boy introduced Jack to the stories of Ernest Hemingway, whose "pearls of words on a white page giving you an exact picture"[116] quickly made him one of young Kerouac's favorite writers.

Under the spell of Hemingway, Jack tried writing some "little terse short stories in that general style"[117] for the *Horace Mann Quarterly*. One of these, a story called "The Brothers," became his first publication. The story, in fact, owes more to pulp detective style than to Hemingway. Its stilted imitation of a "terse" spoken vernacular comes off sounding pseudo-literary and unintentionally hilarious. ("My reward was a terrific swipe in my mouth, and I fell back with millions of myriad stars swimming in my brain.")[118]

1939 track season, Lowell High School: "Jack, the team's best dash man" (courtesy Allen Ginsberg)

OPPOSITE: *Jack Kerouac at Horace Mann, 1939:* " 'Just an innocent New England athlete boy' "

A S at Lowell High, so too at Horace Mann, Jack learned more outside his classes than in them. He spent school days wandering all over Harlem in his "collegiate" tweeds, studying the streets, or playing hooky to see shows all alone in Times Square. The one event of the school day he was careful not to miss was football practice. There he did everything that was expected of him. His season was a roaring success.

Against St. John Prep, he made a game-saving tackle from his safety position, protecting a 6–0 victory that made Horace Mann the "unofficial champs of prep school football in New York City."[119] In the final game of the 1939 season, against Tome, Jack was a "triple threat"—he got off several astounding quick kicks, threw passes, and made a seventy-two-yard heroic punt return. He and Horace Mann were all over the sports pages.

T H E biggest event of the postseason was Kerouac's first complete sexual experience, which did not involve (although it may have been provoked by) the girl he still thought he was in love with, Mary Carney. He received a letter from Mary on November 7, 1939, in New York, suggesting that they "make up." Jack rushed to Lowell, held her in his arms again, and invited her to the spring prom at Horace Mann. As usual, however, he made no move to relieve her of her virginity. Then he returned to New York, where, as soon as he could muster the courage, he went to a "redbrick hotel" in midtown Manhattan with a "red headed older girl" (" . . . a professional whore")[120] and at last lost his innocence.

In April Mary arrived for the spring prom at Horace Mann. Jack prepared carefully, wanting to make a big impression. The uncle of one of the "rich kids" gave him a suit to wear to the prom. His "chicken sandwich" friend gave him the keys to the West End Avenue flat for the night, so he could put Mary up. Jack took the $2 proceeds of a term paper job and sank it into a shave and sunlamp treatment in the barber shop of the Hotel Pennsylvania. Wanting to look like a handsome, dark hero, he sat extra long under the lamp.

The first thing Mary saw when Jack picked her up at her aunt's apartment was the terrible sunburn. His face was "lobster red." They went on to the prom. Mary wore a pink gown, a rose in her hair. Jack held her tight, but they were "miles apart in social fear."[121] The rich girls at the dance snubbed the Lowell girl.

Mary told Jack his face looked awful. She also told him she would never come to New York to live. "Oh Jacky," she said, "come on home."[122]

But all Jack's parents' hopes for him were at stake. Mary went home to Lowell. He stayed at Horace Mann.

A fellow student in Jack's French class, Seymour Wyse, became his musical guide and tutor. Seymour's favorite band was Count Basie's swing orchestra; he had all Basie's records and played them for Jack. Then he took Jack to the Apollo Theatre in Harlem. They sat in the front row and had their "eyes blasted out by the great Jimmy Lunceford band."[123] They also went together to the Savoy Theatre and heard the great Basie's band, featuring Lester Young. Jack wrote a feature article on the Basie band for the *Horace Mann Record*. In the article he eulogized Lester Young's "enormous store of ideas" and "unequalled"[124] phrasing.

In another article on jazz for the *Record*, Jack defined "real jazz" as "music which has not been pre-arranged—free-for-all ad-lib. It is the outburst of passionate musicians, who pour all their energy into their instruments in the quest of soulful expression and super-improvisation . . . a soloist improvises around the melody of a song . . . in order to express himself with . . . originality and personality." This is an early statement of what came to be the central tenet of Kerouac's "spontaneous" aesthetic: when the artist blows free and deep, then—as Jack put it in the *Record* in the spring of 1940—"It gets you—right down to your shoe-tops!"[125]

Springtime passed on an aching wave of broken-heart thoughts for Mary, drowned in a sea of swing notes. Jack finished the school year with a 92 average, but when graduation rolled around, found that he didn't own the requisite white pants, so he couldn't attend. While the rest of the class received prep school diplomas, he lay in the grass outside the Horace Mann gymnasium, listening to the valedictories and applause, trying to read. The books open before him on the grass were the poems of Walt Whitman and a Hemingway novel.

WHEN Jack went home to Lowell in June, it was to a different house. This time the Kerouacs had rented a flat in a house on Gershom Avenue in Pawtucketville. He spent the summer reading, sleeping as much as possible —making up for all those drowsy early mornings doing homework standing up on the IRT train—and dividing the rest of his time between old Lowell pals. With G. J., Scotty, and Roland, he swam naked at Pine Brook woods, played pool and baseball, drank Saturday night beers. With Sammy Sampas, though, he talked about Wolfe, Saroyan, and modern poetry. They sang

"Begin the Beguine"; Sammy yelled the verses of Byron at Jack; Jack, in turn, enthusiastically summarized his recent reading: Hardy, Thoreau, Dickinson, Whitman.

Sammy's love of William Saroyan caused Jack to take Saroyan's books out of the public library. They came as a revelation to him. Saroyan's "funny tone" and "neat Armenian I don't know what" lifted him "out of the 19th century rut [he] was trying to study."[126]

Another favorite of the summer was Jack London. After reading London's life, Jack concluded that this writer was merely "the greatest man that ever lived," and "the greatest union of the adventurer and the writer."[127] He decided that some day, after college, he would become like London, an artist before the mast, sailing the seven seas under a tropic sun, then writing his adventures on deck under moonlight. Following the example of London, every night in his room he printed in block letters, on long strips of paper, any new word he had come across in his reading. He pinned them up over his bed.

PART TWO

A WILD ROAD

．　　　．　　　．

IN September 1940, some Canuck buddies driving to the World's Fair at Flushing Meadows dropped Jack at Columbia. Along for the ride in the rumble seat came the unemployed head of the Kerouac household. Leo whooped and hollered all the way to 116th Street in Manhattan, his son's new address. But once Jack was moved into the dormitory room and it was time to go, Leo shrunk again sadly, giving the boy tearful final instructions to become an All-American and "make your old man proud."[1]

Columbia had recruited Jack to be a touchdown hero; he would never have arrived there otherwise. That much was clear to him. But then why didn't he get to start at wingback—the position Lou Little had told him he would play—in the first freshman game? He sat on the bench watching the team lose to Rutgers and did not get in until the second half. In the second game, with the varsity coach, Little, watching from the sidelines, Kerouac got a chance to show his patented "jack-off" style of running back kicks; he tore off ninety yards in one punt return. But his next runback was not so successful. He jacked off too hard and broke his leg.

45

Lou Little did not believe Kerouac was seriously injured and forced him to practice for a week on a fractured tibia. When Jack complained of the pain, Little accused him of "putting it on." Jack struggled gamely, but began to suspect Little had "some kind of bug against him."[2]

Finally, X-rays were taken; they vindicated the accused malingerer. His leg swathed in a cast, Kerouac became a big man on campus overnight. Every evening he hobbled on crutches to the Lion's Den, a swank mahogany-paneled college restaurant, where he put away expensive steaks chased by double hot fudge sundaes. His injured status allowed him to run up an epic "training table" tab, never to be paid.

The injury also made time for literary pursuits, which football had pushed aside. Kerouac sat at his dormitory desk smoking his aromatic pipe and exploring the works of Thomas Wolfe. Here, he quickly decided, was a better teacher than Lou Little.

Wolfe's expansive and sonorous prose inspired Jack to essay a similar "rolling style"[3] of his own. He began laboring over "Wolfean" stories and journals—stylistic antecedents of his first novel, *The Town and the City*.

The intensive reading of Wolfe's work had a powerful effect on Kerouac's developing imagination, especially in enlarging his sense of the possible spiritual meanings of geography. Wolfe's passages about the "weathers" of America awakened in Jack a sense of "America as a poem," and made him "want to prowl, and roam, and see the real America that was there and had never been uttered."[4] (Later this interest in "weathers" evolved into Kerouac's poetic concept of the "mute unvoiced road"[5] and his related belief that an American writer ought to give tongue to American places.) As soon as he could get around smoothly, Jack "roamed Wolfe's New York on crutches."[6] Over the next several months, he later boasted, he set a Columbia College record for cutting classes. Instead of the " 'classics' of the course," he studied Times Square movies and Harlem street corners. In November, when Lowell buddies G. J. and Scotty turned up in Hartley Hall to visit "big Columbia Zagg," Jack proudly gave them a Wolfe's tour of Lower Manhattan, "stepping smartly with big pipe."[7]

Before throwing his crutches away, he made the acquaintance of one out-of-town visitor who was to figure prominently in his later life. This was a girl from Grosse Pointe, Michigan, named Edie Parker. Staying at her grandmother's home near the Columbia campus, Edie was studying art and dating a former Horace Mann classmate of Kerouac's, Henri Cru. It appears that Cru introduced her to Jack around this time. Not long afterward, she and Kerouac began going out together.

His leg completely healed, Jack went to Lowell for the holidays, paid the customary visits to Mary Carney, had long talks about his football prospects with his father in the "eager kitchen,"[8] got drunk on port wine with G. J. under Gabrielle's Christmas tree—and then hurried back to the greater world of New York, where he now felt more "at home."

THE spring of 1941 Jack devoted largely to his goal of becoming a successful New York journalist–great writer. Aside from toiling away at his own stories, plays, poems, and journals, he ran around the campus interviewing track coaches for college newspaper sports columns, wrote term papers for former "rich kid" connections at Horace Mann, and collaborated with ex-classmate Seymour Wyse on earnest jazz articles ("Lester Young Is Ten Years Ahead Of His Time").

Back on Gershom Avenue in Lowell for the summer, he ignored the chemistry books he was supposed to be studying (having failed that course, he had been told to make it up), and spent his time instead smooching under apple trees with his second-string girlfriend, Peggy Coffey, or hitching to Boston with Sammy Sampas, where they lounged on the Common, listening approvingly to radical orators.

Leo had been drudging off on dusty trains to temporary linotypist jobs in Andover, Meriden, and Boston. In August he secured what seemed to be a steadier position in New Haven. The family dutifully packed up for the move. But New Haven was a disappointment. Once they arrived, Leo seemed distracted, drained of ambition and confidence. He found an apartment in that city's black ghetto, but when Gabrielle saw it, she ordered him to search further. The best he could do was a summer cottage on the ocean at West Haven that would be habitable only for a few more months. By September Jack was happy to have an excuse to leave.

He headed straight to Baker Field and early football drills, where his season immediately began to go wrong. After getting bawled out for showing up a day late, he was told he wasn't going to work out with the first-string varsity backfield. In practice Lou Little made him attempt the tricky "KT-79 reverse deception," Little's pet play. When Jack muddled it, Little told him in front of the whole squad that he wasn't such a "hot runner" after all—"with your big legs . . . I'm going to make you a lineman."

Jack Kerouac and sister, Caroline, Lowell, c. 1940

Kerouac was silently furious: "as if I'd joined football for 'deception' for God's sake."[9]

For months Jack had daydreamed of having a big game against Columbia's rival, Army—and especially against a young athlete who had once slighted him in a shower room episode when they were both at Lowell High and who now was a star at West Point. Leo, who viewed life as a constant vendetta, had encouraged this "revenge" fantasy. Now Jack saw that after all the hard weeks of practice that lay ahead, he probably would not even get into the Army game. This realization prompted what he later called "the most important decision of my life so far."[10] He packed all his pipes, tweeds, and books into a large suitcase and walked out—right past the training table where the coaches were sitting. Lou Little asked him where he thought he was going. Jack mumbled something about taking his dirty laundry over to Brooklyn.

Clinging to a strap on a subway headed downtown, Jack told himself to "go into the American night, the Thomas Wolfe darkness, the hell with these bigshot gangster football coaches, go after being an American writer, tell the truth, don't be pushed around."[11]

He bought a ticket on a bus headed for Thomas Wolfe's south, rode as far as Washington, D.C., then got off, "joyed like a maniac" just to be able to look at "real southern leaves." He was "on the road for the first time."[12] After a night in a flophouse, he got back on the bus, rode to New York, and from there went to rejoin his family in West Haven.

Kerouac's fall from the Ivy League back into the working-class life was dramatic and sudden. Leo could provide no cushion. Jack got a job in a rubber plant in New Haven. He spent a morning making tires. Visions of proletarian joy took mere hours to dispel. At noon he walked out and did not come back. Leo, who had to walk a mile to work at a printing plant while Gabrielle waited on tables at a cafeteria, told him that night to go back to New York. Become a football star, Leo told him, it's your only chance. Jack replied that he was going to be a great writer. "Writer," Leo sneered. "It's Hugo, Balzac . . . not your fancypants Saroyan with his fancy titles."[13]

Jack got a tip from a former Lowell pal about a gas station job in Hartford. For the first time, he left the family to support himself by his labors. He found a cheap rooming house on Main Street in Hartford and rented his first "room of my own."[14] In the morning he "went off to work in oily coveralls," pumped gas, changed tires, and "brooded in the lubrication pit all day."[15] At night he sat down at his small desk under a window facing a bare stone wall and banged out short stories on a rented Underwood typewriter. The stories were written in "the Saroyan–Hemingway–Wolfe style as best I could figure it at age nineteen."[16] The collection he called "Atop an Underwood." None of these stories survive.

Finally, the week after Thanksgiving, he got the news that his parents were going back to Lowell. He threw away his overalls, went to West Haven to help the family pack their belongings on a truck, then rode on top of it all with the family dog back to his home town.

The Kerouacs occupied a first-floor apartment in a two-family flat on Crawford Street in Pawtucketville. Futureless and unemployed, Jack sat at the familiar green desk of his childhood, puffing his pipes, forlornly making fountain-pen entries in a new journal, and reading Dostoevsky's *Notes from the Underground*. Nurturing Dostoevskian ecstatic glooms, he trudged on snowy Moody Street past the brick walls of the mills and sensed "something awful that had not been in Lowell before."[17] That something awful was himself, come home to roost on his "failure," as if in conscious imitation of his father.

O N the last day of the first week of December 1941, Jack went to the Royal Theatre to see Orson Welles's *Citizen Kane*. When he stepped out into the icy street afterward, newsboys were hawking papers with a headline that read JAPS BOMB PEARL HARBOR.

He signed up for a Navy V-2 program that would place him in the Navy Air Force—if, that is, he could qualify for flying school. While waiting for the qualifying exam, Jack went to see the owner of the *Lowell Sun* about a temporary position as a delivery boy and was hired instead as a sports reporter at $15 a week.

The job accidentally occasioned Kerouac's first experiment in extended fiction. By noon he had usually cranked out his daily assignments. Afternoons he spent pounding away on his sports desk typewriter at an autobiographical prose work, "Vanity of Duluoz." (He never completed this work but revived the title for another book twenty-five years later.) Kerouac conceived this writing as an imitation of *Ulysses*—"an attempt to delineate all of Lowell as Joyce had done for Dublin."[18] Excerpts he later quoted, however, make the work sound much less like *Ulysses* than a boyish imitation of Joyce's earlier study of Catholic childhood, *A Portrait of the Artist as a Young Man*.

AFTER about three months on the *Sun*, Jack became convinced that the routine of the sports desk was never going to bring him in touch with the Wolfean "weathers" of America. One day in March 1942, he was told by the sports editor to interview the Textile Institute baseball coach. Considering the assignment beneath his dignity as an artist, he declined, forfeiting his job. Leo blew up. Jack countered by proposing to reenter Columbia as a sophomore in the Naval Reserve; meanwhile he would "study America." "Study mongrel America," Leo snorted. "Do you think you can do what you feel like all your life?"[19]

Jack packed a bag and strode downtown to the bus station. On the way he decided he was headed for Washington, D.C., the doorway to Thomas Wolfe country.

His pal G. J. was doing government construction work in Arlington, Virginia, and had promised Jack a job. Because he had no money for a room of his own, Jack shared G. J.'s double bed and went to work on the Pentagon construction project as a sheet metal worker. It was the hardest physical labor he had ever done. Jack sensed the "gigantic Gulliver-structure" he and the other men were putting up with "their Lilliputian cranes" was a "new Gethsemane."[20]

Kerouac's Washington adventure lasted about two months. He quit the construction job and toiled briefly as a short-order cook and soda jerk at a lunch cart. He moved in for a while with a brunette from Georgia who had introduced herself by slipping him a porno deck at the lunch cart. Finally, he took a bus back to Lowell because he couldn't support himself. Within a week or two, he was off again on several hitchhiking jaunts to Boston, during which, in a series of impulsive gestures probably unrivaled in recruitment history, he seems to have joined every available branch of the military service.

First, he applied for and obtained a U.S. Coast Guard sailing pass. Shortly afterward he thumbed to Boston again, passed the U.S. Marine Corps physical and mental exams, and was sworn into the Marines. Since he had already been accepted in a Naval Reserve program, this technically made him a member of three service branches at once. The evening of the Marine physical, he got drunk in a seaman's bar and passed out; when he revived, some sailors invited him along to the National Maritime Union Hall. He went, and, forgetting about the Marines, took a job as a scullion on the S.S. *Dorchester*, bound for Greenland.

After another terrible binge that left him unconscious, vomit-caked, and wrapped around the toilet bowl of a Scollay Square saloon, Jack was on board the *Dorchester* when it finally raised anchor on July 18, 1942. With his little black seaman's bag—"packed with rags and a collection of classical literature"[21]—he stood on deck and watched the Boston Merchant Miner's Dock slip away.

The *Dorchester* carried 500 Defense Department construction workers and was traveling in a convoy through waters thick with German submarines. Moving in the same convoy, the *Dorchester*'s sister ship, S.S. *Chatham*, was sunk by a sub in the dark waters off Greenland. One thousand men were lost. (The same fate would later befall the *Dorchester*—after Jack had left the ship.)

Kerouac later had two distinct and conflicting ways of writing and talking about his experience on the *Dorchester* (and his merchant marine experiences in general). The first was to insist that it had been a heroic, exciting adventure. This is expressed, for instance, in his boast to Lowell writer Charles Jarvis that he had "sailed the North Atlantic just like Bogey"[22] in *Action in the North Atlantic. The Town and the City* treats the *Dorchester* episode in roughly the same tone. In *Vanity of Duluoz*, however, Kerouac hints that he was miserable for much of the voyage—a "slave" on a "prison ship." In the *Book of Dreams* he admits that "rough seamen who saw my child's soul in a grown up body broke my spirit."[23] And in drunken conversation with a Lowell acquaintance, he even went so far as to reveal he had been "corn holed by a nasty lecherous fatso cook who deflowered me."[24]

Kerouac's journal of the Greenland trip, preserved in *Vanity of Duluoz*, casts him as the lonely, sensitive artist thrust into the company of rude toughs. "I am trying hard to be sincere ... being misunderstood is like being the hero in the movies."[25] When he fries bacon for 500 men, Kerouac imagines himself in the shoes of the cook on a German sub, and finds he harbors nothing but pity in his heart for both his own and the German boy's soul, which makes him "the only real pacifist in the world."[26]

At last the coast of Greenland neared. Jack saw Eskimos in kayaks drifting past the ship; he thought of Thomas Wolfe's line about "morning and new lands."[27] When the *Dorchester* dropped anchor in a fjord, Jack tossed his old Horace Mann football jersey over the side to an Eskimo in a kayak, who handed up the exchange gift of a bone-jointed harpoon.

But the unloading of men and equipment took long, tedious weeks.

Minus its load, the *Dorchester* rolled in heavy seas on its cold mid-September return trip. Once again Kerouac felt trapped inside a "steel jail."[28] During one bad storm, he went up on deck to avoid a big pillow fight among the crew members and practiced Lou Little's halfback drills. For months he had seen nothing but hard work with skillet, mop, and bucket. The regimentation of sea life was making the regimentation of football look better and better.

A night's shore leave in Nova Scotia was the high point of Kerouac's trip, mainly because there were dry, flat saloon floors to stand on. He drank his way through the "cold dusk" to the "cold dog dawn" and, sometime in between, heard "over the radio from wartime America the faint voice of Dinah Shore singing . . . Joy welled up in my heart and exploded fuming into the night."[29]

Jack's exuberant Nova Scotia bender extended unchecked into a second day. Arrested by military police, he was fined two days' pay ($5.50) for going AWOL in a foreign port. Still, at the dock in Boston he was paid $800—the most money he had ever seen at one time, let alone earned.

AT home Jack opened a telegram from Lou Little, inviting him back to Columbia. The old dream of All-American glory beckoned again in a new way; Jack had seen the other side. He gave his mother most of his $800 earnings, telling her to keep $300 for family expenses, and to send him the other $500 in installments. Using Gabrielle—or "Mémêre," as he called her—as a bank for his meager savings was to become a habit with Jack, who always preferred penury to managing his own money.

Two days after stepping off the *Dorchester*, Kerouac was back in New York on the practice field, running through Lou Little's KT-79 reverse. Once again he had trouble getting the hang of the deception maneuver on which the play depended—and quickly found himself on the second string.

The big Army game was coming up. To complicate matters, Leo paid a visit to the campus. He went to the coach's office and buttonholed Little, bringing up two things that had been concerning him for some time. The first was a linotypist job in New York, which Leo claimed he had been promised as part of the coach's recruitment package and which had never materialized. The second was his son's perennial second-string status. According to Jack's later account, Leo accused Lou Little of being a "sneaky long-nosed finagler." Little told Leo that Jack "wasn't ready" to start in the Army game. "Who says he's not ready?" barked Leo. "I say he's ready."[30]

Although the cigar-chomping Leo came stomping out of Little's office, ordering his son to "come on home, these wops are cheating you and me both,"[31] Jack stayed behind for the Army game. Leo's visit hadn't helped; the younger Kerouac didn't get in for a single play.

On the Monday afternoon following the Army game, an autumnal snow flurry blew in. Jack lay in his dormitory room reading books and listening to his favorite symphony, Beethoven's Fifth, on the radio. Glancing out the window at the snow coming down, he knew the practice field would be cold, dank, and muddy. Beethoven and the weather collaborated to help him arrive at an inevitable decision. He didn't go to practice that afternoon—or ever again.

Ten years later, in an attic in San Francisco, Kerouac told his soul mate, Neal Cassady, about the afternoon he had selected writing as his calling in life. "I said to myself 'Scrimmage my ass . . . I'm gonna sit here in this room and dig Beethoven, I'm gonna write noble words,' *you* know— that's the way I quit football (laughing) nothing more logical or less . . . logical."[32]

Sometimes, in low moods, Jack was to look back to this point in his life and say, "somewhere I took the wrong road." It was a time when he had "left [football] disgusting everyone, for to go to heaven deviously I had to cut and dodge institutions, plans, formalities and be silly. . . ."[33]

He knew that quitting football would mean giving up his scholarship. (It was, in fact, quickly withdrawn, and he was handed instead a sizable dining hall bill.) With a sense of self-drama suitable to the occasion, he first went to the room of a dormitory friend, where he got drunk; then he cut across the street to the house where Edie Parker, the girl from Grosse Pointe, was living with her grandmother. Edie and Jack had been seeing a lot of each other. Now they celebrated his defection from organized athletics by making love on a sofa.

Over the next two months or so, Jack shared an apartment with Edie, somewhere near the campus. During this time she seems to have become pregnant and to have had an abortion. "He was very angry about this,"[34] she has said; but Kerouac makes no mention of the pregnancy or abortion in his own "legend" of his life. He *does* say simply that around this time he and Edie began sharing living circumstances, but Edie was "having an affair with another seaman who shoved her thru the turnstiles to save a nickel"[35] and this was complicating their relationship. By Christmas he had had enough of the city. He was now due to be called by the navy.

Once at home he came down with German measles, delaying his induction another month. Alone on Crawford Avenue he returned to his quest for "noble words." At his old green desk he hand printed a "novel" of shipboard life, begun on the *Dorchester*, called "The Sea Is My Brother." ("A dreary attempt at Naturalism with a sea background,"[36] he later termed this work.) The month was a revisitation of the imaginative sanctity of childhood. "I'm alone in the house again with my handprint pencil and pure again."[37]

In January, though, recovered from the measles and still waiting to take a naval air force exam, he did something that forced him to see how much he had changed. He went to see Mary Carney and, playing the experienced man of the world, tried to have sex with her. He was tense and drunk; she fought him off, then laughed in his face. "You look thinner but you're not a kid any more," Mary told him. "You're a kid but you look . . . cold hearted er sumpin . . ."[38]

EARLY in 1943 Jack was inducted into the navy in Boston, but he failed the naval air force exam which he had expected to land him in an officer training program. He was dropped from the flying school class and sent instead to naval boot camp at Newport, Rhode Island. There, ironically, on a routine intelligence test he scored what he later boasted was "the highest I.Q. intelligence rating in the history of frigging Newport R.I. Naval Base."[39] But obedience, not intelligence, was asked of Jack at Newport. He immediately became a "discipline problem."

The sullen, independent streak in Jack's nature, the Canuck recalcitrance, made it hard for him to take orders—especially ones that made no sense to him. He resented being told not to smoke before breakfast; he did not see why he should scrub a deck clean enough to fry an egg on it; he did not like being told to "shut up" by an officer-dentist who was hurting him. Finally, he dropped his weapon in the middle of a drill session and walked off to the library to resume his self-education.

Kerouac's rejection of military authority earned him an ambulance trip to the psychiatric ward of the base hospital. There he complained to doctors of persistent headaches. After checking his I.Q. scores, military intelligence officers interrogated him about possible political motives. But Jack was no antiwar activist. He just wanted *out*, so he could get on with becoming a writer. To explain this to the naval doctors at Newport, he showed them his hand-printed work-in-progress, "The Sea Is My Brother."

The doctors, Kerouac later said, stroked their Vandyke beards and studied his eyes as though he were a madman.

His father, he proudly recalls in *Vanity of Duluoz*, showed up at Newport, "fat, puffing on cigar, pushing admirals aside." Predictably, Leo was convinced he could smell an anti-Kerouac conspiracy in the works. "Good boy," he told his son, "tell that goddamn Roosevelt and his ugly wife where to get off! This is a war for the Marxist Communist Jews and you are a victim of the whole plot."[40]

Sammy Sampas came to see him, but he too soon fell into the growing pool of loss in the center of Jack's life—he didn't survive the Allied landing at Anzio. Jack himself was now sinking deeper and deeper into a kind of deliberate surrender: a giving up forever of his success dream. In April, after he and a "psychopathic maniac"[41] named Big Slim, who had befriended him, were caught stealing some butter knives to use in an escape attempt, the navy shunted him off to another psychiatric hospital, in Bethesda, Maryland.

At Bethesda Kerouac was filed with the hard cases—in a "nut ward with guys howling like coyotes in the mid of night." More military doctors questioned him. He doggedly insisted that he was not a dangerous lunatic but "only old Samuel Johnson," a "man of independence," and a "coward intellectual." He told the doctors that he simply could not live by naval discipline: "I'm too much of a nut and a man of letters."[42] Days and weeks went by; Jack lost track of time.

He had been originally diagnosed as a victim of dementia praecox; this diagnosis was eventually changed to "schizoid tendencies,"[43] and in June 1943 he was finally released from the navy. Officially, it was an honorable discharge with indifferent character, on psychiatric grounds. Unofficially, the verdict of authority was that this Jean-Louis Kerouac was one cog that would fit in nobody's wheel. The machinery had ejected him.

AT this point in his life, Kerouac later said, the "story pivots."[44] Certainly, his navy discharge troubled him for the rest of his life. At the time he seems to have been too shaken to understand what had happened to him. The main thing was that his unhappy fling with Uncle Sam was over. Acting on instinct as usual, he followed the rote pilot in his heart that told him to go home.

By June 1943 Gabrielle and Leo had moved to Ozone Park, Long Island. Multiple anxieties gripped Jack as he rode the el out to Ozone

Park for the first time. Should he have buckled down, tackled boot camp, and "kept going at sea," if only to please his father? Had he grown "old" in the hospital? Worst of all, he had developed some "warts on [his] cock." Were these caused by too much masturbation at Bethesda? A half-conscious memory of the frightening belief, inculcated in his childhood by the Jesuit Brothers, that "self-abuse" causes physical and mental damage, now made him suspect that he might have "syphilis."[45]

The Kerouacs' new apartment was above a drugstore on Cross Bay Boulevard in Ozone Park. To Jack it couldn't but look familiar. His old green desk and all his other belongings of premadhouse days were there. Gabrielle, that paragon of Canuck parsimony, never threw anything out.

Leo was working in the city, downtown on Canal Street, where he once again ran a linotype machine; Gabrielle had a job at a shoe factory in Brooklyn. With both of them on salary and the children gone, the Kerouacs were having an easier time making ends meet. They went out on Saturday nights; Gabrielle even placed Leo's bets at the local bookie. Jack had not seen them getting along so well for years. "It was the happiest time of their entire married life"[46] he later said.

But even his family's warmth failed to save Jack from twisting with guilt. In bed at Ozone Park, he "thrashed in a thousand 21-year-old agonies."[47] After a few such nights, he slung his black seaman's bag over his shoulder, went into New York to the Maritime Union Hall, and signed on as an ordinary seaman aboard the S.S. *George Weems*, bound for Liverpool.

Before sailing, Jack spent several days running around the New York area trying to find Edie Parker. On the Columbia campus he learned that she had gone for the summer to Asbury Park, New Jersey, so he hitchhiked there and found her at her family's four-story seashore mansion. Edie had a bad sunburn, but she was happy to see him again. They walked along the Boardwalk, and when they passed a drugstore, Jack ducked in and bought some Noxzema for her—and also some condoms for himself. Later, at the beach, Edie put her earrings and necklace on Jack for the benefit of her girlfriends, who thought he looked "pagan" and "like a gypsy."[48]

The visit to Edie evidently resolved Jack's anxieties about his wart problem. They agreed to live together when he returned from the sea. Jack sailed for England.

THE *Weems* advertised itself as a death ship by flying the red dynamite flag; its cargo was 500-pound bombs. The obvious danger of the October

1943 crossing hardly concerned Jack. His accounts of the trip comment only obliquely on the potential hazards—the submarine attacks on the return voyage are passed over in a few words. But many other such ships traveling that route at that time never reached port.

The trip would have gone smoothly had not Jack run afoul of the ship's chief mate, "a German with a big scar down his cheek and very mean." Kerouac believed this man "hated [his] guts."[49] Even after Jack contributed to the safety of the whole crew by spotting a mine at sea during his watch duty, the mate continued to make life difficult for him. To escape, Jack fled to his bunk, where, in between snoozes and watches, he worked through Galsworthy's *Forsyte Saga*, which he had brought along as a study guide to England. It gave him "an idea about sagas, or legends, novels connecting into one grand tale."[50]

Storms and submarines tracked the return crossing; Jack kept to himself, and said no more to his shipmates than he had on the trip out—which was practically nothing. But as soon as the *Weems* hit Brooklyn and beer was brought on board, they had a look at another, more voluble Kerouac. Jack got paid, then drunk, then loud, and finally yelled that he was going to "see [his] baby."[51]

He rushed off in the rain and took a subway uptown to 421 West 118th Street, where Edie Parker was sharing an apartment with a woman named Joan Vollmer Adams. Edie came to the door in shorts, told him she thought she had seen the last of him, but then "melted" into a radiant smile. Jack, the sailor home from the sea, dropped his leather jacket over the back of a chair and stayed.

Jack wanted to spend time in New York, but he didn't want to offend his mother—nor to forsake his peaceful room at home. He decided to commute back and forth between 118th Street and Long Island, writing as much as possible in both places.

Through the winter of 1943–1944, he slept mostly at 118th Street. Edie Parker recalls their apartment life together: "We read, took apart the Salem witch-trials in our rap-sessions. We read *Finnegans Wake* together. Jack always figured out the horses in the newspapers. He did this every day—another of his 'self' games. He never bet on the horses. His father, Leo, always did and lost. Jack's horses won—Leo never knew." Edie also recalls that she and Jack began to put their "dreams down on paper and talk about them as soon as we woke up."[52]

In the spring of 1944, Jack and Edie went together to Grosse Pointe, where he met her aunt and widowed father. To Kerouac this trip was a first curious tasting of midwestern upper-class life, a world of rich, blank, "American" kids that Jack had seen only in movies. "I listened to the revelry"—Kerouac wrote in *Vanity of Duluoz*, that document of youth's lost hopes—"and shure did love America AS America in those days."[53]

In May he returned east, apparently ahead of Edie, and there, out of money, began to look for work on a ship. Nothing was available in New York, so on impulse he hopped a bus to New Orleans—but found no ship job there. On the way back to New York, he stopped in Asheville to visit the home of Thomas Wolfe, where he got drunk with "Tom Wolfe's drunken older brother." The whole trip had sprung from "a nutty subliminal desire to see the South."[54] But back in Ozone Park, Gabrielle didn't see the point and was unhappy with her son's new vagabond habits.

On 118th Street Jack got a warmer reception from Edie, who came in from her art class and "whooped" at the sight of his leather jacket on the back of her chair. That night they made love to the drumming of rain on the roof—and then "in start coming the characters of my future life."[55]

THESE new characters—"the Bohemian kids from the neighborhood"[56]— did more than break up the peace of Jack and Edie's ménage. They dropped on Kerouac's shoulders the mantle of laureate: he would be the formal scribe of their whole "generation."

During Jack's latest voyage, Edie had encountered Lucien Carr in the West End Bar, where—she told Jack—this blonde, beautiful young Columbia freshman had been "talkin like Rimbaud."[57] Lucien and his equally beautiful, blonde Westport girlfriend, Celine Young, began using the sofa and shower in the 118th Street apartment. Also, it seems, they were hiding out from David Kammerer, a red-haired, bearded, thirtyish homosexual who was a former scoutmaster of Carr's; Kammerer had been doggedly pursuing Lucien from school to school around the country. (Lucien and others called Kammerer "Swinburne," after the masochistic English poet.)

Jack's first impression of Carr was of a "mischievous little prick."[58] But soon afterward he and Lucien spent an evening getting drunk together in the West End and Lucien rolled him down Upper Broadway inside a barrel—a prank that delighted them both and inaugurated their long friendship.

Within days of Jack's first meetings with Carr, a Columbia friend of

Jack, Nin, Gabrielle, Leo—the Kerouacs on Times Square, June 1943: "They went out on Saturday nights."

Hal Chase, Kerouac, Allen Ginsberg, William Burroughs, Riverside Drive, New York, 1944: " 'The Bohemian kids from the neighborhood' " (courtesy Allen Ginsberg)

Lucien's named Allen Ginsberg turned up. Ginsberg had decided to check out for himself this "workingman proletarian Jack London redneck"[59] who claimed to be a writer.

Jack had risen late, as usual, and was drowsily awaiting his breakfast when the skinny, dark-eyed, New Jersey Jewish boy in horn rims stepped cautiously through the door. The first thing Jack noticed was Allen's extreme youth and intense, slightly ludicrous expression: "sixteen years old with his ears sticking out."[60] Ginsberg was carrying an armload of books. Kerouac sprawled in a chair while they discussed Dostoevsky and the plight of genius. Finally, Jack disdainfully interrupted and hollered to Edie, "Aw, where's my food."[61]

"I didn't like him anyway,"[62] Kerouac later said of this disappointing encounter. But since Lucien liked Allen, Jack subsequently tried to be more tolerant, and soon there was a rapprochement.

Ginsberg, for his part, was by this time floating in what he later described as a state of "erotic *schwärmerei*" and believed he was simultaneously "in love" with Jack, Lucien, and various other people around campus. Kerouac, however, evidently "didn't want to hear" about these erotic feelings, so Ginsberg "had to find another way of expressing them." As he tells the story, the occasion to do so occurred a month or so after their first meeting, when Kerouac helped him move some belongings out of a dormitory room. A long, sincere conversation ensued, which had the effect Allen desired: they became close friends. "I suddenly realized that my own soul and his were akin," Ginsberg recalls, "and that if I actually confessed the secret tendernesses of my soul he would understand nakedly."[63]

Lucien Carr introduced Jack to his "Swinburne," David Kammerer, in the West End Bar. Shortly thereafter, one day when Carr and Edie were off at a life drawing class, Kammerer came by the 118th Street place with a man who wanted to talk to Jack about getting into the merchant marine. The man was William (Bill) Burroughs. He knew Carr and Kammerer from St. Louis; they all came from wealthy families in that city.

Jack, who had been showering, came to the door in a towel and found himself face to face with Kammerer and his companion, a "tall . . . strange . . . patrician thinlipped . . . fella in a seersucker jacket." The visitor snuffled through his nose, "blue eyes saying nothing behind steel rims and glass," and explained to Jack that after trying his hand at bartending and exterminating, he was now considering the sea. He asked a series of "dull questions about how to get sea papers." Sitting there, Jack tried to figure this "wispy" stranger's angle. His immediate supposition was that Burroughs simply "pictured [him as] a merchant seaman who would belong in the merchant seaman category."[64]

Once he got past Jack's wall of "Canuck doubt," Burroughs proved to be a valuable friend and teacher. But Kerouac's first question to himself, upon realizing that Burroughs and the other members of this "St. Louis School" were actually interested in him as a person, was *Why?* He could see that "this handful of rich sharp spirits," as he later termed them, were "the most evil and intelligent buncha bastards and shits"[65] he had ever run into. What then made them pay any attention to Ti Jean?

"Their style was dry, new to me, mine had been the misty-nebulous New England idealist style," Kerouac later recalled. Beneath the misty idealism, however, there was something else in Jack, an underlying quality that he imagined to be his one "saving grace" to his new friends. This was a certain built-in "materialistic Canuck taciturn cold skepticism all the picked-up Idealism in the world of books couldn't hide."[66]

T H E events of the summer of 1944 demonstrated to Kerouac the potential hazards of getting mixed up with the kind of "terrible intelligence and style" his new friends possessed. He later identified this time with a Rimbaud prose poem favored by the group, *A Season in Hell.* Indeed, for him the summer was a period of "playing with fire"—the beginning of his descent into a medium that both repelled and fascinated him.

The fascination was immediate and powerful. These "spoiled rich kids," as Jack thought them, had an ability to be *deliberately perverse* that he had never before encountered. It amazed him. On his first visit to Bill Burroughs' Village apartment, Carr chewed up a beer glass, David Kammerer (who followed Lucien in everything) did the same, and then Burroughs, the thoughtful host, served a whole plateful of razor blades. Another time Jack saw Lucien flip an entire plate of veal parmesan onto the floor in a restaurant. This type of thing Carr described as an *acte gratuit.* The gratuitous act, as presented in *The Counterfeiters*—André Gide's tale of a motiveless, dispassionate murder committed by schoolboys —was much admired by the St. Louis School.

Burroughs introduced Jack to a sort of grifter's realism picked up from a long study of the underworld. Burroughs' only religion was that of "fact." Among other recommended books, Bill gave Jack a copy of the Charles Atkinson translation of Oswald Spengler's *The Decline of the West*—a work of which Kerouac made extensive use in his later writings. Burroughs' unemotional, "factualist" attitude sometimes went too far for Jack, though. For instance, Burroughs once told him he ought to capitalize on his service experience by wearing a merchant seaman's uniform, gaining "soft entry to things" during wartime. Jack demurred, calling the proposition "finkish." Bill countered, "It's a finkish world."[67]

In August Carr got fed up with being tracked by his former scout-master: the pursuit was no longer funny. He told Jack that he *had* to get away. Kerouac, in turn, confessed that Edie had eyes to marry—and much as he liked her, that was getting too close for comfort. Lucien and Jack had just seen the French film *Grand Illusion*. Soon they had hatched a flamboyant plan to imitate the escaped prisoners' flight to Paris. They would land at the Allied "second front" in France, Lucien proposed, stroll on to Montmartre, and "find symbols saturated in the gutters."[68]

Tailed by David Kammerer, they hung around the Maritime Union Hall for a few days, ship hunting unsuccessfully—until Kerouac mentioned he had been on the now-lost *Dorchester*. This got them instant preferment for union cards.

Their union call came swiftly. After frantic goodbyes and picture taking with their girlfriends, they rushed down to Brooklyn to board the S.S. *Robert Hayes*, a liberty ship bound for the "second front." But at the dock the plan collapsed. They immediately got into an altercation with the ship's chief mate and were thrown off the *Hayes* before sailing.

The two young men returned in dejection and embarrassment to their campus neighborhood. After a few beers at the West End Bar, Jack left to go back to the 118th Street apartment. On his way he bumped into Kammerer, who was looking for Lucien. Jack directed him to the West End. A few hours later on the grassy riverside, Kammerer was stabbed to death with a boy scout knife by Carr, who deposited the corpse in the Hudson and then ran to find help.

He went first to see Burroughs, who told him to turn himself in and plead self-defense. Then he went to 118th Street and roused Jack, who accompanied him in burying the dead man's glasses and dropping the bloody boy scout knife down a sewer grate.

After spending the day wandering around the city, imagining themselves as characters in an exotic movie, the excitement wore off; Jack and
Lucien both sensed the party was over. Lucien headed off to see his rich
aunt, then the police. Jack returned to 118th Street to catch up on his
sleep, but he was soon awakened again—this time by city detectives, who
arrested him as a material witness (for not turning in his guilty friend) and
accessory after the fact (for helping get rid of the weapon) in the killing of
David Kammerer.

Jack spent the rest of the night tossing and turning on a hard board
in a windowless cell at a local precinct lockup. In the morning he was driven
downtown to the district attorney's office, where he was told the case against
them hinged on whether Lucien, who had made a self-defense plea—alleging
that Kammerer had attacked him—was a homosexual.

Waiting in the district attorney's office, Jack was shown two New York
newspapers, one headlining the killing as an "Honor Slaying," the other
displaying a photo of Lucien being escorted by policemen into the Tombs
with two books under his arm (the caption said they were *A Season in Hell*
by Rimbaud and *A Vision* by "William Butler Keats").[69]

Jack's testimony to the district attorney was sufficient to free him of
the accessory charge (the murder charge against Lucien would eventually
be reduced to manslaughter) ; but, after a courtroom arraignment, he had
to go back behind bars as a material witness. (Burroughs, also a material
witness, had already been whisked out of town on $5,000 bail by his fam-
ily.) Jack was taken to the Bronx jail and there legally detained in company with the rest of the city's material witnesses to homicide, many of
them crime syndicate veterans.

During his first night in the "Bronx Opera House," Kerouac shivered
under a light blanket, desolately trying to read *Brave New World*. The next
day he got up the nerve to phone his father (who was now employed in a
downtown printing plant) and ask him to post a $100 bail bond. Leo blew
up, told Jack "No [Kerouac] ever got involved in a murder,"[70] and refused
him the money.

Jack's next week in the Bronx jail was the worst in his young life. One
day he was driven to Bellevue morgue in the rain to identify the bloated
corpse of Kammerer. The sight of the corpse brought all his childhood
terror of death rushing into grim focus. Back in the Bronx jail, his cell was
visited by various Mafia tough guys. Jack was sure they were trying to coax
out of him some fatal admission about the "slaying." Finally, he cracked,

called Edie, and made a deal. If she would raise his bond, he would marry her.

The Kammerer killing occurred on August 14. On August 22, the day Paris was liberated, Kerouac and Edie were married by a city magistrate on Chambers Street, with a detective as best man. Jack was still only on half-day loan from jail; Edie's family had not yet wired the bond money.

A week later the money came from Michigan and Jack was sprung. The newlyweds fled the steaming city, bound for a honeymoon in the Great Midwest.

JACK stayed at Edie's house in Grosse Pointe until he had saved enough to pay back her family. He got a night job at a Detroit ball-bearing factory and by day undertook an annotated program of self-instruction in American literary criticism. By the end of September, he had repaid his debt. He told his wife of five weeks that he was going to New York to ship out. Her father fixed him up with a free ride on a truck, and off he went.

While Jack was away, Lucien Carr had pleaded guilty to manslaughter. All charges against Kerouac had been dropped. But a few days after Jack got back to the city, Carr was sentenced to the state penitentiary at Elmira for a term of one to twenty years.

Jack wasn't in a hurry to confront Leo and Gabrielle in his present state of guilt and confusion. His life was a shambles. He hadn't yet published any of his writing, had no job and no prospects, had been mixed up in a homicide, and wasn't quite sure whether he was a married man. Half desperate, he went to the Maritime Union Hall and signed on as an acting able-bodied seaman aboard the S.S. *Robert Treat Paine*, booked for Italy.

Before sailing, Jack went up to the campus to retrieve his Coast Guard seaman's pass. He ran into Allen Ginsberg and Celine Young, Lucien's girlfriend, at the West End Bar. Attracted by Celine's traffic-stopping good looks, some sailors heckled the three of them, and Jack defended his two friends in a nasty men's room fight that followed. Later, feeling "horrible" about the bloody punch-out—he had got the best of it—he went to a hotel near campus to be consoled by Celine. Afterward he felt this to be an act of terrible disloyalty to his incarcerated friend (the "rattiest thing" he had done in "all of [his] life"). Having betrayed everyone he cared about, all that was left to him was the "clean sea"[71]—that long Atlantic run upcoming, which he trusted would wash away guilty memories.

But his special knack for getting on the wrong side of authority sur-

Kerouac and Lucien Carr, Columbia campus, August 12, 1944: "Lucien and Jack had just seen the film Grand Illusion.*"* (courtesy Allen Ginsberg)

Kerouac, August 12,1944

faced again on the *Robert Treat Paine*. From his first hours on board in Brooklyn, the 230-pound ship's bosun made him miserable with constant public taunting and private harassment. Kerouac regarded it all as sexually motivated. He felt another fight coming. When the ship stopped in Norfolk to load supplies, he put on all his clothes in layers, folded his empty duffel bag under his belt, and walked ashore.

"A ship jumper, to add to the rest,"[72] he then skulked back to New York, moved into a small dormitory hotel on the Columbia campus, and, hounded by feelings of guilty anxiety, went into virtual hiding. The next several months he dedicated to a program of deliberate purgation and suffering—a ritual he called "Self-Ultimacy," which included, in its most extreme moments, the writing of notes (brief ones, to be sure) in his own blood.

This artistic self-crucifixion had three essential elements, two of which became important parts of Kerouac's standard procedure as a writer. The first was to write every day—as "a function, a daily duty." He continued this practice for fifteen years. The second was to write "holy" works by candlelight. The third and key element of Self-Ultimacy was the burning of manuscripts. Finishing a page, he fed it to the candle flame. Burning his writings, he believed in the gloomy fall of 1944, would be the one way to assure their *purity*, because it would prove that they had not been "done for ulterior, or practical motives."[73] The flames would guarantee the sincerity. It was not until several years later that Kerouac discovered a more direct method of attaining purity or sincerity: writing straight from the heart, without second thoughts ("spontaneously").

Hedging his bets only slightly, Jack saved a few of his journal pages from the fire. He later used samples of these in *Vanity of Duluoz* to poke fun at his own youthful pretensions. They are an interesting clue, not only to his state of mind at age twenty-two, but also to the huge amount of reading he had been doing: Rimbaud, Yeats, Huxley, Nietzsche, Lautréamont. It was the same kind of reading his friends were doing—not accidentally, since they were providing him many of the books. It was Ginsberg's library card, in fact, that made Self-Ultimacy possible.

Just before the Dostoevskian lower depths swallowed him up for good, a "patrician" friend turned up again in New York and rescued him. Kerouac was working himself into a frazzle over Goethe's *Dichtung and Wahrheit* one night when Bill Burroughs walked in, took a look around, and said, "My God, Jack, stop this nonsense and let's go out and have a drink."[74]

KEROUAC emerged from isolation. After Christmas Edie returned from the Midwest. She stayed briefly with Jack in his room on campus. Then they both moved in with Edie's old roommate, Joan Vollmer Adams, who had a large apartment on 115th Street. There was one more empty room in the apartment, so Jack suggested that Bill Burroughs move in. Burroughs did, and in mid-January of 1945 married Joan Vollmer. By that time Edie had gone back to Grosse Pointe for good.

Jack's reunion with Edie in December and January seems to have been halfhearted at best. Kerouac later said he "sent her home" because he "was of no more use to her as a husband."[75] He told her to get an annulment in Detroit (she did, but not until at least a year later). The specific causes of this final split were economic, according to Jack. He later said that they had been out of money and down to a diet of peanut butter sandwiches.

Herbert Huncke, a hipster and grifter whom Jack met through Burroughs and saw often around Times Square and at the 115th Street apartment, gives a different reason for the breakup. "Apparently Kerouac wasn't too successful with her sexually for one reason or another," Huncke recently told an interviewer. "I think that was the big drawback."[76] Huncke also recalls an occasion around Christmas 1944, when Jack walked in on him and Edie in bed together at 115th Street—"it was perfectly all right with Jack."[77] The implication of Huncke's statements is that Kerouac may simply have lost interest in "the wife of [his] youth."[78] (Jack later referred to his time with Edie as a "comic marriage.")[79]

Before moving into the 115th Street place, Jack had slept overnight several times in Ginsberg's dormitory room. By this time, Jack later said, Ginsberg had begun to "develop" and become a "hipster."[80] He and Allen regularly had long literary talks in the dorm, much like those Jack had once had with Sammy Sampas. Finally, one night when Jack was sleeping on the bed while Ginsberg slept on a pallet on the floor, Allen summoned the courage to make an admission that stunned Jack. "I said, 'Jack, you know, I love you, and I want to sleep with you, and I really like men.' And he said, 'Oooooh, no . . .' "[81]

After his dormitory confession, Allen pressed the sex issue. He thought Jack was "very handsome, very beautiful," and began to pester him about mutually exploring their bodies. Before the end of the year, says Ginsberg, they "wound up in bed together"[82] at least once.

One morning a dormitory official entered Allen's room and noticed

Kerouac curled up asleep on the bed (Ginsberg was sleeping on the floor). The event caused a minor scandal on campus. Though Jack later took pains to dispel it, the rumor flourished that this episode caused Ginsberg's expulsion from the college, which took place not long afterward.

Ginsberg became a habitué at the 115th Street apartment, where both he and Kerouac sat at the feet of William Burroughs, their "great teacher."[83] Burroughs discoursed on everything from the Mayan Codices to morphine, guided them through the works of Spengler and Korzybski, and showed them the bar where Dr. Kinsey had studied the sex life of Times Square. He also suggested that Jack inspect the work of hard-boiled detective writers like James M. Cain and Dashiell Hammett. In 1945, in the 115th Street apartment, Burroughs and Kerouac collaborated on a novel in the Hammett style, originally called "And the Hippos Were Boiled in Their Tanks." The subject of the novel was the killing of David Kammerer and the events leading up to it. Jack, who kept the only copy, apparently prevented its circulation at Lucien Carr's request.[84]

KEROUAC later talked of 1945 as a year of semideliberate disintegration. For Burroughs, Jack said, their involvement with drugs and underworld characters, which began during this period, was "a jaded study"; for Ginsberg it was "a new kind of material for his Hart Crane poetry kick"; but for himself, his whole 115th Street "season"—which lasted nearly a year—later seemed to him a sad, extended indulgence in self-punitive behavior, or "romantic self-torture." When, in between the "endless debauches" of 1945, he visited Ozone Park, he reproachfully envisioned himself "a pale skin-and-bones," too enervated to respond to Leo Kerouac's warnings that Ginsberg and Burroughs would "destroy [him] someday."[85]

Leo himself was being destroyed from within; he had cancer of the stomach. Jack reeled back and forth between dying father and drug binges with friends. Ozone Park and 115th Street: they were "equally dark and inhospitable places of guilt, sin, sorrow, lamentation, despair."[86]

In New York a six-foot, redheaded prostitute named Vicki Russell (whom he had met through Burroughs) taught Jack how to remove the cotton strip from inside a drugstore benzedrine inhaler and swallow it to get high. It was a buzzing, dry mouth, restless kind of feeling. Jack liked it, and began using benzedrine in the city, and in Ozone too, when he wanted to write.

Burroughs and Kerouac, 1945, acting out roles as "hard-boiled detective writers . . . like James M. Cain and Dashiell Hammett " (courtesy Allen Ginsberg)

Jack was involved with Vicki, in an off-and-on fashion, for the next year or two. She introduced him not only to benzedrine, liberated sex, and new jazz but also to a whole different class of ·people—which included musicians, addicts, and petty criminals.

B O P music was a "true religion" of the period, and certain great musicians were its prophets. Vicki dug bop. She kept Jack's photo on her wall next to one of Charlie Parker. Bop hit Jack with "the enormity of a new world philosophy."[87]

> When I first saw the hipsters creeping around Times Square in 1944 I didn't like them . . . One of them, Huncke of Chicago, came up to me and said, "Man I'm beat." I knew right away what he meant somehow. At that time I still didn't like bop which was then being introduced by Bird Parker and Dizzie Gillespie . . . When I first heard Bird and Diz in the Three Deuces I knew they were serious musicians playing a goofy new sound and didn't care what I thought, or what my friend Seymour thought . . . In fact I was leaning against the bar with a beer when Dizzy came over for a glass of water from the bartender, put himself right against me and reached with both arms around both sides of my head to get the glass and danced away, as though knowing I'd be singing about him someday . . . Charlie Parker was spoken of in Harlem as the greatest new musician since Chu Berry and Louis Armstrong. Anyway, the hipsters, whose music was bop, they looked like criminals but they kept talking about the same things I liked, long outlines of personal experience and vision, nightlong confessions full of hope that had become illicit and repressed by war, stirrings, rumblings of a new soul . . . And so Huncke appeared to us and said "I'm beat" with radiant light shining out of his despairing eyes . . . a word perhaps brought from some midwest carnival or drunk cafeteria . . .[88]

Thus began Kerouac's association with what he later called the "Beat Generation."

L I K E a character out of Céline's *Journey to the End of the Night* (which he swiped from a bookstall and read in French during this year of "low, evil decadence"),[89] Jack stumbled forward into his personal night without plot or plan. Finally, on one Manhattan visit, he took too much benzedrine and developed thrombophlebitis—blood clots in his legs. Much of December 1945, he spent flat on his back in Queens General Hospital, receiving treatment under the Veterans' Administration program.

When his legs healed, he went home to help ease Leo out of life. At night, while Leo lay moaning in *joual* in a bed next to his own, Jack twisted in guilt. He decided that he had to become a writer if only to "write a huge novel explaining everything to everybody."[90] He began taking notes for *The Town and the City*, half hoping the book would be a vindication of his dying father.

Down to the final hours, Leo enjoined his son against the art life, making him swear to take care of Gabrielle and telling him to beware of both Burroughs and Ginsberg (the latter of whom he called "that cockroach").[91] A doctor came repeatedly to drain fluid from Leo's swollen abdomen—a brutally painful process. On the day of one such ordeal, Jack and Leo had an argument about how to brew coffee. A little later Leo hunched forward in his chair in what Jack first thought was "pouting repose."[92] In fact, it was death. Jack held his father in his arms for the last time, and as he did, noticed the printer's ink still staining Leo's fingers.

Leo's death plunged him into gloom for weeks. But while Gabrielle did her spring housecleaning, airing out the sickroom sheets, he slowly "settled down to write, in solitude, in pain, writing hymns and prayers at dawn." He began work on *The Town and the City*, which would be "the sum and substance and crop of everything [he had] been through." By it, he hoped, he would be "redeemed."[93] He devoted most of the remainder of 1946 to it.

His trips to the city grew less frequent. His old gang was in transit. Lucien Carr had been released after doing two years at Elmira. Ginsberg had done a turn in the Merchant Marine and gone back to Columbia to write rhymed verse. The 115th Street apartment had broken up; first Bill Burroughs, with Huncke, was busted for drugs and then Joan Burroughs was picked up wandering the streets in a benzedrine haze and sent to Bellevue. The Burroughses had now gone off to Texas to farm marijuana.

IT was from Hal Chase and Ed White, two friends of his who were Columbia students from Denver, that Kerouac first heard of Neal Cassady. In late 1946 in New York, they told him half-mythic tales of a prodigious teenage car thief, "mad genius of jails and raw power," who was a "God among the girls," a "reader of Schopenhauer in reform schools," and a

"Nietzschean hero of the pure snowy wild West."[94] Chase showed Jack a few letters from Cassady written in a New Mexico reformatory. Ginsberg also read the letters and discussed with Jack their chances of ever getting to meet this walking legend.

Around the end of the year, Kerouac heard that the twenty-year-old Cassady had showed up in the flesh, with a new, sixteen-year-old wife, Luanne, in tow. Jack went with White and Chase to the cold-water flat in Spanish Harlem where Neal was staying. Cassady came to the door in the raw. Jack thought he looked exactly like the young Gene Autry. Neal immediately plied Jack and the others with questions, "bobbing, nodding, like a young boxer to instructions, to make you think he's really listening to every word, throwing in even as early as 1947 a thousand manifold yesses and that's rights."[95]

In the weeks that followed, Cassady worked as a parking lot attendant in Manhattan and spent much of his free time pushing schemes to make himself "a real intellectual." He wanted Chase and White to get him into Columbia. When they told him Kerouac was a writer, Neal showed up in Ozone Park—where Jack was busy with *The Town and the City*—and asked to be taught how to write. Kerouac consented. Cassady was a "conman," he could see, but also "simply a youth tremendously excited with life," who "was only conning because he wanted so much to live and to get involved with people who would otherwise pay no attention to him."[96]

Neal visited Ozone Park once or twice a week. He lay on Leo's old bed and read aloud the "entire condensed version of the life of Jack London," just to "accustom [Jack] to his voice and style of reading."[97] The "educational" benefits Cassady got out of these visits came from kibitzing enthusiastically over Jack's shoulder as Jack typed away at his novel.

Kerouac later said they "never became really close"[98] on this first visit of Cassady's to New York, largely because Neal's attention was divided between Jack, Luanne, and his new literary companion (and lover), Ginsberg. Cassady and Ginsberg first met in early December 1946. A month later Kerouac took Cassady to an apartment on 89th Street to meet "a fabulous woman"[99]—Vicki Russell—and to smoke marijuana. Ginsberg, who was also present, engaged Cassady in a heated, soulful dialogue— which stretched across beds, sofas, and folding couches from Harlem to Morningside Heights over the next two months.

Cassady continued his occasional visits to Kerouac in Ozone Park into late February 1947. He and Jack hatched a plan to travel west together, talking it over one warm, early spring afternoon on Cross Bay Boulevard as Jack walked Neal through melting snow to the bus stop.

On March 4, however, Cassady suddenly left New York by bus with Luanne and a stolen typewriter. Kerouac was to follow. He and Ginsberg said their farewells to Cassady at the bus station. They took keepsake photos in a booth, tore them up, and exchanged halves. Lucien Carr later told Jack his snapshot—reconstructed—made him look "just like . . . a dago [who would] kill anybody says something wrong about his mother."[100]

JACK spent much of the spring at the little public library in Ozone Park, studying books and maps on the West and asking "old silver-rimmed ladies" questions about "where to find the Cimarron River."[101]

In June his sister Caroline was married in North Carolina; he made the trip to the wedding with his mother. When he got back to New York he ran into his prep school friend Henri Cru, now a merchant seaman. Cru promised him a job on a ship out of San Francisco. Jack decided to leave immediately, hitchhiking to the West Coast by way of Denver. Ginsberg had already gone west by bus to join Cassady. Kerouac, very tender in the wallet (he was living on his veteran's benefits and Gabrielle's good graces), felt he couldn't afford the bus, and also he wanted to pursue a Jack London hobo-adventurer daydream he had nurtured since adolescence.

After an abortive attempt at thumbing that left him stranded at Bear Mountain on Route 6, Kerouac took a bus back to New York, then another one from there to Chicago, and started hitchhiking again in Joliet. This time he was more successful. He made his first crossing of the Mississippi, and savored "its big rank smell that smells like the raw body of America itself."[102] In Des Moines he slept for a whole day in a railroad flophouse; woke up "as the sun was reddening," not knowing where or who he was; but soon got "the greatest ride of [his] life"[103]—all the way across Nebraska, bundled under a tarpaulin with other hitchhikers on a flatbed truck.

In Denver new divisions had separated Kerouac's friends. One whole group, including Hal Chase, Ed White, and Allen Temko (all campus friends from New York), had taken to disapproving of the street-bred Cassady. This "war with social overtones"[104] made things slightly uncomfortable for Jack. The Columbia group provided him with housing and transportation, creating a conflict of allegiances.

For his part, Cassady had his pool hall gang of lowlife friends. Neal and Ginsberg made up a small, intense subgroup of their own. Luanne was also on hand, and Neal now had a new girlfriend as well, a "striking blond"[105] from Denver University named Carolyn Robinson. He was therefore very busy. The only time Jack spent alone with him on this visit was a trolley ride to see Carolyn perform an ingénue role in Ibsen's *A Pillar of Society*. On the trolley they talked coolly about hot rods and midget car races.

Cassady's time was largely taken up with Ginsberg, who was living in a basement and going through what he termed "Denver doldrums."[106] Neal and Allen soon went off to Texas to help Burroughs harvest his marijuana crop, an episode that resulted in Ginsberg's dejected departure to more "doldrums" at sea and Cassady's driving on to New York with Burroughs to sell the pot.

Deserted by Neal and Allen, Kerouac went on to San Francisco by bus in August. For the first but not the last time, Henri Cru's promise of a ship job turned out to be illusory; Jack ended up camping in a shack in Marin City with Cru and his girlfriend. After drawing a blank on a film script Cru talked him into writing "for Hollywood,"[107] Kerouac joined his friend as a security guard in a construction workers' barracks. They wore guns and badges but stole food from the barracks kitchen at night. Jack wrote long letters to Allen, Bill, and Neal at Burroughs' place in Texas and got one back from Ginsberg (who had been rejected by Cassady) all about disappointment in love.

Kerouac proudly sent most of his Marin City earnings to his mother, but a month of playing hired cop with the bluff, ebullient Cru was all he could stand. At the end of September, he caught a bus to Los Angeles. On board he befriended a young Chicano woman, with whom he spent the next two weeks. He lived with her in a tent and picked cotton in the fields near Bakersfield. This sweaty interlude introduced Kerouac to the real backbreaking labor behind the "fellaheen" dream.

Jack's stamina and pocket money ran out simultaneously. Cramming ten sandwiches in with the bulging notebooks that filled his seaman's bag, he rode a bus as far east as his final pennies would take him—which turned out to be Pittsburgh. From there he hitchhiked. Deep in the night, out of his head with hunger, he hallucinated that a hobo he met on the road was the "Ghost of the Susquehanna."[108] The next night he was in New York, panhandling a quarter for the bus to Long Island.

WORKING late nights at Gabrielle's kitchen table through the early months of 1948, Kerouac gave a final shape to *The Town and the City*, that heart's history of his youth. He had originally intended a book along the lines of Goethe's autobiography, *Poetry and Truth*, but he cast his own tale through a prism of fiction, which dispersed what he thought of as different parts of himself into distinct characters. It was slow going, with periods of painstaking revision. There were also spurts that made Kerouac feel he was at last in command of his writing and riding a creative wave. In a joyous journal entry on March 12, his twenty-sixth birthday, he celebrated a treasure of "4500 words (count 'em)."[109]

John Clellon Holmes, to whom Kerouac entrusted his work journal of this period, has preserved and published fragments that hint of Kerouac's struggle to complete the massive novel, which eventually totaled some 1,100 pages and which Kerouac himself described as "a perfect Niagara of a novel."[110] He also showed the hand-printed manuscript of his novel to Ginsberg, who was awed and began circulating it around New York. Encouraged, Jack hopefully typed a copy and submitted it to Charles Scribner's Sons, Wolfe's publisher.

In June, after some months of silence, Cassady wrote from California that he had dissolved his marriage with Luanne, married Carolyn (who was pregnant), and was now working for the Southern Pacific Railroad. Jack wrote back proposing that once he sold his novel, he would buy a ranch in California on which they would, with Gabrielle and various mutual pals, all live communally. His expectations for the novel were typically unrealistic. Apparently, he did receive some encouragement from Scribner's, if only in the form of stalling. But by June he seems to have grown impatient and to have submitted the manuscript to another publisher, Macmillan. While waiting for word, he went on reworking the novel in the hermetic silence of Ozone Park.

Kerouac's weekend trips to Manhattan were little islands of noise and action. The hot night before Independence Day, he was buying beer to take to a party when he bumped into John Clellon Holmes, who was going to the same party. Holmes already "knew about Kerouac" as the author of "a 1000-page novel that was being passed around 'our' crowd just then in a battered doctor's bag." Seeing the "novelist" in person for the first time, Holmes thought Jack looked less like an artist than a T-shirted "young John Garfield back in the neighborhood after college."[111] The two aspiring writers hit it off immediately.

Neal Cassady: " 'Mad genius of jails and raw power' " (courtesy Carolyn Cassady)

Luanne Henderson Cassady, 1945 (courtesy Carolyn Cassady)

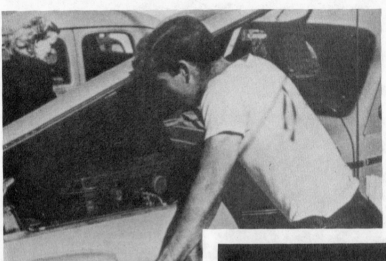

Neal Cassady, Carolyn Cassady in background, 1948: "He had dissolved his marriage with Luanne and married Carolyn." (courtesy Carolyn Cassady)

John Clellon Holmes, 1948: "The two aspiring writers hit it off immediately." (courtesy the unspeakable visions of the individual)

O N September 9 Kerouac received a form rejection slip from Macmillan in the mail. The same night he completed the revised final chapter of his latest draft. Evidently this went to Scribner's, which was still considering the book. "Tonight I finished and typed the last chapter," he wrote in his journal. "The work is finished."[112]

Having written his own American novel, he now began his first systematic consideration of the competition. In this fall of 1948, he began attending classes at the New School for Social Research, paid for by his veteran's benefits under the G.I. Bill. He enrolled in Elbert Lenrow's course on the Modern American Novel and in a creative writing course given by Brom Weber. With Holmes he also audited a course on Melville and other nineteenth-century American writers, taught by Alfred Kazin.

In a course paper for Lenrow, Kerouac concentrated on the neutrality and objectivity of Theodore Dreiser's novelistic reporting, which may have particularly appealed to him because he was then under the sway of "Factualism," an off-the-cuff literary program developed by William Burroughs. Factualism called for the cool, detached, hard-eyed approach of a Dashiell Hammett or James M. Cain. In early November 1948, Jack began a naturalist-factualist account of his 1947 travel experiences. His narrator was "Ray Smith," a name he later used for the first-person narrator of *The Dharma Bums*. Producing about 1,500 words a day, by Thanksgiving he had 32,500 words. This was the first version of *On the Road*. After submitting it for his New School creative writing course in early December, he abandoned it; on second look it gave him a feeling of "emptiness & even falseness."[113]

He now decided to seek "deep form"[114] as he believed it had been achieved by Melville in the great harmonic symbol of the whale in *Moby Dick*, which Kerouac was reading in Kazin's class. Only in the "metaphysical" depths of writers like Melville and Shakespeare, Kerouac concluded, could the strongest emotion be found. He made long-range plans to employ deep form in another new work first projected around this time—a tale of his childhood fantasy hero, Doctor Sax.

Despite the interest of the influential critic Alfred Kazin, who had read *The Town and the City*, Scribner's finally turned the book down in December 1948. An unhappy Kerouac told Holmes the time had come for him to "choose between the drawing rooms full of Noel Cowards and the rattling trucks on the American highways."[115]

Though Kerouac quickly sent the manuscript to yet another publisher, Harcourt, Brace, the Scribner's rejection continued to rock him in stages. On December 15 he wrote a letter to Ginsberg that showed he half-consciously connected Allen—his unofficial "agent"—with his sense of humiliation and defeat caused by his book's failure to be accepted. In the letter Kerouac charged Ginsberg (and Burroughs as well) with laughing at his idealism. He told Ginsberg he hated him and wanted him to die or go mad. If his book didn't sell to a publisher, Jack threatened, he himself would simply have to die; he couldn't face going back to work in a gas station.

I N October Cassady had tried by letter to persuade Jack to come to California. When that effort failed, he took a more drastic step. Packing into a new smoked-silver '49 Hudson his ex-wife Luanne, a buddy named Al Hinkle, and a young woman he had ordered Hinkle to marry so they could add her savings to their slim traveling budget (she lasted only as far as Tucson), Cassady left his second wife and infant child behind to roar across America and pick up Kerouac.

Jack had informed Neal by phone that he would be spending the holidays visiting his sister and her family in North Carolina with his mother. A few days after Christmas, there was a commotion outside Jack's brother-in-law's house. When the in-laws looked out, they saw a muddy Hudson parked in the sand road and a seedy roughneck standing next to it scratching his belly under a filthy T-shirt. Slumped in the car, Luanne and Hinkle looked "like dead people . . . victims of [Neal's] frantic tragic destiny."[116] Jack experienced a moment of horror, mistakenly (but understandably) assuming the car to be stolen.

Cassady, who wanted simply to *move*, proposed they leave right away for New York to transport some furniture of Nin's to Ozone Park, then return for Gabrielle, and make the whole drive a second time. The proposal was absurd, but Jack accepted. "I went with him for no reason,"[117] he later admitted.

As darkness fell and the Christmas lights came on, they bundled up and "whaled" north in Neal's Melvillean Hudson. Kerouac and Cassady crossed "oceans of rain and the desolation of the wilderness and of the Dark Cities" twice in thirty-six hours, "and in all that time [Neal] just talked and talked and talked."[118] They stopped long enough in between trips to get the car radio fixed, then loaded Gabrielle in the back and again turned north. The weather was terrible, but Cassady, now propelled into the night by "wild bop"[119] on the radio, floated the big car over road ice like a dream boat.

They deposited Gabrielle in Ozone Park, slept for a day, then cruised up and down Manhattan between stops of a three-day New Year's weekend party, which culminated in a trip to Birdland to hear the blind British jazz pianist, George Shearing (whom Neal was sure was "God"). At that point the "tea [they] were smoking" briefly convinced Jack that "everything was about to arrive—the moment when you know all and everything is decided forever."[120]

Cassady got a temporary job parking cars. After a short breather in Ozone Park, Jack came back to track Neal's movements around New York. His notes in his work journal for early January suggest that in following Cassady, Kerouac now thought he was involved in some kind of religious pilgrimage. Neal brought out the ingenuous, childlike side of his nature, which, in turn, generated belief.

NEAL and Luanne were spatting. Jack was anxious. Ginsberg's "great forum" at his York Avenue apartment (where they were all staying) had collapsed. And Allen was delivering stern admonitory lectures in "a tone of voice which he hoped sounded like what he called The Voice of Rock"— warning Jack, Neal, Luanne, and Al Hinkle that "the days of Wrath are yet to come."[121]

It was time to go. Once they had collected Jack's latest veteran's benefit check and called Burroughs in Louisiana (he told them to hurry: Hinkle's wife had turned up at his place), they all piled into the Hudson again and headed toward the deep South.

At the time of their visit to his bayou retreat, William Burroughs' life style consisted of injecting morphine, reading the Mayan Codices, and shooting guns at benzedrine inhalers; his wife, Joan, meanwhile, ate the benzedrine and got up every day to shake lizards out of dead trees at dawn. Happy as he was to be getting rid of Helen Hinkle ("this ain't a hotel"), Burroughs remained unable to understand why his friend Kerouac would bother to go riding around the country in company with a half-crazy cowboy con man and a couple of ordinary grifters. In between nods he scrutinized them all curiously, snuffled down his nose (*"thfump*, like a sound in a dry tank"), and asked them exactly what they thought they were doing. "I want you to sit quiet a minute," he said to Neal, "and tell me what you're doing crossing the country like this." Of his former "pupil," Jack, he asked bluntly, "What are you going to the coast for?"[122]

There was no reasonable answer Kerouac could make. The only answer was to *move*. On January 28, 1949, practically without funds, the Cassady caravan left for California. After several thousand miles of north–south rambling—which now seemed to Jack a mere preamble—Neal swung the big car due west at last.

They crossed the Mississippi "at a place called Port Allen" and entered the West by a back door of dark mystery swamps, "a manuscript of the night we couldn't read."[123] The next afternoon, in West Texas, Luanne sat in the front seat between Cassady and Kerouac, and they drove naked into the setting sun. Neal stopped long enough in El Paso to run off after dope with "a young crazy reformatory hepcat"[124] they met; Jack and Luanne waited for him in the bus station.

The long miles had robbed the road of a little of its magic. When they hit San Francisco, Cassady did something that made the bottom drop out of Kerouac's trip. He simply dumped Jack, Luanne, and the Hinkles on a street corner (O'Farrell and Grant) and went off to pursue his "tragic destiny" elsewhere. This abrupt and unexpected abandonment by his "brother" caused Jack to "lose faith"[125] in Neal for about six months, he later said.

"Neal will leave you in the cold any time it's in his interest," Luanne consoled him. They spent two days together in a flophouse; Jack finally got to make love to her, and he told her about his continuing dreams of Dr. Sax. Then she left him broke and flat; Jack angrily suspected it was to take up love for hire. There ensued "the beatest time of [his] life."[126] Half starving, he wandered the streets of San Francisco in a daze. Back at the flophouse, Neal—at last—showed up and took him home.

Kerouac "relaxed a few days"[127] with family-man Cassady. As soon as Jack's next check came from his mother, though, he was on a bus headed back east, carrying fifteen carefully made sandwiches. There was a sullen goodbye scene at the bus station—Neal showed up with Luanne; they were hungry and wanted some of Jack's sandwiches. Jack refused. He later felt remorse over his lack of generosity and confessed to Ginsberg that five of the sandwiches had gone bad before he could eat them.

Kerouac left his return bus trip out of the story of his travels as told in the published version of *On the Road*. In fact, though, he kept a detailed journal of the trip. It was a continuation of his close study of American geography. Alone and with "nothing to do but read the land," he spent most of the long ride looking out the window and reflecting on "the source of the rainy night we cross on tidal highways, the snow North, the West that makes Mississippis." At Three Forks, Montana, "where the Madison and the Gallatin and the Jefferson rivers in strange confluence act to form the cradle and beginnings of the Father of Waters," he decided he had located "the source of everything."[128] On the bus he conceived the image —later used in several books—of a log floating from Three Forks downriver all the way to the gulf, joining with twigs from the Ohio in a single continent-binding flow. Then in an all-night saloon in Butte, where the bus stopped for several hours, he watched a card game presided over by a bulbous-nosed old blackjack dealer who reminded him at once of his father and of W. C. Fields. This scene, preserved in notes jotted at the bus depot, later became the great Doctor Sax–Old Bull Balloon pool game in *Dr. Sax*.

As Kerouac's voyages so often did, this trip came to a close on a note of desperation—the stealing of some meager groceries in Pennsylvania. But by mid-February he was back in Ozone Park, feeding at Gabrielle's ample table. He had come home only a week or so beyond the date he had originally promised his mother.

THAT March Kerouac began to try to focus on his "poetic" visions and dreams of Doctor Sax and to make notes on them, but he soon decided the work was too subjective, too much influenced by Ginsberg's pseudomysticism (Jack and Allen had been exchanging mutual dream revelations of "hooded strangers").[129] He then began a second version of the *Road* book, inspired by his recent journey. This time he approached his travel material from a "metaphysical" or Melvillean depth perspective. In this new version, Ray Smith—former hero of the factualist version—was reduced to the role of third-person narrator. The hero was now Red Moultrie, a young ex-convict and man of experience, who pursues an unidentified spiritual "inheritance."[130] In his journals Kerouac quotes John Bunyan's *Pilgrim's Progress* to indicate his novel's new direction.

On March 29, four days after his first journal entry on the state of this "Red Moultrie" version of *On the Road*, Kerouac's work was temporarily interrupted by a letter from Robert Giroux, a young editor at Harcourt,

Brace. *The Town and the City* had been accepted. Jack fell to his knees in the Ozone Park kitchen and said a "prayer of Thanksgiving."[131]

Not only would Harcourt publish the book but also they were willing to pay Jack an advance of $1,000. It was the first money he had ever earned as a writer. The money itself meant less to him than did its effect on Gabrielle, whose excitement over his earnings made Jack feel like he had fulfilled his father's last pleas that he take care of his mother. "Ah, Ed, I feel good," Jack wrote to his friend Ed White in Denver in a letter announcing his good fortune. "Just think what it means to me and the family."[132]

The pleasure of the sale was mitigated for Kerouac by his discovery within only a few weeks that the editing of his novel would not be in his control. He later complained that his 1,100-page manuscript had been "cut to 400 pages by Harcourt Brace and thereby reduced from a mighty . . . black book of sorrows into a 'saleable' ordinary novel."[133] Kerouac did play some part in the editing—which took place during April 1949—but the final decisions on cuts were in the hands of Robert Giroux.

ON April 5, 1949, Ginsberg learned from Burroughs' wife that Bill had been arrested on a drug charge in Louisiana and that a federal search of their bayou retreat had uncovered letters from Ginsberg about a marijuana deal. Ginsberg, now working as an AP copy boy while awaiting his Columbia graduation, instantly got nervous about his own letters and journals, which were full of detailed information about the illegal activities of a group of amiable criminals (Huncke, then fresh out of prison; Vicki Russell; and her current boyfriend, "Little Jack" Melody), who had begun storing stolen merchandise in his York Avenue apartment.

On April 20 John Clellon Holmes threw a party to celebrate the sale of Kerouac's book to Harcourt, Brace. Jack showed up beforehand at Allen's apartment and invited all present—Allen, Huncke, Vicki, and Little Jack—to the party. Kerouac then left; the others were to follow.

Earlier that afternoon, according to Huncke, he and Jack Melody had "pulled a caper"[134] and stashed guns, jewelry, and fur coats at the York Avenue apartment. They drove to the party in a stolen car. Afterward, on the way home, Allen persuaded Little Jack to make a side trip to Long Island so that he could hide his guilty notebooks at his brother's house. Little Jack made an illegal turn en route, alerting a police officer, and in the subsequent chase, crashed the car, spilling Ginsberg's papers all over the street. The driver and passengers fled from the stolen car, but with the aid of Allen's notebooks the police traced them back to the evidence-laden apartment, where they were all arrested. Huncke and Little Jack each got five years in jail. With the help of his lawyer brother and his analyst, Ginsberg "made a deal"[135] (as he wrote on June 16 to Holmes) and agreed to accept psychiatric care. Charges against him were dropped. He was admitted to the Columbia Psychiatric Institute as an inpatient in June 1949.

Ginsberg's arrest shocked Jack and frightened him. It was another good reason for getting out of New York, where the "hassles" were getting too close for comfort. Coming at the time of his temporary financial good fortune, it helped him decide to take the major step of moving away from New York with his mother. In May he convinced Gabrielle to quit her job in the Brooklyn shoe factory, brought her to Colorado on a bus, and spent his entire $1,000 advance on a two-month fling at becoming a "patriarch" in "Middle America."[136]

He leased a $75-a-month clapboard bungalow in one of the cheap tract subdivisions west of Denver. There were no paved roads near the property; spring rains were heavy. Neither Jack nor Gabrielle could drive. With all his friends out of town, Kerouac had to tote their groceries through a quagmire. "It was doomed to failure, of course," Kerouac's friend Ed White later said of Kerouac's patriarch experiment. "Jack wasn't terribly practical."[137]

A large part of Kerouac's reason for coming back to Denver was to study the scenes of his "brother" Neal's past life. In search of inspiration for his *Road* book, which he now associated with Cassady, he trailed Neal's "ghost" through the principal Cassady haunts, even taking the same parttime job Cassady had held—hauling watermelons in the downtown fruit market.

By late June, Jack's patriarch experiment was "collapsing around him." Gabrielle wanted to go to Radio City, not sit alone trapped in mud. She wrote to the shoe factory in Brooklyn and asked for her job back. On July 4 Jack gave up and packed Gabrielle off to the East. His advance money now gone, the whole trip had come to look like a "huge madness."[138] Kerouac stayed on anyway, writing and wrestling with watermelons, until a scheduled visit from Robert Giroux, who arrived in Denver on July 15.

With the editor he worked on final proof corrections of *The Town and the City.* Jack introduced the urbane Giroux to hitchhiking on a day trip into the mountains around Central City. But even during that excursion, Kerouac couldn't dispel an impression that Giroux—who wasn't much older than Jack—was "a bored old Tiresias." The Giroux visit made Kerouac's own courting of success and fame suddenly seem contemptible to him. After seeing the editor off on a plane, Jack walked and hitched back to Denver from the airport, brooding that "nothing in the world matters; not even success in America . . . just void and emptiness awaits the career of the soul of a man."[139]

Later that night he walked through the purple dusk of Denver, under drooping trees, and stopped to watch a softball game: "earnest glad young athletes rushing pell-mell on the dust."[140] No bored Tiresiases, these earnest, frantic amateurs reminded Jack of Neal Cassady. He had just received his first letter in months from Cassady—an urgent, confused note, begging Jack to come to the Coast.

"I WAS burning to know what was on his mind and what would happen to me," Kerouac wrote later of his July 1949 gamble to shoot for more "pilgrimages" with Cassady, "for there was nothing behind me any more, all my bridges were gone and I didn't give a damn about anything at all."[141] He rolled into San Francisco by bus, went straight to Cassady's small house—it was two o'clock in the morning—and was greeted by a stark naked Neal holding aloft a fractured, infected thumb (it had been broken on Luanne's head).

Neal seemed to have become—"by virtue of his enormous series of sins"—a sweating, distracted imbecile-saint, "the HOLY GOOF,"[142] castigated by friends, welcome nowhere. Jack proposed a way out: they would drive to New York, collect his royalties (at this point he was still in the throes of a vast illusion about future income from *The Town and the City*), and then keep on going all the way to Italy. They headed east in a Denver-bound drive-away Plymouth.

Ignoring the driver and two other "tourist" passengers, Jack and Neal talked up a back-seat benzedrine storm. Jack had recently told Holmes that all the dialogue in novels should be *confession*; now he and Cassady traded long confessions that reached all the way down to "the substance of our lives."[143]

That night in Sacramento, "the gangbelly broke loose" in Neal's homosexual encounter with the owner of the "fag Plymouth." Kerouac watched, peeking through the crack in a lavatory door, and later described the "Olympic perversities" he witnessed. The episode was another expression of the mythic dimension of Cassady's male urge, which made Neal—as women had told Jack—a "machine in the night." Jack was fascinated and "horrified."[144]

Jack and Neal, who had driven most of the last 1,000 miles, were both exhausted on arrival in Denver, and when Jack dropped a remark in a restaurant that betrayed his disapproval of Neal's "slambanging big sodomies" in Sacramento, Cassady's eyes teared with chagrin. Jack quickly apologized and told his friend by way of explanation that he didn't "have close relationships any more" because he didn't "know what to do with those things."[145]

After two hectic nights in Denver, during which Neal "stole cars and raised Cain with idiots,"[146] they picked up another drive-away—a '47 Cadillac limousine to be delivered to Chicago—and took off over the plains, evidently just ahead of squads of investigating police. The confusions of Denver outdistanced, Cassady "smashed onwards" in the Cadillac, "hurling toward the dawn" at 110 mph. He now seemed to Jack like something out of Melville, a "mad Ahab at the wheel," battling the "groaning continent."[147]

By the time they walked away from the battered Cadillac in Chicago, the two young men felt nearly as "beat" as the car. Even so, they sought to "dig the street of life" and followed "bop musicians" around the city until dawn, when they staggered with their "wretched baggage"[148] onto a Detroit bus. In the Motor City Jack looked up Edie Parker, his ex-wife, to whom he had written from Colorado in May. If not a reconciliation, he certainly expected at least a few nights on clean sheets. Things had changed since 1944, however. Jack and Neal got to chat briefly with Edie on her manicured lawn in Grosse Pointe, but as Neal put it, Jack and his ex-wife "were no longer on the same team." Shortly afterward the travelers were shaken down by police (alerted by the Parkers' neighbors, who thought the two rough-looking young men were "casing joints"), and they ended the night by flopping among derelicts in a cheap downtown movie house, "both as miserable-looking as anybody else."[149]

A few nights later Jack and Neal staggered into Gabrielle's new apartment in Richmond Hill, Queens, "all petered out in the dark of Long Island." They walked nervously around the block a few times, the blind impulse to move still twitching. But "there was no more land."[150]

There was also no European trip. Jack's "Italy" money, he now had to admit to Neal, was "nonexistent." Cassady went on into the city, ostensibly to face his "prophetic" future, live on Skid Row, and write his autobiography (to be edited by Jack). A few days later, however, Jack saw him at a party. There he introduced him to a dark-haired model named Diane Hansen. Within an hour Cassady was "kneeling on the floor with his chin on her belly and telling and promising her everything and sweating."[151] Cassady went on to father this woman's child and to commit bigamy with her. He disappeared from Kerouac's life for the next ten months.

COMMERCIAL prospects for *The Town and the City* were bright. Jack boasted in a sanguine self-promotional note to Charles Sampas of the *Lowell Sun* about an advance sale of 20,000 copies. Harcourt was putting $7,500 into advertising. An English publisher, Eyre and Spottiswoode, had also accepted the book.

On February 26, 1950, a week before the publication of *The Town and the City*, Kerouac wrote a long, ingenuous letter to Ginsberg, who was now at his family home in Paterson. In it Jack outlined his personal role in the "salvation" of the country. There was a new America coming that would be unlike any now known, he prophesied. He didn't want to be unprepared for it. As a result, he was cutting out weekend parties and cocktails, abandoning his failed love life, writing steadily, and trying to keep in shape at the Richmond Hill YMCA.

As for his novel, he had only the highest hopes. Unfortunately, *The Town and the City*—published on March 2, 1950, with a dedication to Robert Giroux, "Friend and Editor"—got only mixed reviews, sold poorly, and, except for the sharp good looks shown by a well-groomed "John Kerouac" in the newspaper advertising photo, made no splash at all.

Kerouac reacted against both Harcourt—which had trimmed the book's "guts"—and the book itself, which he now decided had "a dreary prose to it when all's said and done."[152] Gabrielle was unhappy, and Jack dejectedly told friends the failure of *The Town and the City* had even hurt his love life. He was too poor to ask girls out on dates. He wrote to John Holmes in the spring of 1950, that if he now stayed in New York it could only be as a commercial hustler—and he refused that alternative. It was time to leave. Bill Burroughs had invited him to visit Mexico City. Jack decided to take him up on it.

Kerouac as young author, early 1950 (photo by Elliott Erwitt)

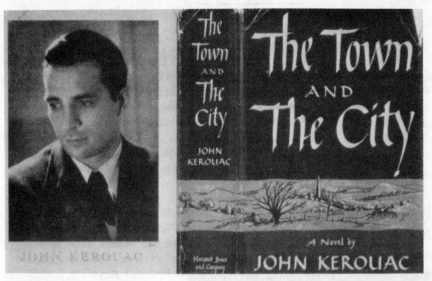

OPPOSITE: *Kerouac, early 1950*
(photo by Elliott Erwitt)

ABOVE: The Town and the City,
published March 1950

RIGHT: *Kerouac the young author
signing copies of his book at a Denver
bookstore, July 1950* (photo by Justin
W. Brierly)

IN late June 1950, Kerouac traveled by bus to Denver, where he spent a week with his friends Ed White and Bev Burford. He planned to continue south to Mexico by rail—but Cassady suddenly arrived in a '37 Ford jalopy and announced he was taking Kerouac to Mexico (he was also planning to obtain a Mexican divorce from Carolyn, so he could marry his New York girlfriend).

On their "last great trip," Cassady for once aimed the car south. Entering Mexico, he ecstatically announced they were leaving "everything behind" and entering "a new and unknown phase of things."[153] As Neal idled the Ford through villages, Jack gazed out the window in ecstasy at "hillbillies, paisanos, cats of the pampas, campo people." This was the universal "fellaheen" of which Spengler had spoken—it was an "Indian thing." In one village where they stopped to buy marijuana and women, Jack experienced what he later called his greatest "vision" of Neal—"the one great occasion when I saw . . . everything not only about him but America, all of America as it has been conceptualized in my brain." They smoked a "great rugged cigar" of pot, and as Neal drove slowly through dusty streets in search of a local whorehouse, Jack suddenly saw his friend glow "like a sun" and become "all rosy as a rosy balloon and beautiful as Franklin Delano Roosevelt."[154]

But after a week of "bawdy nights and bordellos and wines"[155] in Mexico City, Jack fell ill with amoebic dysentery, and while he was only half conscious, Neal again deserted him. Cassady had not obtained his divorce, but he had bought marijuana and was in a hurry to get back to the States.

Neal got only as far as Lake Charles, Louisiana, where the rear end dropped out of the Ford. He flew on to New York and there entered into a bigamous union. Jack, meanwhile, was nursed back to health by Bill and Joan Burroughs. He spent his days talking and playing fast-draw pistols with Burroughs, his evenings wandering around Mexico City, usually in a "marvelous marijuana hallucinated" state.[156]

Other nights in Mexico, a great Spenglerian atom bomb apocalypse haunted Jack's dreams. He began to envision himself as the "Great Walking Saint of On the Road,"[157] a pilgrim who would cross an otherwise doomed America to pay for its sins—perhaps in the final moments of history.

At the end of the summer, Jack wrapped two-and-a-half pounds of strong marijuana in a silk sash, tied it around his waist, bound his waist in a broad Mexican belt, and left for the border. At Laredo he crossed over, diverting a border guard's attention by offering him a drink from a bottle of tequila.

BACK in Richmond Hill, Kerouac was soon telling correspondents he felt more disenfranchised than ever in this lost America he had dedicated his life to writing about. He felt, he said, almost like a small black child. Accordingly, he started *On the Road* again—now in a vernacular dialect, using as first-person narrator a young black boy from the south ("Pictorial Review Jackson"), who travels across country. But after toiling at it for a month or so, Jack decided he wasn't meeting his own story prescriptions— "saying what [he] had to say, and saying [it] simply," in the "sincere tone" of an "angel-author"[158]—and once again put the work aside. (After his death, it was published as *Pic.*) He told Holmes he was tired, dissatisfied, and impatient with the stalled *Road* project. It "resisted [his] head," he complained. By December Holmes was advising him to forget his false starts, begin again in a reverent mood, and simply write down everything he could think of, "in its natural order, in the beauty of its happening."[159]

ON October 12, 1950, one of Jack's New York friends—a wild, suicidally inclined individual named Bill Cannastra—had died in a bizarre mishap: his head was cut off when he stuck it out a subway train window. Jack temporarily occupied Cannastra's vacated loft on West 21st Street. There he took up with an ex-girlfriend of the deceased man, Joan Haverty, who had been hanging around the loft since Cannastra's demise. She was twenty, attractive, and possessed, Jack intuitively felt, "the pure innocent dear eyes [he] had always searched for and so long."[160] (He later told friends he had been "overwhelmed"[161] by her beauty.)

Kerouac barely knew the girl, but that didn't stop him, a few days after he met her, from taking her to a judge and marrying her. The event took place on November 17, 1950. Lucien Carr, who was now working for United Press, was best man. The marriage stunned Jack's friends. They gathered in the former Cannastra loft, where the newlyweds were living, for a spur-of-the-moment wedding party.

Both Jack and Joan went to work, he as a part-time script synopsizer for a motion picture company, she as a salesgirl in a department store, then later as a waitress. Within a month domestic joy was wearing thin. Joan didn't appreciate her double role of working girl and housewife, especially since Jack's idea of the latter was based on no less demanding a standard than Gabrielle. (At five in the morning, Kerouac awakened his new wife and asked her to bake him a spice cake—and when she refused, informed her that his mother would have done it!) Kerouac's later accounts suggest he felt himself to be making a sincere effort; but he eventually became convinced that the marriage had taken place on false pretenses and claimed that he had privately "realized [he] didn't love or like her at all eight days before [their] marriage."[162]

In December the newlyweds moved in with Gabrielle to save on expenses and also to allow Jack to concentrate on his writing. But the Richmond Hill place proved too small for two women who were in essential competition over the same man. Joan couldn't speak *joual* with Gabrielle; Gabrielle resented Jack's speaking American with Joan. After a few weeks Jack grudgingly gave in to Joan's demand that they move back to New York. They rented an apartment in a brownstone on West 20th Street. Lonely and hurt, Gabrielle gave up the Richmond Hill apartment, quit her job, and went south in an ill-fated and short-lived retreat to Nin and the in-laws.

FOR a while Kerouac clung to unrealistic hopes that the marriage would work out. His big plan for the winter was to migrate to California with Joan—"bringing all our beat furniture and broken belongings with us in a jalopy panel truck."[163] There, with his putative literary earnings as capital, they would share a place on the land with Neal Cassady.

Jack and Neal wrote back and forth about this and many other matters. The correspondence was hardly limited to practicalities, however. Cassady's letters had begun to provide Kerouac with valuable stimulus and example. They were profuse, awkward, oddly inspiring. Cassady said that when writing, he felt "like Proust . . . Remembrance of your life and your eyeball view are actually the only two immediate first hand things your mind can carry instantly."[164] Neal's letters, containing his own "eyeball view," were heavily autobiographical. Indeed, he told Jack that, contrary to the prevailing literary style of the time ("to create fiction"), everything he said should be taken "as straight case-history."[165]

Kerouac expected Cassady to arrive in February; then they would all return in the "frantic truck" to the Coast by way of Denver, stopping there to pick up Neal's father. But, riding free on a brakeman's pass, Neal blew into New York a month ahead of schedule. Jack hadn't saved a dollar of the "truck money." Cassady stayed only three days—two more than it took Jack's wife to get tired of having him around.

Within weeks of his return to San Francisco after this whirlwind visit, Cassady typed a long, candid letter to Kerouac, crammed with "Proustian" recollection, about his youthful experiences with women. It became known as the "Joan Anderson letter." (Though the original was soon lost—by Ginsberg, to whom Jack loaned it—an excerpt survives in the posthumous collection of Cassady's literary fragments titled *The First Third.*) Kerouac had by this time begun to write Neal's life story as the centerpiece of yet another version of *On the Road*—this one with a revived "Ray Smith" as third-person narrator.

When the Joan Anderson letter arrived—around the end of February —Jack was working on the elaborately crafted "metaphysical" scenes of Cassady's young manhood that appear as pages 57–70 in the published version of *Visions of Cody*. Within the next few months, and largely under the influence of the "prophetic" letter, he moved toward a more direct, "confessional" style. Later he said he had "got the idea for the spontaneous style of *On the Road* from seeing how good old Neal Cassady wrote his letters to me, all first person, fast, mad, confessional, completely serious, all detailed, with real names."[166]

In March, while Joan went out to work, Jack stayed home and read Henry Murray's edition of Melville's *Pierre*. One line in Murray's introduction, selected by Kerouac for underlining, stated: "Melville was not writing autobiography in the usual sense . . . he was writing the autobiography of his self-image."[167] His selection of this sentence indicates perhaps how Kerouac's plans for *On the Road* had finally locked into focus. He had decided to go back to the beginning, as Holmes had proposed in December, and start his *Road* story—by now reduced in his mind to the several major trips with Cassady—all over again, as a Cassady-style "confession." But now, while Cassady would be the book's ostensible hero, Kerouac would place *himself* in the center as narrator. He would be "Sal Paradise," a young man who spends his life "shambling after [the] people who interest [him]."[168] The book would be the "autobiography" of his own "self-image."

IN writing the April 1951 version of *On the Road*, Kerouac made an important change in his physical working circumstances. To pour the story out "in natural order," as John Holmes had suggested, Jack wanted above all a great *speed* of composition. A fleet, hundred-words-a-minute typist, he could fill a page with single-space prose in minutes. But changing pages broke the flow of his thoughts. To remedy this he took some sheets of onionskin art paper (left behind at 21st Street by Bill Cannastra) and glued them together into a long scroll. Around April 5 he began typing on this scroll, letting it uncoil onto the floor in front of him as he worked.

Spurred on by benzedrine and coffee, he wrote at breakneck pace in a flat, terse, slightly formal narrative style. The style was influenced by Cassady's "fast, mad, confessional"[169] letters, by the headlong narrative pace of Louis-Ferdinand Céline, and by the factualist tradition (Hammett, et al.), as promulgated by Burroughs and practiced earlier in the 1945 Burroughs–Kerouac collaborative novel.

When he showed it to Holmes on April 27, the typescript was a single 175,000-word paragraph, fully punctuated and containing all the characters' real names. On May 7 Ginsberg wrote to Cassady that he had read the manuscript, praised its "dewlike writing," but suggested it still "needed an ending."[170] Kerouac continued to work at the book.

To complicate matters, Joan announced that she was pregnant. When Jack told her that he couldn't earn enough yet to support a family and suggested she get an abortion, she threw him out. To friends and his mother, he began a series of denials of paternity that eventually, when Joan produced an offspring, became a kind of defensive campaign.

About May 10 Kerouac moved a few blocks to Lucien Carr's loft. Carr has said that he gave Kerouac a roll of teletype paper from his UPI office and that Jack typed on it all day and much of the night for several weeks.

In the first flush of joy over his creation, Kerouac appeared at Robert Giroux's office, carrying a roll of what Giroux later called "rubbery sheets, like Thermo-fax paper . . . teletype sheets pasted together." It took some moments for Giroux, who had never seen anything quite like the 100-foot unparagraphed typed scroll that Jack insisted on unraveling across the floor of the editorial office, to register Kerouac's seriousness about submitting the novel in this form. "He said, 'I don't make any corrections,' " Giroux later recalled. " 'That's the way it will be.' "[171]

The unorthodox state of the typescript may or may not have influenced Harcourt's rejection of the book, which was almost immediate. Giroux briefly encouraged Jack's hopes by saying the book was "like Dostoevsky," then quickly explained that the sales department was against it.

Mentally and physically spent after the long athletic feat—six weeks' nonstop typing—of writing his book, Kerouac now hit a spiritual low point as extreme·as the joy he had experienced only shortly before. To John Holmes, who saw him just after the Harcourt rejection, he seemed desolate: "It was quite a blow to him."[172]

In June Holmes's literary agent, Rae Everitt of MCA, read Jack's book. He had now reduced it to the more acceptable format of 8½-by-11-inch pages. Still, Everitt told him—through Ginsberg, who acted as intermediary—that she thought it "would be hard to sell" and needed "lots of revision"[173] under an editor.

Despite his low spirits, Kerouac insisted on doing things his "own way." Instead of revising, he stubbornly began working on "inserts" for the *Road* book. These were further scenes of Cassady's childhood, describing the appearance of Neal "on the poolroom scene in Denver at a very early stage."[174] But this new portrait work turned away from the linear, kinetic style of the rest of the book toward a more involuted and elaborate prose, resembling his efforts immediately preceding the April scroll. (Kerouac's insert work of May–June 1951 can be found on pages 47–56 of *Visions of Cody*.)

AFTER several months of daily typing, constantly pushing himself further, Jack's health finally failed. In late June of 1951, thrombophlebitis flared up in his legs and made him an invalid. Because there was no one in New York to take care of him, he went to stay with his mother and sister in Kinston, North Carolina, for the rest of the summer. It was like stepping into a vacuum. He caught up on his sleep and, his legs propped up to restore circulation, read hungrily—Melville, Lawrence, Blake—but did no writing aside from correspondence with friends. As an ailing and penniless guest, he gradually began to feel like a burden on his relatives. In August he returned north to enter Kingsbridge Veterans' Hospital in the Bronx for about a month.

The summer's inactivity forced Jack to pause and reassess the direction of his work. He decided it had separated into two divergent currents: one moving toward a subjective, lyrical vision—the "metaphysical" strain in his Dr. Sax notes and in the "vertical" portrait work on Neal's childhood; the other toward a more historical, external perspective—as in the April *Road* with its speedy "horizontal" narrative. He continued to seek a unifying element that would merge these two currents into a single stream. "Deep form"—a resolution of both metaphysical vertical depth and horizontal narrative movement—still obsessed and eluded him, as evidenced in a July 14 letter from the South to Holmes: "When I get to be so pure you won't be able to bear the thought of my death on a starry night," Kerouac wrote, "it will be when I'll have come to know and tell the truth (all of it, in every conceivable mask) and yet digress from that to my lyric-alto knowing of this land...a deep form bringing together of two ultimate and at-present-conflicting streaks in me."[175]

With a new, blue Eversharp pencil to change his luck, Kerouac started a hospital diary. Begun as a record of the "lostness" he felt (he had lost wife, family, dreams of success), the diary became a way out of it. Kerouac had been reading Proust. In his diary he attempted, like Proust, to remember his own life, to store up in words an interior strength gathered from memory that would allow him to go on in the world. He was convinced that "re-remembering [his] soul in the hospital . . . for [his] big personal knowledge Odyssey structures,"[176] had rescued his creative life.

In the early fall of 1951, Kerouac was released from the hospital. He went to Richmond Hill, where Gabrielle had resettled in the same apartment building, though in a much inferior apartment—smaller, noisier, and at the same rent—directly under the former one. Jack blamed himself for her unhappy declension, wishing he had never married and thus not disrupted his former comfortable life with his mother. The whole mess, he thought, had been caused by his "own stupidity that the ghost of [his] father never warned or curbed."[177]

At this low ebb of his personal life, his writing, for which he had sacrificed everything, was all he had left. For the next year, despite the vicissitudes of circumstance, he wrote at levels of depth and intensity that seemed to justify all the hardships that had gone before.

PART THREE
WRITER

* * * *

O N C E he had been out of the hospital a few weeks, Jack got his street legs back and roamed all over New York in his "red October shirt," with his "beat" copy of Proust under his arm ("because I'm really reading it") and "portable breast shirtpocket notebooks slapping."[1] Though his poverty and "lostness" sometimes plunged him into numbing despair, there were other moments when he felt weirdly purified, as if life could take no more away from him. "Everything belongs to me because I am poor,"[2] he wrote in his notebook. As if in proof, his powers of observation and expression bloomed as never before.

A meeting with a prospective publisher contributed motivation to write. Ginsberg introduced Jack to Carl Solomon, who was then working in an editorial capacity for his uncle, A. A. Wyn, publisher of Ace Books, a cheap paperback house. (Ginsberg and Solomon had met while both were patients at Columbia Psychiatric Institute.) Allen's first achievement as liaison between Wyn and Solomon and his own writer friends was to bring in Burroughs' "factualist" novel of drug addiction, *Junkie*, which Ace accepted. Solomon extended an offer to Kerouac of a $250 advance for an option on three books, tentatively beginning with *On the Road*. Although it took Jack months to collect his advance, and Ace eventually rejected several of his books, at the time this offer encouraged him considerably.

October was always Kerouac's favorite month. Now, with notebooks at the ready, he wandered the city, straining to take in—and instantly to articulate on paper—everything he saw or heard. On October 18 he went to Birdland to hear bop alto player Lee Konitz, whose sound he considered the supreme evolution of the heroic modern lyric mode innovated by Charlie Parker. Konitz's "lyric-alto" style at this Birdland performance, Kerouac said later, "inspired me to write the way he plays."[3] To Jack, who was now searching for a new prose voice, the free phrasing and speedy independent ideation of Konitz's bop solo lines seemed translatable into a literary procedure based on "the flow of words and the releasing bop-sound at the end of a prose rhythm paragraph."[4]

"Sketching" was what Kerouac called his new rapid notational approach. The candid, spontaneous prose it produced became the root of his mature style, that highly personalized Proustlike but American private monotone, which he called "Modern Prose indeed."[5]

"Sketching" got its name from Kerouac's artist friend Ed White, with whom Jack dined one night in a Chinese restaurant on 124th Street. "Just sketch in the streets like a painter but with words," White suggested. A few days after the Chinese dinner, on October 25—later memorialized by Kerouac as "the great moment of discovering my soul"[6]—the meaning of White's proposal came to him "in full force" and he began "sketching everything in sight." Thereafter, the revisions of *On the Road* he was planning for Solomon took a "turn" from "conventional narrative survey of road trips etc. into a big multi-dimensional conscious and subconscious character evocation of Neal in his whirlwinds."[7]

Beginning on October 25, Jack "sketched" on location in the streets, at subway stations and cafeterias. He found the whole phenomenal field—with its cargo of associations in imagination and memory—activating in front of him "in myriad profusion." "You just have to purify your mind and let it pour the words," Jack later advised Ginsberg in summarizing the principles of sketching, "and write with 100% personal honesty both psychic and social etc. and slap it all down shameless, willynilly, rapidly." The new kind of bop-trance composition that resulted was—Kerouac sweepingly concluded—"the only way to write."[8] Sketching was at first strictly an on-the-spot technique, but it quickly developed into a rapid notational method for transcribing from memory and imagination as well. Kerouac's experimental work during the final months of 1951 is documented in the early pages of *Visions of Cody*.

The best and purest evidence of the original sketching impulse are the New York and Long Island sketches of October and November (*Visions of Cody*, pages 3–38). These were scribbled by Kerouac in exhausting ten- and fifteen-minute bursts. Each was a dense, detailed "solo" of attention ("Blow as deep as you want to blow,"[9] he reminded himself). Sitting in a cafeteria, for instance, he tried to capture the situation at all levels—from the Dutch still-life particulars of surface optics (light reflecting off shiny glass, metal, and glazed food inside cafeteria cases) to the psychological, existential nuances of behavior, the loneliness exhibited by people eating in public.

On his peripatetic sketching expeditions around New York, Kerouac carried *The Remembrance of Things Past* both as talisman and manual; he envisioned himself as the priest of a new Proustian-American prose, a "great rememberer," whose function was "redeeming from darkness"[10] minute particulars both visual and interior. In this mission the notational prose itself became a source of illumination, a perceiving instrument that, like the neons and reflective surfaces of the cafeteria (or like "Proust's Combray Cathedral . . . a great refractor of light"),[11] made perceptible the details of a world.

BY the end of November 1951, two things impelled Kerouac to make a decisive life move. First, his mother gave notice that she would quit her shoe factory job at the end of the year and once again go to North Carolina to live with Nin; Jack wasn't invited. Second, he ran into his seagoing friend Henri Cru, who—as in 1947—promised him a sailing job, this time aboard the S.S. *President Adams*, bound for the Far East.

Jack spent a mournful night in Richmond Hill, packing up his few personal possessions and listing them emotionally in his notebook. As he packed he listened to his sleeping mother's labored breathing in the next room. The "tragedy" of the Kerouacs, with their long string of sad "moving-days" (he dreamed of them endlessly) was a choking lump in his throat.

But it was "time to leave home and go to the last coast."[12] Jack planned to get on the *Adams* as a deck hand in New York. After a few days of hanging around the pier, however, he missed the boat; there were no jobs, and he watched forlornly as the *Adams* slid away. Unfazed, Cru told him jobs would open up in San Pedro and urged him to meet the *Adams* there. Cru even offered a loan of bus fare. Short on options, Jack accepted.

KEROUAC was in San Francisco a week ahead of the *Adams'* Christmas Eve arrival in San Pedro. He stayed that week with the Cassadys at their small house at 29 Russell Street on Russian Hill. Neal arranged for him a job tossing mail sacks in the baggage room at the Southern Pacific depot. Jack, who had almost no money, spent an entire day's pay ($10) on one celebratory bash with Cassady. Neal drove them in his old green jalopy "across tracks and beyond junkyards" to some housing project shacks, where they drank bourbon and wine and "oolyakoo'd" with two black sisters from Arkansas (Carolyn Cassady "had fits").[13] Jack wound up with "a sudden awful cold of the virus X type California style."[14] Nonetheless, a few days later, using Neal's railroad pass, he rode a Southern Pacific caboose down the coast to Los Angeles.

In "bleary sorrow,"[15] he hiked from the Los Angeles railroad yard to a downtown skid row hotel and there collapsed for twenty-four hours, sleeping and dosing himself with bourbon, lemon juice, and Anacin. His fever brought visions of the travels stretching out behind and ahead of him, relentlessly criss-crossing an America that had no end. He recovered in time to meet Cru and the *Adams* in San Pedro on Christmas Eve, but once again it was a "comedy of errors": he didn't have enough seniority, and all the deck-hand jobs went to men with longer records in their union books. He spent the wee hours of Christmas morning in silly alcoholic pranks with Cru; then Cru and the *Adams* sailed away without him. Hung over in San Pedro, Jack had $14.50 in his pocket and no one to care about, or to care about him. (He loved only his "own skin,"[16] Cru had told him.)

He went back to the one place where he was welcome, the Cassadys'. Two days after Christmas 1951, he moved into their barnlike, half-finished attic. Neatly arranging his notebooks and papers, he began to write more "inserts" he hoped would add vertical depth to *On the Road*.

The work sent on from California by Jack, along with passages from the 1951 *On the Road* and Jack's earliest inserts (about young Neal in the pool hall), were sufficient to elicit, through Ginsberg's persistent collection efforts, the long-awaited $250 advance from Ace. With the money came little else but confusion, however. Solomon's positive comments on work Kerouac sent were often followed by contradictory negative ones. In letters he called Jack an "idiot" and a "work-shirker," insisted *On the Road* was unreadable and "unintelligible,"[17] and kept deferring final acceptance of anything. Jack managed to interest Solomon in Cassady's autobiographical piece, *The First Third*, but then suffered the humiliation of having Solomon write patronizingly to Neal, advising him to ignore Jack's literary advice and example.

At this time Kerouac and Cassady were supposed to be writing books for Ace about the same subject: Cassady's life (of course, Jack's book was also—as he had told Solomon—"about himself"). Their main literary study, accordingly, was Neal's favorite writer, Proust. They read aloud to each other nightly, sometimes from Shakespeare or the Charles Atkinson translation of Spengler but usually from *The Remembrance of Things Past*.

Listening to Neal's halting and heartfelt rendition of the auto-biographical epiphanies of Proust, Jack slowly realized his still-developing "book about Neal" was ceasing to be a realistic, literal study of Cassady in rapid movement through space and was becoming instead an entirely different work—a "vertical" illumination of Neal's life in all its interior cross sections, each one a sedimentary deposit of the past. At least in terms of his own perception of the work, it was certainly true that "Proust impelled the beginning of *Visions of Cody*."[18]

Writing night after night in his attic, Jack kept digging deeper and deeper into the "Neal book," as he had begun thinking of his new work about Cassady. Material was readily at hand. Jack typed up tape recordings of their conversations, preserving Cassady's surprising verbal hesitancy on the tapes—and so revealing another vein of Neal's character, something that would have been impossible to display so well in expository prose.

Sometime in the early months of 1952, Kerouac recognized that the inserts he was working on really made up a second book, a vertical *sequel* to the horizontal 1951 *Road*. However, in dealing with his publishing contacts, Ginsberg and Solomon, he continued to represent the two projects as one. The reason for this was evidently his hesitation to abandon *On the Road* until he had actually produced the work that would supersede it. As the vertical book neared completion, he gradually rejected the earlier *Road*, both in his mind and in his dealings with Ace. He was preparing, he believed, an entirely new *On the Road* that would render all earlier versions—including the 1951 scroll—obsolete.

When Ginsberg, probably speaking at least in part on Solomon's behalf, expressed reservations about the shocking chunks of prose he kept getting in the mail from Kerouac (some of which Allen considered too frankly erotic to be published in the censorship climate of the fifties), Jack responded adamantly that he wouldn't change a word. The absolutism of his position made perfect sense aesthetically but was economically and professionally suicidal.

It is hard to speak seriously of Kerouac's professional life as a writer at this time, however, because, though he was writing constantly, he had almost no sense of any relation between that fact and making a living; if he had, he certainly would not have written as he did. It wasn't that Jack was uninterested in the dollars-and-cents side of things, but rather that he had an understanding of it that was as obscure as a Trobriand Islander's.

He immediately sent the $250 Ace Books advance to his mother and lived for his first few months on Russell Street virtually without money. Then—and only after the major ground-laying labors of the new "Neal book" had been done—he accepted another mail- and baggage-handling job with Southern Pacific, set up by Cassady.

Even at that, he worked for a living only a few nights a week. Other nights, alone in his attic with "typewriter clacking," he mused about the "working people" in neighboring houses and wondered what they thought of his nocturnal typing. Though he gave himself headaches with his long stints at the typewriter, and for his efforts was "less paid than a Mexican in New Mexico,"[19] Jack had no doubt he was doing the right thing—he had at last "absolutely attained the quintessence of [his] voice."[20]

But in the burnt-out dawns, when the typing was over but the benzedrine jangle lingered, Kerouac sometimes sank into self-pitying anxieties about his personal life. When in early February he heard from New York that Joan Haverty had given birth to a girl (Janet Michele), he asked his journal if he really did "have a baby daughter somewhere,"[21] but didn't trouble to find out more—fearful, probably, of being stuck with a dependent. The mere thought of being somebody's "lost" father reminded him of all the accumulated "loss" in his family. He brooded over his mother's orphaned childhood, the deaths of Gerard and Leo, and his own long quarrel with his sister and his in-laws over his writing (they thought he should get a job and "stop wasting his time playing around").[22]

ON February 8, 1952, Cassady celebrated his twenty-sixth birthday: "Tragic Saturday in Frisco," Jack later called that day. Kerouac spent it working at the railroad yard; on his way home he stopped for beers at 3rd and Howard ("the wildest bar in America")[23] and there ran into one of the "oloyakoo"-ing black sisters from the housing project. Much deeper into the evening, he lured Neal out of Carolyn's arms with a drunken phone call saying he was in jail. They went off together with the sisters. But when, in an attempt to continue the party, Jack later tried to sneak one of the girls into "his" attic, Carolyn caught on. The resultant domestic scene reduced a guilty Jack to fretful contrition. Carolyn was surprised—and moved—by the sincerity of his remorse.

In an ironic twist, the "Tragic Saturday" episode not only temporarily fortified the Cassady marriage (Neal was on his best behavior for weeks afterward), it tied Jack more firmly into the family bond. During Neal's work shift, Jack now took to sitting in the Cassady kitchen with Carolyn, sharing sips from his daily bottle of cheap sweet wine and blurting out the tale of his "tragic" family and failed marriages.

When Cassady went off for two weeks to a railroad hold-down in San Luis Obispo, he implicitly encouraged Jack and Carolyn to become lovers. Confused, Jack held off till Neal came back. Cassady then repeated the signal more explicitly. This time Jack dutifully (and eagerly) acted on it. For the next several months, the two men traded shifts as Carolyn's lover. Once "Neal saw that Jack and I weren't going to love him any less, everyone relaxed,"[24] Carolyn later wrote.

For a few months, until the tension grew too great for both men, it was a successful three-way relationship. Jack had fallen heavily for Carolyn, whom he described to Ginsberg as "Ideal Mother Image."[25] Her companionship gave him the kind of emotional security he rarely felt when away from Gabrielle. Carolyn recalls that Jack's writing "didn't isolate him very much. Even when he'd go to his attic or his room to write, he was aware of being with us and frequently broke his concentration to come share the current work . . . He liked to talk to us about the book he was working on, quote from it, read to us and generally share his excitements."[26]

IN this ideally supportive atmosphere, Jack completed his "Neal book," or what is now *Visions of Cody.* His last spasm of effort, concluded in early April 1952, was a capsule account of all his major travels with Neal— "four trips in 40 states,"[27] compressed into 160 typed pages (pages 338–398 of the published book, beginning "I first met Cody" and ending "Adios, king"). Sending it off to Solomon, who had rejected everything he had so far submitted, Jack proposed that this 160-page tale of the road trips be published as a self-contained short novel in two editions, hardcover and paperback, under the title *On the Road*. Simultaneously, he also submitted the same book to Harcourt.

Throughout April Kerouac worked at organizing all the writing he had done at the Cassadys' and began assembling it together with the fall 1951 "sketched" material from New York into one giant manuscript of more than 600 pages. (This he typed six weeks later in Mexico City and sent to Ginsberg as the latest *On the Road* to be submitted to Ace.)

LOOKING for a second opinion, Jack sent the 160-page road trip novella and other excerpts from the new work to William Burroughs in Mexico City. For once the usually taciturn Burroughs replied in entirely positive terms: "excerpts from your novel sound mighty fine."[28] Burroughs subsequently wrote to Ginsberg that these new manuscripts indicated to him that Jack had "developed unbelievably" in his writing and clearly possessed "a tremendous talent."[29]

Burroughs' encouragement prompted Kerouac to conceive a third novel (for the Ace deal—the other two being *Road* and the still-unwritten *Sax*), which he first proposed in a letter of April 8 to Ginsberg. This would be a book about Burroughs in South America. Between the lines of the letter, Kerouac's growing unhappiness with the Ace deal was apparent. He asked Ginsberg to come clean with him; was Solomon an idiot? He also charged in the letter that John Holmes was plagiarizing him in *Go*, a novel named after one of Jack's own rejected manuscripts, and he reported anxiously that the authorities were bugging his mother on behalf of Joan Haverty, who was trying to sue him for child support. (Allen's lawyer brother, Eugene Brooks, had agreed to provide Jack with legal defense.) Kerouac suggested to Ginsberg that his publishing and personal problems were helping turn him into an alcoholic in his San Francisco attic.

Around this time Robert Giroux of Harcourt, Brace rejected Kerouac's latest version of *On the Road*. Ginsberg, acting as agent, suggested that this rejection was due to Kerouac's new material being "too personal and subjective."[30]

The failure of either Solomon or Giroux to appreciate his new work took the edge off Kerouac's creative surge. Carolyn Cassady recalls that while Jack often seemed to consider himself "the best" of writers, he sometimes tumbled from such peaks of confidence into bad depression, caused by "his reception or lack of it."[31] This was one such valley. In letters to Ginsberg, Jack now hinted for the first time of discontent with his living circumstances at the Cassadys'. Neal's stubbornness, intractability, narrowness, and pitiful attempts at thrift all annoyed him.

The strain of maintaining their ménage-à-trois had finally begun to affect the Cassady–Kerouac relationship. He and Neal were fighting for the first time in their lives, Jack sadly told Allen. After an argument over peyote and French poets (Jack's friendship with a Berkeley surrealist poet, Philip Lamantia, disclosed in him socio-literary aspirations Neal obviously didn't share), Jack thought Neal was acting "dead."[32]

Around May Day the Cassadys left on a trip to Tennessee, with the Mexico City-bound Jack riding along as far as Nogales. The drive to the border, Carolyn later wrote, was a "romantic agony," fraught with "unbearable"[33] tension between her and Jack. Jack sensed (as he told Ginsberg in a letter a few days later) only "sad hostility"[34] between himself and Neal, his erstwhile soul brother. After standing for some moments by the wire fence, watching the Cassadys wave and drive away, Jack slouched under the eyes of "sinister" and "severe looking"[35] U.S. border guards into Mexico, feeling like a kid sneaking out of school at last.

BILL BURROUGHS, once again Kerouac's host in Mexico City, was at the time of this visit beset by legal problems. The previous summer, in a drunken game of William Tell, he had accidentally shot his wife. The Mexican authorities' ongoing investigation of Joan's death made him touchy about Jack's habit of smoking grass in the Orizaba Street flat. Kerouac, who had acquired several ounces of top-grade *sensimilla*, which he liked to use while writing, solved the problem by shutting himself up in the toilet down the hall. There he sat "on the closed toilet seat [on] a little tile toilet," smoked his joints, and as he "hallucinated,"[36] scribbled away in pencil on children's notebooks held in his lap.

At the beginning of the first notebook, he printed: "*A novella of children and Evil, the Myth of the rainy night*"—a title he later changed to *Dr. Sax*. The whole tale—one that he had been devising for years—took him a month of afternoon writing sessions, in Burroughs' flat and in the hall toilet, to complete.

The novel was a unique mélange of past, present, and impossible. Into the personal "Shadow" material from his youth ("angles of my hoop-rolling boyhood," he described it to Ginsberg, "as seen from the shroud"),[37] Kerouac mixed a kind of *Weird Tales* subplot drawn liberally from Aztec symbology, which he was now studying under Burroughs' tutelage. In the middle of his story he placed Doctor Sax, picturing him as a Burroughs-esque, effete, magisterial dabbler among narcotic "jars of eternity" and "herb powders."[38] Kerouac was clearly conceiving his fictional "doctor" as a cartoon enlargement of the real Bill—as a sort of contemporary magus, pitted in cosmological struggle, with the whole conscious universe at stake. To Jack the Burroughs-Sax figure represented the last incarnation of what Spengler had called "Faustian man"; this novel, Kerouac said later, was his attempt to write "the third part of *Faust*."[39]

The real power of the novel, however, lay in its jewel-perfect evocation of thirties Lowell. Consciously emulating Proust (that "old teahead of time"),[40] Kerouac uncoiled his story from a single memory image—the "wrinkly tar sidewalk" outside the Kerouacs' Moody Street apartment. Beginning there he spontaneously elaborated all the associations the image brought back to his pot-hallucinated mind. ("Don't stop to think of words," he told himself, "just stop to think of your picture better.")[41]

Sax was saturated with clues relating the guilt-ridden sexual frustrations of Kerouac's youth (when he had, by masturbation, "discovered sex on the night [his dog] Beauty died")[42] to adult tensions that were all too similar. The tension-frustration-masturbation cycle of Jack's adolescence, as described in *Sax*, had survived into maturity intact. It was now accentuated by semivoluntary literary poverty. In Mexico City Jack abandoned masturbation only when he had a few extra pesos to spend on a teenage whore from Organo Street, and that was seldom. Though in letters to pals he described lavish prospective sex idylls with women in France and Italy (to be met on wild sea voyages), in private he was now nearly paralyzed with fear that his wife was suing him for nonsupport. It exaggerated his inclination to dread the machinations of all women.

His romance with Carolyn Cassady, as fulfilling as any he had ever experienced, had been too complex in its implications. On June 3 he wrote to Carolyn from Mexico, attempting to address "the emotional complexities" of their relationship. In fact, he steered around them and shifted part of the blame to Neal, who was, he said, "incapable of dealing with such big abstract problems as love and mystery." But Jack finally had to acknowledge that for him, too, love was "lost in a tangle of shrouds." He now

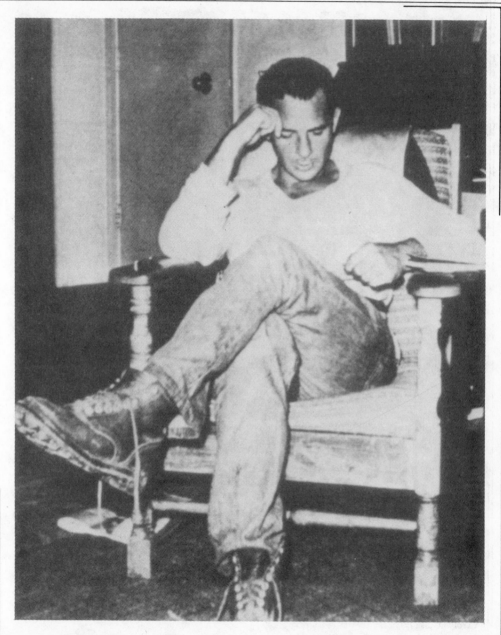

Kerouac at the Cassadys', San Francisco: "The one place where he was welcome"
(courtesy Carolyn Cassady)

Cassady, Kerouac, c. 1952: "Kerouac and Cassady were supposed to be writing books . . . about the same subject: Cassady's life." (courtesy Carolyn Cassady)

Cassady at work, sketched by his wife (courtesy Carolyn Cassady)

Neal Cassady, Cathy Cassady, Jack Kerouac: "The family bond" (courtesy Carolyn Cassady)

TOP: *"It was a successful three-way relationship."* (jacket photo courtesy Carolyn Cassady; *Heart Beat* published by Creative Arts, 1976)

BOTTOM: *Cartoon drawn by Kerouac while at work on* Dr. Sax: *" 'Angles of my hoop-rolling boyhood . . . as seen from the shroud' "* (courtesy Carolyn Cassady)

declared himself ready to forsake all claim to Carolyn and (he added self-dramatizingly) to accept "loss and death."[43] But between the lines, his letter exudes anything but the Olympian resignation it proposes. The truth that his choice of a solitary writing life and his long habit of emotional dependence on his mother were factors that would forever prevent him from enjoying a satisfactory prolonged relationship with any woman was now dawning on him, and it was not easy to face.

O N Burroughs' typewriter Jack typed up the final 600-page manuscript of his October-to-April "Neal book." While typing it he wrote to Ginsberg that he was already certain its "flood of language" was "inspired in its entirety, like Joyce's *Ulysses*."[44] By the end of May 1952, he had mailed the book to Ginsberg. On June 3 he wrote in elation to John Holmes that he felt he had at last found the "deep form" he had spent four years searching for.[45]

Kerouac was convinced that in *Sax* and the "Neal book" he had arrived at the height of his powers as a writer. But in the weeks that followed, the days without mail piled up like slow months in Burroughs' Mayan calendars. By June 20 he could wait no longer, and wrote to Ginsberg. Had Allen received his manuscript?

Ginsberg had indeed received it and was slow to comment because he harbored serious doubts. When he finally replied, it was in terms that turned Jack's sweet savoring of his work into a taste of ashes. "I don't see how it will ever be published," Ginsberg told Kerouac. "It's so personal, so full of sex language, so full of our local mythological references." Allen charged Jack with writing out of his mind—"crazy (not merely inspired crazy) but unrelated crazy," admonished him for "just crappin around," dismissed the book psychologically as "just a hangup," and finally demanded impatiently, "What are you trying to put down, man?"[46]

Stung, Jack reacted angrily—but not openly. In dealing with Ginsberg and Ace, he adopted a new stance: defensive, cautious, bristling with "Canuck doubt." Instead of sending them *Dr. Sax* (which was completed by June 20), he lied and told them it was only half done. (Later, however, when he had cooled off, he did submit *Sax* to Ace—and it was rejected.)

Still reeling from what he considered to be a betrayal by Ginsberg, Jack now wrote to Holmes that though he had been producing "concentrated marble-fist writing," it had come out of a "hallucinated, clairvoyant type trance"—at the conclusion of which he was starving (he had lost twelve pounds from his usual 170), alone, and absolutely without prospects. "What have I got?" he moaned. "I'm 30 years old, broke, my wife hates me and is trying to have me jailed, I have a daughter I'll never see, my old mother after all this time and work and money and hopes is still working her ass off in a shoe shop, I have not a cent in my pocket for a decent whore." He had finally hit bottom—all because he had trusted "dirty bastard publishers." He was not only the "loneliest writer in America" but also, in his own opinion, "probably the greatest"—and yet "the most despised bum."[47]

Kerouac's Mexico stay ended in a nasty slide into humiliation. Multiplying the rancor he already felt over his literary misfortunes, his only raincoat was stolen, as was a letter from his mother containing $10 that he needed to get his shoes and seabag fixed. Down to his last five pesos, he had nothing to eat and was no longer getting along with Burroughs (who thought he had turned "surly").[48] On July 3 he wrote an enigmatic note to the Cassadys, advising them that they would not hear from him again for a long time because he was going off to live in an adobe shack in the countryside of Mexico—"to sink into natural oblivion with myself, dog, indians." He instructed Neal and Carolyn to let his mail "dust under a floorboard."[49] A few days later he borrowed money from Burroughs and left by bus for North Carolina to join his family.

J A C K stayed about six weeks in the South—as always the uneasy, penurious guest among skeptical relatives. In late August Neal broke two months of silence between them by writing to Jack from San Jose, where he had moved his family into a big house. He urged Kerouac to come to California, become a student brakeman on the Southern Pacific, and live with the Cassadys. As a lure he sent Kerouac an expired railroad pass along with a thousand-word letter of instruction on how to deal with every conductor between Rocky Mount and San Jose. Pass or no pass, Kerouac feared a debacle in forgotten rail yards of the South. Cassady then wired him $25, giving him enough for bus fare. Once again Jack headed west.

That September he worked for the railroad as a student brakeman, ran around a little with Neal, talked about Proust and read *Dr. Sax* aloud to him—as in the "good times" of six months earlier. On most days, however, they worked different railroad shifts. When Neal was out on the day shift, Jack made love with Carolyn. (She later described this as their "golden" time together.)[50]

But with early October the first winter rains came; there was less work on the railroad, more periods of sitting around at home for the men—and increasing tension between Neal and Jack, not only over Carolyn but also over the much less interesting question of money. Jack had not as yet received his first railroad check and, except for a $50 check from John Holmes, had to get along on the Cassadys' dwindling generosity.

Writing to Ginsberg on October 4, Cassady complained that Kerouac was stubbornly brooding over imagined insults and "refusing to smoke (almost)." Calling him "the lonely fucker . . . of Carolyn, who blows him," Neal said that Jack now acted "morose," and talked only of moving "to way down there on skid row" in order to "write."[51] In the next few days, the situation deteriorated even further. Jack's threat to buy a hot plate and do his own cooking caused a quarrel with Neal. The petty dispute quickly escalated; Jack took his things and left. He called Neal from San Francisco, drunk, but Neal angrily hung up on him.

Shortly after Jack moved into a $4-a-week room in a skid row hotel, the Cameo. "Bitchy people, I hate people, I can't stand people any more,"[52] he grouched to Allen.

KEROUAC'S falling-out with the Cassadys and the general misanthropy he expressed variously at this time were by-products of the bitterness he increasingly felt over his rejection by New York publishers. On October 8 he focused his outrage over his failure in a letter to Ginsberg. He openly accused Allen of mishandling his career. In failing to sell the 1951 *On the Road*, he charged, "agent" Ginsberg had not taken advantage of recent "pocket book styles and the new trend in writing about drugs and sex." Ginsberg's criticism of the "Neal book" Jack dismissed as mere jealousy. Not only Ginsberg but also Holmes and Solomon would give their "right arms" to "be able to write like that," Kerouac said. Looking back he now saw his whole career in New York as "one long almost humorous chronicle of a real dumb lil abner getting taken in by fat pigjaws."[53]

Kerouac had arrived at the end of that period in his life when the word "young" could be used to qualify the "writer" that he had so emphatically become. As he told Ginsberg between the threats and invective of which the letter was largely composed, he felt like an "old man."[54]

ALTHOUGH the work both exhausted and terrified him, Kerouac stuck with a Southern Pacific brakeman's job all that bitter fall of 1952. The money he made compensated for the job's drawbacks; it bought him precious independence from other people. He salted away most of his $600 monthly salary, storing it up in traveler's checks while surviving like a man in a voluntary poverty experiment and talking to almost nobody.

His move to the city forced him to put in an extra fifty miles of train time every day, commuting to and from the main San Jose yards on a local out of downtown San Francisco. This ride became his "library." He stuffed his books and papers into his tattered black seabag—the same one he had dragged all the way from Greenland to Mexico—and became a rolling writer.

His work consisted of daily runs up and down the Coast Division of the Southern Pacific between San Jose and the Gilroy substation at Watsonville, about a hundred miles south. His duties en route included setting brakes and switches and giving flag signals. Unable to overcome his fear of "those merciless wheels,"[55] he particularly dreaded getting on and off moving trains.

At night, in the Cameo, he sipped rotgut port and poured onto paper his spontaneous prose paean to the working man's life, "October in the Railroad Earth." This was a 15,000-word exercise in "experimental speedwriting," intended to "clack along all the way like a steam engine pulling a 100-car freight with a talky caboose at the end."[56] Indeed, it did just that, in long, limber sentences like those loose-jointed locals that make all the stops. This piece captured basic local "weathers" in a rugged prose that evoked American landscape not as background but as a foreground character with a pastoral beauty and bulk of its own. Artistically, Kerouac had turned his isolation into gold.

But the abuse of unfriendly conductors, the constant danger, and the long hours of standing on trains all day—which made the phlebitis in his legs flare up—finally wore Jack out. One Saturday in December, after a chewing-out from a French-Canadian conductor, he walked off the job and kept on going—first to San Jose, then to Mexico.

KEROUAC stopped for a week at the Cassadys' on his way south. He asked Carolyn to follow him to Mexico City for a visit, a request surprising enough to throw the Cassadys into a quandary. Neal finally proposed that Carolyn should visit Jack in Mexico—but only after he, Neal, was allowed to go first to drop Jack off and pick up some marijuana. Carolyn agreed. Jack told her they would "be together again in two weeks."[57]

The long drive south took its toll on Neal. After they had smoked strong local grass in a dead-end village somewhere in Chihuahua, he asked Jack to take over the wheel. Kerouac was a terrible driver even when "straight"; on this occasion, stoned, he had a recurrent problem with the clutch. Convinced Jack was deliberately screwing up, Neal got angrier and angrier. At last he repossessed the wheel, called Kerouac "rattle-brained,"[58] and drove the rest of the way to Mexico City himself, blocking Jack out with the "blank wall"[59] treatment that Kerouac always hated.

Neal rushed right out of Mexico City with his pot, barely saying goodbye to Jack. Out of one of his traveler's checks, Kerouac put down $12 for a month's rent on a two-room adobe blockhouse atop the building where Burroughs had lived on Orizaba Street. As soon as Neal was gone, Jack started a little novel in French with a plot about himself and Cassady meeting in 1935. He had little to do but write; Burroughs had departed for South America (jumping a local bail bond in the process), leaving Kerouac with no one at all to talk to. Fearful that the Mexican police would come around looking for Bill, Jack got nervous about his own legal situation in regard to Joan Haverty. He imagined invisible authorities closing in on him and instructed correspondents not to use his real name on mail.

After only a few days, Kerouac admitted in a letter to Carolyn that he was "unbearably lonely." He begged her to come and "dance the Mambo"[60] with him. Carolyn showed the letter to Neal, who went into "paroxysms of grief"[61] over the thought of his wife's departure. But before Carolyn was able to write and tell Jack their deal was off, Jack's own nerve collapsed. He ran off to New York for Christmas, announcing to Carolyn in a brief, scribbled note that he was "hung up in the night."[62]

JACK spent Christmas of 1952 with his mother, who was back in Richmond Hill. On New Year's Eve he went into the city for a party at his ex-classmate Jerry Newman's recording studio. Ginsberg, whom Jack hadn't seen for six months, was there. Jack got very drunk and high and later, in the bleak dawn, broke down in tears in the back seat of a taxi with Allen.

Ginsberg gave his sad account of the evening and of Kerouac's current state in a letter to Cassady, announcing that Jack was writing at home in "very hard and long solitudes," then on Manhattan visits "flitting from soul to soul like hornet-bee." Jack's "condition of withdrawal from life," Allen suggested, was making him too preoccupied "with self as subject matter"[63] in his writing.

"Self as subject matter" did indeed preoccupy Jack. Who else's life did he know? His new book, he told Neal and Carolyn, was one he had often said he would write—a serious study of his love affair with Mary Carney at age sixteen. Sometime shortly after the holidays, he wrote a first chapter on the typewriter in Richmond Hill, then completed the rest of the work by hand, in less than six weeks. Dissatisfied with the final one-fourth of the book in its original "spontaneous" form, he went back and completely rewrote that part in early February. "Springtime Mary" was his original title for this manuscript; he later changed it to *Maggie Cassidy*.

In February 1953, acting on a professional tip from Holmes, Kerouac submitted this manuscript and two others (*On the Road*, *Dr. Sax*) to a literary agent, Phyllis Jackson of the MCA agency. She evidently passed all three directly on to Viking Press. Viking editorial adviser Malcolm Cowley took Kerouac to lunch. Confronted with the "publishing world" in the person of one of its most eminent statesmen, Jack's arrogance melted into awe. If he removed the fantasy parts of *Sax*, Cowley casually told him, the remainder—the boyhood tales of Lowell—would make him $50,000. But after much talk, Viking was willing to advance Kerouac only $250 for an option on an unspecified book. Jack, who had heard Holmes was getting nearly one hundred times that much for *Go*, considered this advance "peanuts," though he took the money.

In early spring 1953, Jack visited Quebec to look for his "fellaheen" roots among his own people, the Canucks of the Caughnawaga Valley. His search, however, took place almost exclusively in various taverns located near the corner of Ste. Catherine and St. Laurent streets in "Montreal, Russia"—a fantastic "Northern Gloomtown." There, amid the "beer, smoke, talk" of the "bleak wintry city" (a "cathedral of the world"), he endeavored to discover "something Breton and lost" in his forever-displaced soul. He briefly thought he had found it when a "teary old lush in the Papineau tavern" told him he should drink "le sang du caribou" (caribou blood). Suddenly he felt like "Ti Jean the happy saint back among his loyal brothers at last."[64] But another night in Montreal he went to a Ste. Catherine Street bordello, had sex with a whore, and then passed out. After hours of disturbing nightmares, he awoke "sneering at the ceiling . . . making horrid gestures with [his] hand at hole void of red room." Before they escaped him, he scrawled in his notebook as much as he could remember about his bad dreams: "something . . . about 'the deception of the female.' "[65]

Finally, in the grim light of his hangover at the end of the trip, Kerouac saw his fantasy of living in Quebec for what it was. Reporting on the trip to Ginsberg, he gruffly wrote off Canada in a single scatological phrase.

I N mid-April Jack returned by bus to California and the Southern Pacific, this time working on a hold-down in the Southern Division out of San Luis Obispo. He braked and switched through long afternoons in dusty gravel spurs in the mountains around Santa Margarita, an area he later memorialized in *Mexico City Blues*, 146th Chorus: "The Eagle on the Pass/The Wire on the Rail."[66] The work absorbed his days, but by night his railway flophouse in San Luis Obispo was a lonely place. In a May 7 letter to Ginsberg, he related that though the railroad life was peaceful, it was also tedious—and he was as miserable as he had been in New York. His mind seemed to be in a tightening spin at the lip of a whirlpool.

Impatient with Phyllis Jackson's unsuccessful efforts to sell the books, Kerouac turned again to the friend he had recently tried to drive out of his life and sheepishly solicited Ginsberg's services as an agent once more. Ginsberg dutifully attempted to fetch *Dr. Sax* and *Maggie Cassidy* from "the female member of the family, Mrs. Gabe of Richmond Hill." But Gabrielle, who did not want Ginsberg in her house, proved "hard to reach"[67] (as Ginsberg snidely reported to Cassady). For the time being, Kerouac's manuscripts went on collecting dust.

Jack's plan for the end of the summer, when the hold-down was over, was to go into the California wilderness and learn to survive by himself, fishing, hunting, and making Indian acorn mush, in preparation for his final departure from civilization. By the end of May, however, he could take no more of the railroad life. With $300 in his pockets, he walked out on the hold-down. His first stop was the Cassadys' in San Jose. There Neal was glumly hanging around the house while recuperating from a foot injury. Jack felt like the proverbial fifth wheel and quickly proceeded to San Francisco.

He spent a few nights at the Cameo, did some heavy drinking with a bar pal of previous North Beach stays, Al Sublette, then began looking for work. At the maritime union hall, he picked up a bedroom steward's job aboard the S.S. *William Carruth*—bound through the Panama Canal to the Gulf and beyond. After downing thirty beers and ten whiskies in an all-night presailing binge with Sublette, he barely made his ship and began the southern voyage in that "shuddering void" phase of alcohol poisoning marked by "nerve-ends being slowly living deathly cut in the center of the gut."[68]

IN a letter to Ginsberg at about this time, Cassady had described their intractably independent "brother" Kerouac as "the thing from another world"[69]—a joke based on *The Thing*, a 1951 science fiction movie about a hulking space monster. On the *Carruth* Jack lived up to Neal's description. His tour of the "kitchen sea" was dismal from start to finish. He slogged through it in an alcohol-benzedrine stupor, saying as little as possible and mostly "staggering around the tragic darkness of the slavish alleyway with brooms, mops, handles, sticks, rags sticking out of [him] like a sad porcupine." The work was dirty and demeaning enough; even worse, the ship's discipline reminded Kerouac ominously of the navy. Officers told him not to smile while he served their eggs; "I'm not the smiling type," he answered grimly. After a Wagnerian passage up the Mississippi delta in a lightning storm, Kerouac walked off the *Carruth* in New Orleans with his pay in his pocket and his duffel bag on his shoulder. Though he had announced he was quitting ship, no one on board said goodbye to him as he sauntered down the gangplank into "the silence of the afternoon."[70]

BACK in Richmond Hill in July, Kerouac swore to cut down on drinking. He typed up his railroading prose and tried to restore himself with "day-long meditations around the house."[71] Out of the $600 he had saved from the railroad and ship jobs, he contributed to Gabrielle's rent and even bought her a television set. He fixed her supper and a martini after her day at the shoe factory, then washed the dishes and sat out with her sipping Tom Collinses under the summer moon.

But after staying on his best behavior for a few weeks, Jack gave in again to the lure of the city. He began hanging around the San Remo Bar in Greenwich Village, headquarters of a set of unconventional persons called by Ginsberg "a circle of seekers"[72] and by Kerouac "the Subterraneans." The habitués of the San Remo, as Jack saw them, were a new wave of "bohemian kids," pseudosaints of a late, mystical stage in cultural evolution (they understood "the Wig and Europe Sadness of us all"). Though Jack suspected the bearded Village sophisticates regarded him as "some kind of hoodlum,"[73] he was attracted by their tastes in drugs and women.

He usually slept the night at Ginsberg's apartment. The East 7th Street flat was, in fact, a common haven—not only for Jack but also for many of Allen's other friends, including Lucien Carr, Allen Ansen ("Austin Bromberg" in *The Subterraneans*), and the youthful, pixyish street criminal-poet Gregory Corso ("Yuri Gligoric"). In September 1953, when William Burroughs returned to the country, acquitted at last of Mexican manslaughter charges, he too took up residence at Ginsberg's.

This was one of Kerouac's periods of general dependence on Allen. These alternated with periods of surly standoffishness. Jack's extreme sensitivity—or paranoia—sometimes registered "great waves of dark hostility . . . hate, malice"[74] emanating from his friend. Yet Ginsberg now not only provided him with weekend housing but also sent Kerouac's manuscripts by messenger service to publishers all over New York.

Although his efforts to get Kerouac published mostly came to nothing, Ginsberg did discover new interest at Viking. Malcolm Cowley, who had rejected both *Sax* and *Visions of Neal* (as the 600-page "Neal book" was now titled), wrote to Ginsberg in July 1953 that he was still considering the 1951 *On the Road*—brought to him six months earlier by Phyllis Jackson—and considered Kerouac "the most interesting writer who is not being published today."[75] But in-house editors at Viking did not yet share Cowley's enthusiasm for *On the Road*; no deal materialized.

Meanwhile Kerouac watched other writers less gifted than himself basking in success. It particularly irked him that Holmes had reportedly received $20,000 for *Go*, while he himself was constantly broke. One night at Ginsberg's apartment when Jack was staying there, Holmes dropped in. Torn between jealousy and embarrassment, Jack hid in another room, eavesdropping resentfully on Holmes's conversation about bop music, all the while telling himself "I'm the bop writer!"[76]

With the years of failure, common literary envy had begun to eat at Kerouac. By mid-1953 he was increasingly obsessed with what he considered a foolish "adolescent literary vision" that made him both chase after and resent famous writers. In *The Subterraneans*, his "confessional" account of the events of that summer, he writes—somewhat painfully—of drunken meetings with two writers of his generation, both much more famous than he was: William Gaddis and Gore Vidal. The source of his interest in such men, Jack admitted in his book, was purely "literary avidity, envy."[77] Kerouac's version of the Vidal encounter, fuzzily mentioning a visit to the well-known writer's "suite in some hotel," with Jack

TOP LEFT: *Kerouac and Ginsberg in Ginsberg's apartment on East 7th Street, New York: "He usually slept the night at Ginsberg's apartment."* (courtesy Allen Ginsberg)

BOTTOM LEFT: *Burroughs and Kerouac, 1953: "The East 7th St. flat was . . . a common haven."* (courtesy Allen Ginsberg)

ABOVE: *Kerouac on fire escape, East 7th Street, 1953 (note brakeman's manual in pocket)* (courtesy Allen Ginsberg)

waking the next morning hung over on a couch, is one of the few deviations from strict truth in the novel. Kerouac left out the fact that he had, as Ginsberg wrote to Cassady, acted "boastfully queerlike"[78] with Vidal. And Vidal later commented that Kerouac had written about the evening with "astonishing accuracy . . . until the crucial moment when Jack and I went to bed together at the Chelsea Hotel, and, as he told me later, disingenuously, 'I forgot.' "[79]

SINCE the "golden" summer of 1952 with Carolyn in San Jose, Jack had experienced a "lack of love for a year almost."[80] Just how much he had been missing came home to him when he began reading the works of Wilhelm Reich, the subterranean god of sexual therapy. To Carolyn he wrote in August 1953 that he had "one vastly tho unimportant sounding thing" to tell her and Neal: "for God's sake read and dig Wilhelm Reich's *Function of the Orgasm* before it's too late, he has discovered that *all* neurotic and somatic physical problems arise from lack of straight genital potency, man cock, woman cunt (vagina not clitoris orgasm), and if you concentrate on that and work out details with (I say) or without Reichian doc you will soon find everything opening out and getting simpler . . . Reich is simple as bread or pornography."[81]

Kerouac attempted to put his Reichian theories into action during a late summer affair with a black girl from the San Remo crowd ("one of the most brilliant gals in their orbit"). "Mardou" was the name he gave this girl in his writing. In bed he gave her the benefit of his Reichian teachings. Eventually, he claimed, they attained together "Reich's beclouding of the senses"—"exchanging existential and loveracts for a crack at making it." He went on at so much length about the cosmic meaning of the theory of the orgasm, however, that the girl (who had already been through professional analysis) finally told him not to "pull that Reich on [her] in bed."[82]

Echoing Ginsberg, Mardou told Jack he was too old to be living with his mother. He responded by proposing to divide his time between Gabrielle and the girl. With Gabrielle, Jack confessed to Mardou, he had a sense of "well-being" and security that he couldn't get elsewhere. When he stayed an extra three hours at Mardou's place to make love to her one more time, he had "visions of [his] work neglected, [his] well-being . . . smashed."[83]

The relationship gradually collapsed, sabotaged by Kerouac's own confused mental state. At the end there were scenes of drunkenness and petty jealousy, resulting in part from Jack's "literary avidities"; after being ambiguously encouraged by Jack, Corso emerged as interloper and rival in the love affair. Jack and Mardou drifted apart. "I don't want to live in this beastly world,"[84] he told her on their last meeting, the day she revealed to him her dalliance with Corso.

"SOMETHING is sick in me, lost, fears," Kerouac wrote after his autumn affair with Mardou. He went back to Richmond Hill but found to his dismay that the familiar "feeling of well-being at home," which he needed "to be straight,"[85] had vanished. There were long, cold nights in October and November when he "just sat in [his] room, hurting." He was, as he wrote later, "suffering . . . from the grief of losing a love, even though [he had] really wanted to lose it."[86] There were now also sad, drunken, loveless visits to the city, when tastes of new drugs (heroin, dolophine, barbiturates) dragged him into slow crawls through the depths of the American chemical synthetic night.

During the three nights of the October harvest moon, he stayed up till dawn in Richmond Hill and typed out ("like a long letter to a friend") his account of the affair with Mardou. His plan was to produce a true, painful testament, like Dostoevsky's *Notes from the Underground*—"a full confession of one's most wretched and hidden agonies after an affair of any kind."[87] His methodology was to sit down at the typewriter, "start at the beginning and let the truth seep out."[88]

Written in desperation to objectify emotions torn from the heart, *The Subterraneans* was the triumph and epitome of the "spontaneous" writing technique Kerouac had been refining for the past two years. The first-person prose of this novel achieves a unified sound like a great bop solo. It has a tensile strength that bears strains and torques of complex feeling; its extended sentences hold together despite sudden shifts of mood. "The prose is what I believe to be the prose of the future," Kerouac later stated in a blurb for the published book, "from both the conscious top and the unconscious bottom of the mind, limited only by the limitations of time flying by as your mind flies with it."[89]

WRITING a whole novel in seventy-two hours was an achievement in itself. Jack later called it "really a fantastic athletic feat as well as mental." In the three nights of composition, he lost fifteen pounds.

Both the ordeal and the outcome impressed his friends. After Ginsberg and Burroughs had read the typescript, they asked Kerouac to give them a statement on the details of his new prose technique—something more specific than his usual mumbled explanations about imitating a jazz soloist who takes deep breaths and blows chorus after chorus. Kerouac responded by putting together a nine-point list of the "Essentials of Spontaneous Prose," which remains the clearest statement of the compositional principles that guided his work from late 1951 on. In it he prescribes the "mental state" necessary for true spontaneity: "write without consciousness in semi-trance . . . write excitedly, swiftly, with writing-or-typing-cramps, in accordance (as from center to periphery) with laws of orgasm . . . *Come from within*, out—to be relaxed and said."[90] Like almost everything else that came into his life, the theories of Wilhelm Reich had been processed out again as aids to writing.

IN Richmond Hill Kerouac brooded over his life, "feeling guilty for writing *Doctor Sax, On the Road*, a sheepishly guilty idiot turning out rejectable wild prose madhouse enormities." He dreamed "immense sagas all night long, fantastic nightmares." In one particularly horrifying and recurrent dream, his father, looking washed-out and indifferent, returned to life in Lowell. The dream had a haunting quality of sadness to it; Jack recognized that his father's "true soul" in the dream was like his own: "life means nothing to him—or, I'm my father myself and this is me."[91]

After conducting a brief romantic attachment on East 7th Street, Ginsberg and Burroughs had split up—Ginsberg heading for Mexico and Burroughs for North Africa. With his friends gone, Jack had nobody to talk to in New York. "God is alone, and I'm better off because of it," he wrote to Carolyn. In the coming "Apocalypse of the Fellaheen,"[92] he had decided, it would be worth more to him to know how to grow potatoes and strawberries than to know about advances and reprint rights.

Neal Cassady, worried about his friend, wrote urging Jack to come west and take a parking lot attendant's job in San Jose: "forget God (no such thing), forget being farmer (far too late, or soon)."[93]

Kerouac accepted. He made plans to hitchhike west at Christmas with Jack Eliot, a "singin' cowboy" pal from the Village—but then slumped into a paralytic depression that stretched into months, delaying his departure for California until the first week of February 1954.

PART FOUR
WANDERING BHIKKU

• • •

THE final weeks in Richmond Hill were a time of difficult reflection. The idealistic dreams of Kerouac's youth had faded. "It's all a big crrrock, I wanta die,"[1] he moaned.

At the Richmond Hill Public Library, studying Thoreau, he stumbled on a reference to Hindu philosophy that led him to look up Ashvagosa's *Life of the Buddha*. He started reading it while walking home. Under a street lamp, he stopped in his tracks. A single phrase had "hooked [him] on the true morphine of Buddha": "REPOSE BEYOND FATE."[2]

He ran home to experiment. Within hours he was deep in his "first meditation." Closing his eyes, holding his breath and concentrating on fighting off thought, he suddenly felt "ecstasy" and "saw golden swarms of nothing."[3] He decided he had achieved nirvana.

Jack carried his new meditation habit with him on the bus to San Jose, as he had once carried ten sandwiches. But this time he meant to spread the blessings. Crossing the country, he meditated assiduously and read Buddhist texts to bone up on important tenets of the dharma with which to enlighten the Cassadys. When he arrived, however, he was dismayed to find that their San Jose kitchen had turned into a metaphysical Chautauqua show. The Cassadys couldn't be enlightened about Buddhism because they were on a new religious kick of their own. Neal had found an Edgar Cayce book in the back seat of a car at the parking lot where he worked. Both Cassadys were now firm proponents of soul transmigration.

Neal in particular had suddenly become religious and was preaching reincarnation and karma, as Jack soon reported in a letter to Ginsberg. Talking as fast as a short-order cook on diet pills, Cassady dished out rapid-fire "scientific" evidence of Cayce's doctrine of rebirth, threw in a speedy side order of Gurdjieff and Ouspensky, and topped it all off by trying to persuade Jack that the inhabitants of Atlantis had possessed the secrets of atomic power. This new Neal made Kerouac think of Billy Graham.

The two months of this visit were a steady downhill slide into mistrust. The "religious" argument hung in the air. Neal expected Jack to pick up work at the parking lot, or else a brakeman job, and stay on as a boarder until Ginsberg's arrival from Mexico. Hoping for satori, Jack guzzled Neal's benzedrine and goofballs, then sulked off to his room to meditate and sweat over notes on Buddha's life, while Neal, rapping frenetically about soul travel, held the floor in the kitchen. Finally, in March, within the space of a few days, Jack and Neal had two bitter quarrels, both of a type later described by Carolyn as "like lover's fights—petty, heartrending and caused by other factors under the surface."[4]

One was a dinner table argument about who would get to eat some pork chops. Guilt over his poverty made Jack sensitive that Neal, who paid the food bills, was secretly begrudging him his meals. The second was about the division of, and payment for, a pound of marijuana they had bought together. At the last minute Neal whisked some powdery leaf residue into his pocket; Kerouac blew his top and announced he was moving out. He asked Carolyn to drive him and his gear into the city, but her car wouldn't start. The red-faced Cassady had to come out and push them down Santa Clara Boulevard in his old clunker, bumping them hard, "not just to give [them] a start but to chastise [Jack] for being so greedy"[5]— and for leaving. Carolyn finally chauffeured Jack into San Francisco, where he blew the $10 he had saved in the pot dispute with Neal on wine and wound up passing out in an un-Buddhalike heap on Al Sublette's floor in North Beach.

KEROUAC rented a $3-a-week room at the Cameo. There, in between binges with Sublette, he sat in a rocking chair by the window, sipping tokay and muscatel, looking down on "bebop winos and whores and cop cars"[6] and writing speedy, wine-blurred "sketch poems" he later called "San Francisco Blues." He also labored over a 100-page compilation of reading notes on Buddhism ("Some of the Dharma"), which he had typed in San Jose. After a week of this, his small savings and his ability to tolerate the life of a wandering religious hobo ran out. On April 23, 1954, he was back in Richmond Hill. As Cassady wrote in a snappish note to Ginsberg, Jack had followed his "sudden" departure from San Jose by "even more suddenly return[ing] to New York and [was] home with mama now."[7]

IN case Kerouac was tempted to believe he had surmounted ego, all he had to do to learn otherwise was observe his own reactions to the continuing cold shoulder he got from publishers. In the spring of 1954, he submitted his 1951 *On the Road* to Little, Brown. He now retitled it *The Beat Generation*, in hopes of capitalizing on the notoriety the term had gained after John Holmes—who had first heard it from Jack—had appropriated it for the title of a much-quoted *New York Times* piece. By May Kerouac was already dreading another rejection. The editor handling his book at Little, Brown—Seymour Lawrence—had previously turned down (with what Jack considered an insulting note about "craft") Kerouac's favorite chapter on his father's death from *The Town and the City*. "Fuck these little Seymour Lawrences of America/these pissyass misinformed minimizers,"[8] Jack exclaimed in a letter to Ginsberg written while he was still awaiting the Little, Brown verdict. Not long afterward, he got his *Road* manuscript back from Lawrence—with another note about "craft" that made him see red.

There was a single encouraging development. Malcolm Cowley, though still unable to get Jack published at Viking, now managed to persuade Arabelle Porter of *New World Writing* to buy excerpts adapted from both the 1951 *Road* and 1952 *Cody* manuscripts. (Jack titled the excerpts "Jazz of the Beat Generation.") In a summer 1954 *Saturday Review* article, Cowley gave Kerouac an added boost, crediting him with coining the term "Beat Generation": "it was John Kerouac who invented the phrase, and his unpublished narrative 'On the Road' is the best record of their lives."[9]

The $120 from *New World Writing* was Kerouac's first payment for published writing since 1950; in the past four years of work, he had received only the two small advances from Ace and Viking. It was clear to him that what he needed was a good professional agent. In May 1954, through the recommendation of Robert Giroux, he finally got one—Sterling Lord. Lord's first move on Kerouac's behalf was to submit *The Beat Generation* (the retitled 1951 *On the Road*) to E. P. Dutton.

THAT spring of his return from California, Jack aspired to a state of Buddhist renunciation. He planted tomatoes, potatoes, and beans in the yard at Richmond Hill and boasted to Carolyn that he was turning down sexy phone calls from beautiful girls to till the soil, meditate, keep up with his Buddhist readings and scrapbooks, and type his dreams. He wrote to Ginsberg about the "bliss of heaven" ("we're already there and always were"),[10] enclosing tips on meditation technique and copious bibliographies of Orientalia. To Bill Burroughs Kerouac wrote that he was giving up sex and embarking on a new life of Buddhist chastity, tempered only by occasional masturbation. From Tangier Burroughs wrote back on a realistic note, suggesting that Jack was taking absolute chastity too far.

Kerouac's reductivist life style had economic as well as philosophical bases. He spent at least two early summer days riding "endless els" all the way to the Brooklyn waterfront to work as a brakeman on the New York dock railway. But the job was too much for him; he developed phlebitis in his right arm. Recuperating, he worried about his inability to contribute to the rent and tried to reduce his expenses to zero by living in total seclusion, tending his garden and writing day and night.

Inevitably, however, the city beckoned. There he quickly found out that he was not "Buddha" after all but (as he wrote to Ginsberg) "a dehumanized beast." He had a brief, scary early summer affair with a "junkey girl," and on one occasion got "sillydrunk" in the San Remo and "disgusted [him]self a la Subterraneans"—making him realize that despite his desire for a "quiet life" he was now dangerously "weak for booze."[11]

In the summer of 1954, Kerouac sat in his mother's parlor, sneaking joints and watching the McCarthy hearings on television. He supported McCarthy's pursuit of "traitors" in Washington, but at the same time he was working on a story that probably would have made the Wisconsin senator break out in spots: it undermined not only government but modern civilization altogether. This was "CITYCitycity"—a science fiction cartoon-nightmare about a futuristic planetary metropolis, overpopulated to the point of total loss of individuality and remote-controlled by a governing elite that regularly and methodically "eliminates" whole neighborhoods, blasting them out of existence at ten seconds' notice. The hallucination of nuclear holocaust hangs over this story much as it does over the later part of the *Book of Dreams*, on which Kerouac was working at the same time. The nihilistic sci-fi tale, "very tea-head writ,"[12] was Jack's 1954 dope vision of the decline of the planet, prophetic in that it anticipated a Vonnegut–*Blade Runner* world view still at least thirty years in the future.

POVERTY and personal loss, Spengler and the sutras, had converged in Kerouac's mind. An atomic apocalypse was near, he was sure; it was the end of the Faustian-intellectual West. In October he was writing to Ginsberg that Buddhism was a faith of the fellaheen—the peoples who came before or after, but always *beyond*, cultures and civilizations. He couldn't follow Buddhism in New York but told Allen he hoped soon to pursue it in stone wastelands and desert places. He described plans to take camping equipment into the Mexican wilderness for three months of solitude and meditation.

The escape to the wilderness was both a fantasy and a threat. Kerouac was growing more and more dissatisfied with all his social associations, and his announcements of the "wilderness plan" implied that he wanted to cut himself off from them for good. But, in fact, he was hardly less alone in Richmond Hill than he would have been in the desert. What contact with people he did have only seemed to him to confirm the pointlessness of believing in or relying on illusory emotional "self-natures." For his efforts to show compassion, he often got callousness in return. When Bill Burroughs, for example, came through from Africa on his way to the West Coast to see Ginsberg, for whom he now carried a torch, he made a stop at the Kerouac home in Long Island to pump Jack for news of Allen. To Jack, who was uneasy about bringing up his friends' homosexual affairs around the extremely intolerant Gabrielle, it was a very uncomfortable visit. When Burroughs left he took Jack's last $30 in cash and didn't hurry to pay it back. A few weeks later Kerouac received an angry note from Ginsberg, who had heard of the visit from Burroughs and thought Jack had been indiscreet in discussing their affair. Jack exploded back in a ten-page letter that took both Ginsberg and Burroughs to task for involving him in the secrets and subterfuges of their relationship. He charged Allen with treating him like a dumb Canuck—and suggested that Ginsberg was the Devil.

JACK tried to escape from the interpersonal mess of the present into the past, through the keyhole of a new recollective writing project—a delineation of "Lowell in its entirety" in Proustian, "deliberate prose." This work soon bogged down, but before it did, he made a pilgrimage to Lowell to refresh his memory. He stayed at a skid row hotel near the railway depot and spent several days hiking around town. He saw several old chums; they looked right through him, as though he were a ghost. Other passersby stared at him, convincing him that in the eyes of Lowell, his "New York" clothes—Japanese plaid shirt, pale blue jacket, white crepe sole shoes—made him seem "dazzling and effeminate."[13] He felt, in fact, less dazzling than *beat*—and on a late afternoon visit to the church of his confirmation, Ste. Jeanne d'Arc, he fell into a prolonged meditation on the meaning of that term. He decided that it meant not only "poor, like sleeping in subways," but "beatific, illuminated."[14]

Back in Richmond Hill Jack grasped at Buddhist austerities like a drowning man grabbing a spar. On December 19 he told his diary that he had reached "the lowest beat ebb" of his life. He was now thought of by others as "a criminal and insane and a sinner and an imbecile," he believed, and was himself "disappointed & endlessly sad." The year 1954, he wrote, had not only "delayed" his goal of enlightenment but also had robbed him of his "purity."[15] Kerouac could forgive anything in himself, as long as his behavior remained "pure"; now he was sure that, in all his tumbles into the mud and evil of New York, he had lost even that. To top things off, in December a policeman appeared at his door in Richmond Hill and served him with a nonsupport warrant sworn out by Joan Haverty. Enlightenment had never seemed farther away.

OVER the holidays, while Gabrielle went south to visit Nin, Jack lingered in Richmond Hill, trying to "exert [his] intelligence" to "secure the release of [his] bodhisattva from the chains of the city."[16] In practice this meant a discipline of meditation, benzedrine, and much midnight toil over manuscripts. He retyped *The Beat Generation* for Knopf, submitted it through Sterling Lord, and got back a quick verdict from Knopf editor-in-chief Joe Fox, who dismissed it as not even a "good novel." Jack considered Fox's rejection note "contemptuous."[17] A few days later *The Subterraneans* was also rejected—by Seymour Lawrence at Little, Brown.

By New Year's the steady work at his typewriter caused Kerouac's chronic thrombophlebitis to flare up. He wrapped his legs with elastic tape, was told by a doctor to give up cigarettes, and for some weeks had to type his manuscripts on a board stretched across his bed. The work went on regardless.

On January 18, 1955, Kerouac limped into a New York courtroom to respond to Joan Haverty's suit for nonpayment of child support. He was legally represented by Ginsberg's brother, Eugene Brooks. Jack still hadn't seen his nearly three-year-old daughter but before the court hearing was shown pictures of her. ("Looks just like me, especially frowning square-browed photo," he reported later to Ginsberg, "so may be mine.")[18] The judge ruled Kerouac medically disabled. His case was suspended for a year. Kerouac had come to court carrying an armload of typed notes on Buddhism, ready to go to jail.

IN the early spring of 1955, Jack went south to help his brother-in-law build a house in Rocky Mount, North Carolina. Gabrielle again decided to move to North Carolina. She sank her life's savings in Nin's TV business and became her daughter's housekeeper. Jack stayed on until summer.

He converted the screened-in back porch of his sister's house to a writer's cell, with cot, typewriter, and desk. There he worked on two new literary projects that were religious in nature: *Buddha Tells Us*, an American version of the *Surangama Sutra*, and *Wake Up*, a life story of Buddha. Renunciation of the material world was not a subject New York publishers wanted to buy into, however. Jack had to postpone a planned May trip to California because he didn't have the $20 it would take him to get to New Orleans, where he could start hopping Southern Pacific freights. His books were floating around New York, but as he told Carolyn in a letter, he didn't even have a nickel to buy a popsicle.

In April, after keeping Kerouac in suspense for months, E. P. Dutton finally rejected *The Beat Generation* (*On the Road*). Although it was far from his first rejection, Kerouac felt the blow of this one particularly strongly; Sterling Lord had held high hopes for Dutton. Now weeks went by without mail from Lord—or from Ginsberg, who was supposedly shopping for a publisher for *Sax* in San Francisco. Depressed, Kerouac sought fortification by writing to Burroughs and Cassady. Neither replied.

Jack sank into nonrenunciatory solo bouts with "white lightnin" (corn whiskey), which gave him very bad dreams (H-bombs and frightening adventures on scaffolds and girders). When there was again a long silence from Lord, he wrote to the agent suggesting that they forget doing any more business together. There was no reply. On May 20 Kerouac wrote to Ginsberg that he feared he would soon go crazy or even kill himself.

In the last week of May, he finally spent his last $2 on an unsatisfactory phone call to the agent. Lord reported only bad news: *Buddha Tells Us* had been turned down by Giroux. When Kerouac complained about the agent to his sister, she stepped in and notified him she was taking over his business affairs.

Before that could happen, however, a few lights at last started showing up on the dark switchboard of Kerouac's career. Through Malcolm Cowley's efforts, a story called "The Mexican Girl"—actually a chapter adapted from the 1951 *On the Road*—appeared in *The Paris Review*. Along with the *New World Writing* excerpts (from *Road* and *Cody*), which came out almost simultaneously, the *Paris Review* appearance caused a new surge of interest in *Road* at Viking Press. Viking senior editor Keith Jennison called Lord and offered to try to raise a $1,000 advance on the book.

Trusting that this time the negotiations were finally for real, Jack made a late-June trip to New York to work out a deal. When he got to the city, however, he was swept off his feet by confusing talk—Li'l Abner in Gotham—and did more spinning than negotiating. At the last minute Dodd, Mead seemed ready to snatch *Road* (still titled *The Beat Generation*) away from Viking. Feeling a sudden power, Jack drank Viking's liquor and tried to convince Cowley and Jennison to finance him (at a modest $25 a month) to go to Mexico and write a new, Buddhist-style *Road* (featuring Ray Smith as wandering bhikku). But Jennison couldn't raise even that much, and Cowley told Jack that Viking was interested only in the original *Road* and would accept no substitutes. Jack rode the bus back to North Carolina wondering whether anything had been accomplished—and with phlebitis-swollen legs from too much city benzedrine, nicotine, and alcohol.

In July 1955 Cowley arranged a small literary grant for him; Kerouac also received payment for the *Paris Review* story. A few hundred dollars wasn't much to show for the many promises that had been thrown his way all spring, but it was enough to get him moving in the direction he wanted to go—away from civilization, toward Mexico.

LEGS still aching from hitchhiking over boiling, no-traffic Texas roads, Jack moved into the same "mud block" he had occupied in 1952 on the roof of the Orizaba Street house in Mexico City. Bill Garver, a garrulous, aging junkie who occupied the ground-floor apartment, welcomed the company. Garver filled their long, idle hours with stoned monologues, while Jack snoozed or worked on an extended sequence of free-associating, spontaneous poems—the 242 "choruses" of *Mexico City Blues*. Garver also put Jack to work, sending him to fetch morphine from a female drug connection who lived in the slums of the city. With this woman, Esperanza Villanueva, whom he saw as a sort of Aztec priestess-Billie Holiday-Madonna, Kerouac conducted the chaste, desperate courtship chronicled in *Tristessa* —a tale he now began writing by candlelight in his rooftop cell but did not complete until the following summer.

As the empty weeks went by, Kerouac felt abandoned to "Love's multitudinous boneyard of decay."[19] Worries about his soul and his mother troubled his sleep. He reminded himself that every living being was only "born to die"[20] and, disgusted by his unsuccessful pursuit of the junkie waif, swore off sexuality for the thousandth time.

AFTER about six weeks as "a mad genius in a hovel,"[21] Jack set out on another grueling hitchhiking trip, across Durango, Chihuahua, and Texas. The late September heat burned his skin, leaving his face parched and chapped: truck drivers who stopped to pick him up would have had a hard time identifying him as a major American writer.

From Los Angeles he hopped a Southern Pacific night freight, practicing meditation to ward off the chill, and, following the *Diamond Sutra*'s prescriptions about charity, shared his cheese and wine with a fellow "religious wanderer." The grateful hobo offered him in return a slip of paper that "solidified [Jack's] beliefs":[22] it contained a prayer of Ste. Thérèse. Even luckier, the next day Kerouac, the neophyte Buddhist monk, got a perfect ride all the way from Santa Barbara to San Francisco in a new Lincoln driven by a good-looking blonde in a bathing suit.

His destination on this trip was Berkeley, where Allen Ginsberg, now a University of California graduate student, was renting a small rose-trellised cottage in the leafy back yard of a house on Milvia Street. Allen had just written "Howl," a work that reflected his serious study not only of Kerouac's spontaneous writing mode but also of "the myth of Lester Young as described by Kerouac."[23] (Jack had, in fact, suggested the poem's title in a letter from Mexico.) Now "a big learned Buddhist"[24]—at least in the eyes of his surprised friend—Jack sat on the rickety porch of the cottage and chanted the "three Refuges of Buddha," which, says Ginsberg, "he used to croon, sort of like Frank Sinatra."[25]

Ginsberg introduced Kerouac to a young Berkeley neighbor, Gary Snyder. A sturdy, compact, goateed backwoods boy from Oregon, the twenty-five-year-old Snyder was not only a poet and Buddhist scholar but also adept in anthropology, Indian lore, and wilderness skills. He revered the "Zen Lunatics of China"—poet-monks who had lived in solitude, the original back-packing "dharma bums"[26]—and wanted to live like them.

In Gary Jack saw an interesting new kind of hero—one who came out of the American backwoods and frontier past but had adapted equally to the prospect of the coming apocalypse. The orderly, purposive Snyder seemed to have no madness in him, no self-destructive frenzy. This was, in short, a character exactly the opposite of Kerouac's greatest previous hero, the disorganized, frustrated, headlong, ineffectual—yet somehow glorious —Cassady.

The difference was pointed up dramatically to Jack when he went down to visit Neal in a new Los Gatos home bought with railroad-injury settlement money. Once a fabulous "roman candle exploding . . . across stars,"[27] Cassady now seemed burned out, like a spent comet, his tension wasted in crazy pothead schemes to beat the horses. After a short stay in Los Gatos and one bad, rocky drunk in the city, Kerouac staggered back across the bay and moved in on Ginsberg just in time for a big poetry reading Allen had arranged.

This was the historic Six Gallery reading, held on October 13, 1955. The gallery was a converted auto repair garage. Kenneth Rexroth, polymathic, acerbic major-domo of literary San Francisco, acted as master of ceremonies. Kerouac circulated in the crowd, collecting coins in his cap for jugs of California red wine and cheering the readers on with "go's" and "yeah's," as though they were bop soloists. Though the poetry of Michael McClure, Philip Lamantia, Gary Snyder, and Philip Whalen was enthusiastically received, the real climax of the evening was Ginsberg's incandescent performance of "Howl." "'Howl' just blew things up completely," Rexroth later said; "that night was . . . the birth of the San Francisco Poetry Renaissance."[28]

The very success of Allen's reading, however, caused an immediate division in the "Renaissance," by challenging the local preeminence of Rexroth as a poet. The rift first emerged not long after the reading at one of Rexroth's regular Friday afternoon "at-homes." Kerouac and Ginsberg were drunk. Rexroth reprimanded Kerouac for acting loud and called him a "punk." Ginsberg responded by boastfully informing his host, "I'm a better poet than you are."[29] Kerouac, who had unwittingly precipitated the whole scene, became persona non grata in the Rexroth salon.

J A C K lived in Berkeley for the next six weeks. He slept at Ginsberg's but spent most of his time with Snyder, who introduced him to tantric love games, even sharing a girlfriend. (Kerouac had just "gone through an entire year of celibacy," the result of his conviction that "lust was the direct cause of birth which was the direct cause of death.")[30] Gary also coached Jack in "dharma bum" lore. The climax of Kerouac's apprenticeship was a late-October climbing trip to Yosemite.

"It was all new to Jack," poet-librarian John Montgomery, who went along on the expedition, recalls. "He seemed to have little idea of how to react."[31] Montgomery reports that for all Jack's unfamiliarity with mountains, he appeared "light on his feet" and climbed like a "Basque," with "that powerful frame and an intensity."[31]

Enthusiastic about the Yosemite trip, Kerouac, under Snyder's guidance, equipped himself with full Berkeley-style hiker's kit—bed roll, frame pack, pup tent. Certain he would soon be using all this gear in his flight from the mechanized police state—which would anyway be annihilated before long by the H-bomb—Kerouac took as straight fact Snyder's comment to a store clerk that he was "outfittin' me friends for the Apocalypse."[32] Jack's plan was to vanish with his survival kit into the southwestern wilderness in early December 1955. His final week in the Bay Area was spent with the Cassadys. He visited Carolyn in Los Gatos and was present one evening when a local Unitarian bishop dropped in to see her. The roving Neal happened to be at home; Ginsberg was there also. The bishop had brought his elderly mother, adding a further note of absurdity to a scene that was comical to start with. The ensuing dialogue later went into Jack's play "The Beat Generation," which, in turn, became the film *Pull My Daisy.*

Neal no longer lived at home with the family. He divided his time between work, race track, and a new girlfriend in the city, Natalie Jackson. Natalie was an emotional young woman, highly strung and prone to dangerous fits of depression. Neal, who often relied on Jack as a stand-in (Kerouac even went to the track and placed bets for him), requested him to "sit with" Natalie one work day. Not realizing the extent of her illness—

she had already once tried to slash her wrists—Jack was unable to deal with the girl's irrational fears. When she began raving about a "big new revolution of police," he responded by telling her about the coming "rucksack revolution." His calm Buddhist sermons got nowhere, and he experienced the frustration he "always" felt when he "tried to explain the Dharma to people."[33] That evening, after Neal's return, the disturbed girl went to the roof of the building, attempted to cut her own throat, and then fell or jumped to the street below.

Natalie Jackson's suicide blew Kerouac's Buddhist pieties back in his face. His reaction was to flee the city and head for his desert retreat. From San Jose he hopped the night freight south. Though in *The Dharma Bums* —that testament to positive thinking, Zen-hipster style—he spoke of sleeping "warm as toast" on this leg of the trip, Jack's later description in a note to Cassady indicates that, in fact, it was a cold ordeal. To avoid prying railway cops with flashlights, he was forced to jump off and on moving cars at every stop. Aching legs folded uncomfortably beneath him, he shivered trying to meditate in the speeding blackness. His phlebitis acted up again. Desperate for relief, he tried a tip from a traveling bum he met the next day in skid row Los Angeles. The bum advised him to stand on his head for a few minutes every day. Kerouac decided the bum was "buddha";[34] henceforth, and for the rest of his traveling days, he did headstands, often in the midst of company.

In the Los Angeles rail yard he couldn't board the daily Yuma-bound freight because it was all box cars, no flats. After a sad hike through industrial Los Angeles, he took a bus to Riverside, where it took him some time to locate a riverbank campsite out of range of police. The next day he hitched across the desert into Mexico. There it took only hours to discover that his plan to camp out would probably get him either arrested or robbed or both. Dharma boy scouts weren't welcome on either side of the border. Bouncing back and forth across the U.S.-Mexico line, Kerouac finally picked up a long ride east with an intercontinental trucker.

IT was a flat, lonely homecoming to Rocky Mount. Kerouac had hoped to spend the holidays with his mother, but he had hardly arrived when Gabrielle was called away to her own stepmother's funeral in Brooklyn. When Nin and her family subsequently left on a trip to Florida, Jack was left alone in the house.

Natalie Jackson's suicide elided in Jack's dreams with the funeral his mother was attending—"big gay cities have huge sad cemeteries right outside, need 'em."[35] For the past year he had often wished to be "safe in heaven, dead."[36] Now, though, death appeared to him not as a final security and relief but as a blank horror. Something dark and lost washed up into his reveries: a rainy day in Nashua, the shoveling-under of Gerard.

On a bleak New Year's Day 1956, he sat at Nin's kitchen table and began filling the first of several tiny pocket notebooks with the story of the last year of his brother's life, reconstructed from his few dim memories and from some old letters of Leo's that he had kept among his papers. On the first notebook he printed "Saint Gerard The Child," a title that later became *Visions of Gerard.*

He wrote in long benzedrine stints through most of the first fifteen nights of January, working in a half trance, revising only one night's work. On completing each session of writing, he walked across a cotton field into the pines for dawn meditations with his brother-in-law's hound dogs.

Visions of Gerard was an elegaic "poem of death," as Kerouac called it. Its place in the "one vast book" of his life that he was already projecting— the "Duluoz legend"—was to fill in the years of earliest childhood, the period preceding *Dr. Sax.* The style of *Gerard* was consciously "windblown and Shakespearean";[37] Kerouac had been reading *Henry V* just before composing it.

Once he had typed the pencil draft, he decided he had produced a major work. "It's a beaut, my best," he wrote Carolyn, "real cracky teeth closing down on great awful final statements about the grave and all. Enuf to make Shakespeare raise an eyebrow." He planned to ship it on to "the publishers"—but shrugged that they wouldn't "care anyway."[38]

T H E warm wind of early spring began to make "the pines talk." Fretful by day, Kerouac tried to invite transcendental visitations at night. On March 12, 1956—his thirty-fourth birthday—he performed what he later described as his "first and last 'miracle.'"[39] That day his mother came down with a bad cough and sore throat. At night, when she continued to cough, Jack sat up in his sleeping bag on the cold back porch (where he always slept with the windows wide open) and tried to "hypnotize" himself to discover the cause of her illness. Three images floated before his mind's eye: a bottle of Heet liniment, a brandy bottle, and some white flowers. He went to his mother's room, found some white flowers on her table, removed them, and the next day brought her the Heet and brandy.

Gabrielle's cough and sore throat disappeared. A local doctor "verified" Jack's cure.

His feats of healing notwithstanding, Jack survived in Rocky Mount only on the tolerance of his family, which was variable at best. Thus he was delighted when a letter came offering him a job as a $230-a-month summer fire lookout in the Skagit River area of the Cascade Mountains in Washington. (Gary Snyder had recommended him.) As a lookout Kerouac would, in effect, be his own boss; the fact that the region was marked on road maps as uninhabited made the offer doubly attractive.

Jack had another reason to go west. Still up in the air was the editing of *On the Road* with Malcolm Cowley of Viking. Having already made one mistimed trip to New York to meet Cowley only to find that the editor was spending the spring term at Stanford, Kerouac now hoped to catch up with him in California before heading north to the Cascades.

Meanwhile, though, he had to borrow from Gabrielle to begin his own latest trip west.

HITCHHIKING out of the South in a late March heat wave put a strain on Kerouac's faith in the dharma bum ethic. Rain-soaked in Georgia, he dipped into his slim wallet for a bus ticket to El Paso; from there he caught Southern Pacific freights to San Francisco, where he learned Cowley had just returned to New York. Jack had once again misconnected, holding up his own career by that stubborn, involuntary faculty of "unconscious sabotage" which many of his friends considered his most infuriating personal characteristic (it was William Burroughs who first gave it that label).[40]

Kerouac spent the spring in Marin County, camping at Snyder's small Victorian-style Corte Madera cottage. Close editing on a collaborative basis proved impossible by mail, so Cowley did most of the work in New York. Kerouac began writing letters to obtain releases from the people whose real stories would be in *On the Road*, even if their real names—which he had been ordered to change—would not.

In Corte Madera he also started two new writing projects. One was *The Scripture of the Golden Eternity*, an American version of the *Diamond Sutra*, begun at Snyder's instigation. This was a carefully revised, largely conventional effort. The second was *Old Angel Midnight*, a prose transcription of "the sounds of the universe," which began with the ambient noise "swimming through [the] window"[41] of the Corte Madera cottage on a

Friday afternoon and extended into a multilingual collage that included not only natural sounds but also thoughts, phrases, and bits of neural gossip.

Kerouac first thought proudly that in *Old Angel* he was updating Joyce in spontaneous prose (" 'a spontaneous Finnegans Wake' with the sounds of the universe itself as a plot").⁴² But when John Montgomery came to visit him at the cottage a few weeks into the work, Jack admitted that "all [he] could write was gibberish."⁴³ And writing to John Holmes in May, he confessed that his "doodling with an endless automatic writing piece" had begun to "rave on with no direction." He wished, after all these years, that he "could get rid of this . . . compulsion to write."⁴⁴

Weekends at the Corte Madera place were usually taken up with visiting parties of friends of both sexes—a "regular classic scene of angels and dolls having a kind of flowery time in the void." But Jack, still agonizing over celibacy and convinced that "sociability [was] just a big smile and a big smile [was] nothing but teeth,"⁴⁵ shrank from the social action and in mixed company was most often to be found off in a corner beating rhythm on a cooking pot while the party rolled on around him.

In the months since he had seen him last, Snyder seemed to Jack to have grown "serious and sad."⁴⁶ Kerouac was made uncomfortable by Gary's advice that he shape up as a Buddhist and stop drinking so much. Indeed, alcohol was rapidly replacing meditation as Jack's mainline to illumination. One friend he made that spring was the poet and editor Robert Creeley, then living a hand-to-mouth existence in San Francisco. Creeley had previously been sent Kerouac's "October in the Railroad Earth" and had accepted it for his *Black Mountain Review* even before his first meeting with Jack, which took place in May 1956. Kerouac and Creeley had much in common—both were northeast Massachusetts natives with French Canadian blood—but the main bond between them that spring was that both were intense, engaged drinkers. With Creeley Jack never got told to sober up and head for the Zen Center. Both men possessed, Creeley now suggests, "a kind of characteristic shyness that made [them] seem on the edge of things. . . . I always felt very at home with Jack," Creeley says, "because I think we both drank to deal with that social shyness."⁴⁷

Kerouac came to Creeley's aid in a San Francisco bar fight and subsequently suggested that the injured poet come out to Marin with him to recuperate. Creeley occupied the large main house on the property (the landlord was away), while Jack slept in the small rear cottage, which he

TOP: *Poets Robert Creeley and Robert Duncan, Mallorca, 1955: "One friend he made that spring was the poet and editor Robert Creeley."* (courtesy *the unspeakable visions of the individual*)

BOTTOM: *Kenneth and Marthe Rexroth: "Creeley fell in love with Kenneth Rexroth's wife."* (photo by Arthur Winfield Knight, courtesy *the unspeakable visions of the individual*)

had to himself, as Snyder had left for Japan. "We had about five dollars," recalls Creeley, "which we invested in gallons of port wine. We ate corn-meal dodgers, which Jack cooked in slices of onion, for vitamin C. We had this really specific sense of what would make us very healthy—while we drank ourselves to death. And we got cigarettes, of course, etc. And we sat on the porch in that old-fashioned manner of New England, in chairs, drinking our port wine. Jack loved to put ice cubes in it, and sort of sip it, and watch the passing parade, which was slow at that end of the street. We'd muse on life and literature, and play the records that were in the house."[48]

Back in the city Creeley fell in love with Kenneth Rexroth's wife, Marthe. When Kenneth went out of town, Bob took Jack along on a visit to the Rexroth flat. When Rexroth returned, he presumed Jack's "complicity" in adultery and included Kerouac with Creeley as objects of his jealous rage. "I am Creeley's friend," Kerouac wrote to Holmes, "and Rexroth has conceived a great hatred for me."[49]

"Jack was certainly supportive to me and knew of my relations with Marthe, whom he liked," Creeley recalls, "and he was particularly disappointed by Kenneth's reaction." The Rexroth "reaction," Creeley suggests, first took the form of revisions in an article the well-known critic was then preparing for the *Nation*. The article was intended to introduce underground writers to a national audience. "The first report was that Rexroth was doing this extensive article, the first real advice of the so-called San Francisco Renaissance, and that he had called Jack the peer of Céline. That was the first draft. And then that was revised to say, 'he is in the great *tradition* of Céline.' And then, by the third draft, in what was finally printed, it's been diminished again—that he, you know, 'follows in the footsteps of . . .' "[50]

In the article, published in February 1957, Rexroth announced a new "Bohemian" literary movement that had only two interesting prose writers: Henry Miller ("who stays to home in Big Sur") and the still-unpublished Jack Kerouac. But Kerouac received very mixed praise: Rexroth called him "the most excited Buddhist I ever heard of," mourned his "lapses into pages of terrifying gibberish," and finally adjudged him "too frantic . . . for even my middle-aged taste."[51]

In late June 1956, Kerouac hitchhiked north to his fire lookout, happy to be putting the complications of human relationships behind him for a while. He never saw either Creeley or Rexroth again, but the latter's enmity was to affect his career permanently.

JACK had nine weeks to spend on Desolation Peak—"sixty-three days and nights to be exact." His duties—taking weather readings, keeping an eye out for lightning strikes, and making daily radio reports—took very little of his time. He cooked his own meals and carried buckets of snow for drinking water. The great gulping spaces of freedom that remained—and for which he had longed—loomed up like uncrossable canyons. Surrounded on his lookout by frightening "black mountain shapes gianting all around," he yelled metaphysical questions across gorges, sang show tunes at the top of his voice, yodeled "what is the meaning of the void?"[52] The enormous silence only yawned back.

By late August he was reduced to playing his old solitaire baseball game for hours at a time, cooking Chinese meals not out of hunger but to trick forth memories of restaurants in Lowell, and rerunning the ancient derbies and handicaps of his "Turf." The sheer weight of time on his hands became a mirror of emptiness that made Jack's whole life feel insubstantial. When he went outside to do his daily push-ups, he was afraid one particularly menacing nearby peak—Mount Hozomeen—would crush him into the ground.

With two weeks to go, the weather turned bad. He was soon telling his notebook he no longer knew what to do with himself, that his mind was "in rags," and that he wanted "to come down RIGHT AWAY." Finally, he "murdered a mouse"[53] he had found hiding in one of his Lipton's soup packages—a small act of violence that broke personal vows of mercy and kindness going all the way back past his discovery of Buddha to the long-departed holy Gerard. The mouse murder left Jack sobbing and wondering what had happened to him.

Solitude had taught him only lessons he didn't want to learn. It was with great relief that he came back down to "the world" in September 1956.

FROM Seattle Kerouac drifted down to San Francisco, where he stayed variously at the Bell Hotel, with the Cassadys in Los Gatos, and with Ginsberg, who was living in Peter Orlovsky's Potrero Hill housing project apartment. Ginsberg had adopted the role of politico-literary organizer and was now involved in a new scheme of building a big "united front" to join East and West Coast poets. Problems hounded this enterprise. First there was the reaction of Rexroth against Kerouac and friends, then the grumbling and defection-from-the-front of another local subfaction led by Robert Duncan. Jealousies were rife over who were the *real* "San Francisco poets," now that the *New York Times* had written about them and *Mademoiselle* was coming to town to take their pictures. "All this fighting" had to stop, Ginsberg announced; all the poets had to be "hand in hand in paradise and no bullshit." Allen's gang consisted of himself, Peter Orlovsky, Gregory Corso (the new brooding "dark angel" of the group), and the undependable Kerouac, who couldn't help grumbling that whatever was "percolating in [Ginsberg's] brain" went "beyond [his own] non-political intelligence" and that anyway Allen was "too serious and concerned about the outcome of everything."[54]

The role cut out for Jack in the big "united front" was that of the intense, instinctive, romantic, slightly simple-minded writer-bum; this was clear from the first round of publicity photos taken by *Mademoiselle*. At the photo session Corso gave Jack a silver crucifix on a chain and told him to "wear it outside your shirt and dont comb your hair." Jack's unkempt appearance in the photo was only slightly modified by *Mademoiselle*, which airbrushed out the crucifix. For public consumption, Jack was to be Li'l Abner-on-the-Road, no matter how hard he tried to be a serious writer. At a high-class dinner for poets in the home of a prominent San Francisco poetry patroness, he was kidded by a street-wise Corso about the discomforts of riding freight trains. Kerouac responded ingenuously that he rode only *first-class* freight trains, a reply that brought down the table in hoots. But Jack hadn't meant to be funny.

Kerouac was of little use to Ginsberg's "united front"; poetry-politics-wise, all his actions had a retrograde effect. Drunk, he unintentionally stepped on the toes of at least two local bards, Robert Duncan and Michael McClure. After a week of war among the jealous rival "fronts," Jack opted for flight and headed once again for his Mexico City retreat, "to meditate upon the world without being imbroglio'd in its actions."[55]

On the floor of the adobe rooftop shack on Orizaba Street, he dropped his sleeping bag, lit a candle, and almost immediately started work. Sipping midnight cups of cocoa, he scribbled in pencil on nickel notebooks by candlelight; when a candle sputtered and died, he stopped working. Writing only "for Fame of self" and "because [he] was Ti Jean,"[56] he began the rambling, episodic autobiographical inventory later to become Book

One of *Desolation Angels*; then switched to a more intense, lyric mode ("ingrown toenail packed mystical style")[57] and completed a second part of *Tristessa*, the story of his continuing strange relationship with Esperanza Villanueva.

He wrote the latter even as the unhappy events unfolded. Esperanza had fallen on her head in a junkie nod, nearly killing herself. During her recuperation, Jack went out to make a morphine "run" for her in the slums of Mexico City. When he came back she gave herself a shot that put her "out like a light." After weeks of abjectly following her around, Jack told himself "now was the time" and got his "little no good piece." (He later censored his description of this bleak seduction out of *Tristessa*, because when he showed the manuscript to Lucien Carr's wife, she told him it would "spoil the book.")[58]

The "peacefulness" of Jack's month of writing in Mexico City (September–October 1956) was shattered when Ginsberg arrived with entourage (Corso, two Orlovsky brothers). Allen was fresh from a first triumphant removal of his clothing at a reading in Los Angeles and brimming with visions of future conquests. Interrupting Kerouac's sleep on the "solitary roof," he admonished Jack to wake up and rejoin the united front immediately. "Why don't you come to New York with us now . . . It's time to make it . . . to *influence* American civilization!" "All that literary stuff is a drag," replied the twice-shy Kerouac. Ginsberg insisted that it was *"time"*: Jack would soon be "dancing naked on [his] fan mail."[59]

Finally, Kerouac's resolve to maintain creative austerity buckled, overmatched by Ginsberg's powers of persuasion. Jack suffered through the long, "horrible trip," knee to knee with five other men in a drive-away car. At the end of it he stood shivering on a frozen November sidewalk in Manhattan. It may have been *"time,"* as Allen said, but Jack wasn't sure he was ready for it. His mind a blank from lack of sleep, he coughed like a sick junkie from too much smoking and half-believed he had tuberculosis. He was down to 155 pounds, the lowest weight of his adult life. When he noticed his "hollowed cheeks and really sunken eyes in a cavernous eye bone"[60] reflected in a store window, all he could think about was death.

Kerouac spent several weeks hanging around New York, waiting to see what was going to become of *On the Road* at Viking Press. In early December he learned that Viking had finally agreed to the $1,000 advance requested by Lord (it would be paid, however, only in $100-a-month installments). Jack signed a contract. The book was scheduled for fall 1957.

Mexico City, 1956 (standing: *Kerouac, Ginsberg, Peter Orlovsky;* in front: *Corso, Lafcadio Orlovsky*): *"Ginsberg arrived with entourage."* (courtesy Allen Ginsberg)

Viking's in-house editing of the manuscript continued. Kerouac later charged that the published version was an emasculation of the 1951 book, but, in fact, Viking's 1956 editing left the story largely intact; paragraphing was added and some of the cross-country travels were removed or spliced together.

After a brief round of celebrations, including a meeting with Salvador Dali at the Russian Tea Room—at which Dali pronounced Jack "more beautiful than Marlon Brando"[61]—Kerouac headed south to catch up with his mother and celebrate a family Christmas at Nin's new home in Orlando, Florida.

JACK'S old wooden rolltop desk, on which he had written at least four books, was waiting for him on the porch of his sister's house in Orlando. Trying to work, he sat and stared down at it, drifting off into thoughts of how he had "worked as hard [on his writing] as any man in the world"[62] and still had almost nothing to show for it. On Christmas Eve he drank martinis with his relatives in front of the television set. When Gabrielle dozed off in a chair, Jack drew pictures of her aging, weary face in his sketchbook.

Not long after New Year's, he informed her he was taking off once again. This time he would go to New York, borrow ship fare from Ginsberg, then sail to North Africa. Gabrielle—still unhappily housekeeping for Nin, living on social security, and missing her own home—was "almost crying" when he left. Jack promised to move her to California by the fall. His new book would buy them a house, he said, where they would live together as in the old days, and "be glad."[63]

Back in the city Jack walked into a modest spotlight, powered by Ginsberg's busy connectings of wire to wire in the New York media. Their recent West Coast notoriety had enabled Ginsberg to interest several publications in himself and his "Beat" gang. *Life* wanted a photo story. For the session Allen produced himself, Kerouac, Corso, and two Orlovskys. Jack got drunk and high, combed his hair, did headstands, and told jokes for the unsmiling photographers. From *Life* Allen led the "madcap" group to the *Village Voice*, where they spent half an hour cutting up Marx-Brothers-style for a friendly reporter.

Although Jack performed for Ginsberg's publicity campaign, it was only reluctantly. From a cheap New York hotel room, he wrote to Edie

Parker, whom he hadn't seen since 1949, and told her that he wanted to escape reality "to go into simplicity" but found it difficult because Ginsberg "never lost track" of him, even when he tried to "hide." "I can't keep up with the hectic 'fame' life he wants."[64]

In the hotel he began typing his previous summer's Mexico books for publishers, but even with potential "thousands of dollars hidden in [his] pack," he couldn't afford the room for more than a couple of days and wound up calling Ginsberg. Allen suggested that he contact Corso's "uptown girl." Jack phoned the young woman, Joyce Glassman, told her he was "starving," and asked her to "meet [him] in the Howard Johnson's and buy [him] two frankfurts."[65] Glassman not only bought Jack's hot dogs but also provided him with a place to stay and became his sometime city consoler and protector for the next few years.

Mademoiselle came out, plastering Jack Kerouac's darkly handsome visage all over newsstands in New York. At the same time, editor Don Allen of Grove Press accepted *The Subterraneans* for *Evergreen Review*, an influential new magazine. Jack went from friend to friend to get final libel clearances for *On the Road*. After drinking heavily at nearly every stop, he was badly hung over when, on an early February morning, he boarded a Yugoslavian freighter bound for Tangier.

Kerouac's expectations of peace, quiet, and solitary studies in his stateroom were washed away by a series of winter storms in the Atlantic. At the worst of the bad weather, he felt the ship "pitching like a bottle in the howling void,"[66] and then experienced what he later told friends was a "Catholic-like" vision of God. His "Buddhism vanished in a crap of green fear" (as he later told Holmes in a letter), and over the "raging black sea" he saw a "white glow," representing "God's snowy arms."[67]

The rough Atlantic crossing was symbolic of what was to come. On this trip, Kerouac later wrote, a "great change took place in [his] life . . . turning from a youthful brave sense of adventure to a complete nausea concerning experience in the world at large."[68]

On the roof of the Villa Mouneria in Tangier, where Burroughs had a "dingy" main floor pad, Kerouac rented a room for himself with a patio facing the sea. He began keeping a diary, but instead of writing any new books of his own, spent most of his time helping out with a work-in-progress of Bill Burroughs'. This was an amazing blend of letters, notes, and transcriptions of satirical "routines" like the ones Burroughs acted out for Jack every afternoon over brandy. At the time the work was called "Word Hoard,"[69] but Kerouac suggested a new title: *Naked Lunch*. He typed up the first two chapters of the manuscript—the whole first section of the book—and for his efforts was rewarded by Burroughs with a kerosene stove, which took the ocean chill out of his rooftop cell. Toking nonstop on marijuana and hashish as he worked, Kerouac inhaled an overdose of imagery from Burroughs' frightening prose; at night he had terrible dreams of "endless bolognas," reaching all the way into his "entrails,"[70] being pulled out of his mouth.

Jack found Tangier pretty dreary. Nevertheless he cased the city thoroughly on long, lone afternoon walks in the Medina or along the beach, where he watched Arab brakemen man a dingy railroad. Back in his room he enjoyed abundant kif, codeine, sleeping pills, Cinzano, Spanish benzedrine, and even, now and then, a $3 veiled whore.

The surfeit of cheap drugs and alcohol eventually made Kerouac feel jumpy, introverted, and "bugged" in Morocco. There was one pivotal bad experience. He swallowed a ball of black, sticky Moroccan opium (given him by Burroughs) and spent twenty-four hours in a depressed stupor so gloomy it made him decide to put an end to all his traveling and "Go home—make a home in America."[71]

While in Tangier he was also "bugged" by new publishing problems. Sterling Lord sent him galley proofs of the forthcoming *Evergreen Review* version of *The Subterraneans*. Editor Don Allen, Jack angrily charged after inspecting the proofs, had "pulled a Giroux on [him] all over again, and presented [him] with an eight pound baby 60 percent cut with all the long sentences cut up into little faggish sentiments." Jack turned Allen's rewrite job down cold, calling it a "castration," and shot off an angry ultimatum to Lord, ordering that his work henceforth be published "as it is or not at all."[72] Lord forced the replacement of *The Subterraneans* with "October in the Railroad Earth" in *Evergreen*. When Grove Press then went ahead with *The Subterraneans* in book publication, Don Allen was again Jack's editor, but the manuscript was restored to its original state.

ALLEN GINSBERG brought the "united front" to Tangier in March, but for Jack the arrival of Ginsberg and Orlovsky, originally intended as a "big triumphant reunion in Africa," came "too late." Kerouac was by this time useless to the "front"—grumbling, discontent, sequestered on his roof. One

Kerouac in Tangier (courtesy William Burroughs)

Kerouac, Orlovsky, and Burroughs in Tangier, 1957: "Ginsberg brought the 'united front' to Tangier in March." (courtesy Allen Ginsberg)

night Ginsberg insisted that Jack come down to Burroughs' room to meet "a big bunch of hipsters and chicks from Paris." These studiedly "cool" visitors—the men in goatees, the girls "with long thin legs in slacks"—struck Kerouac as "an enormous drag." Even as *Road*, his chronicle of the Beat Generation, was on the brink of publication, he was "already sick of the whole subject."[73]

In early April his check from New York arrived and he caught a boat to Marseilles, then struggled on, through dismal hitchhiking failures and a stream of café vermouth, toward Paris. His Parisian stay consisted of frantic tourism, hiking from bar to church to bar to museum with rucksack on his back. Down to his last few dollars, he hunched over a table full of empty vermouth glasses in what seemed like the world's bleakest bistro and wrote in his notebook, "All the Martinis . . . are for death."[74]

His remaining money barely got him across the channel. He had only $2 left and was refused entry to England until he showed a customs officer the *Nation*, with Rexroth's article mentioning his name in the same breath as Henry Miller's. He hurried on to London, where he picked up an advance from the British publisher of *On the Road*. During his ten days in London, he looked up his old jazz buddy, Seymour Wyse, who was shocked by the volume of Jack's drinking. But Kerouac reeled from monument to monument, oblivious. At the British Museum he investigated his family coat of arms in a book on heraldry. The highlight of his stay, however, was a visit to St. Paul's, on Good Friday, for a performance of the *St. Matthew Passion* by full choir and orchestra. Buoyed by the noble music, he cried—partly out of exhaustion, partly out of joy—and saw his own "mission."[75]

T H E "mission" was to move his unhappy mother from Florida to a new home in the West. Jack had no house lined up in California, nor even a forwarding address. Upon his return to America in May 1957, he told the movers to deliver their belongings to poet Philip Whalen's cottage in Berkeley, then escorted his mother west on a transcontinental bus.

The trip via New Orleans and Juarez was a bleary, dusty grind. Both Kerouacs survived by gulping countless aspirins with cokes. In Berkeley Jack went out and found them an apartment. But Gabrielle was ill-disposed toward Berkeley from the first; she hated the fog, feared earthquakes. By June she was telling Jack she felt "lonely and idle" and wanted to go back to New York. Put off by the furor over "the banning and impounding" of Ginsberg's *Howl* in San Francisco, Kerouac wrote to Holmes that he agreed with his mother: "NEVER COME TO CALIFORNIA . . . silly place for old people."[76]

The obduracy and inattention of publishers continued to irritate him as well. Though San Francisco was a city of poets, and though *Howl*—dedicated to "Jack Kerouac, new Buddha of American prose"—had already sold out three printings as a City Lights book, Kerouac found he couldn't get poet-publisher Lawrence Ferlinghetti of City Lights to accept *Mexico City Blues*. This rejection of his best book of poetry especially disappointed him. For such "negative shits"—critics and publishers—he now had, as he wrote to Holmes, one thing to say: "fuck em all, I know better."[77]

Their furniture had barely arrived from Florida when Jack decided—after six weeks in California—that he could take no more of living as "an imbecile poet trapped in America with a dissatisfied mother in poverty and shame." The last event of importance to occur during his Berkeley stay was the arrival of advance copies of *On the Road* from Viking. Coincidentally, the book's hero, Cassady, happened to be present when Jack unwrapped the package. Neal glanced at the book noncommittally, and when the time came to say goodbye, "for the first time in [their] lives failed to look [Jack] in the eye."[78] Kerouac put Gabrielle back on the bus and they rode across country again.

I N late July of 1957, they landed back in Orlando. For $45 a month Jack rented his mother a small bungalow apartment two blocks from his sister Nin's house. He set up to work on the tin-roofed back porch, looking out at some dusty orange trees, but the tropic sun beat down without mercy; his porch was an oven. He tried to read Spengler again and to begin books expressing his "visions" of Burroughs and Snyder, but the proximity of his in-laws and the heat made work impossible. After only a couple of weeks in Florida, he impetuously jumped on a bus to Mexico City. This was, he later said, "one of the great foggy mistakes of my life."[79]

Having recently spent four days on a bus from Berkeley to Orlando, he now spent another three and a half getting to Mexico City. There he stayed just ten days. He went to Orizaba Street, only to learn that Bill Garver had died. Then he went looking for Esperanza, couldn't find her, and assumed that she too was dead. He checked into an expensive hotel, felt plunged in "marble" gloom, and soon came down with a fever. While he tossed and turned in delirium, sweating holes in his "dharma bum" sleeping bag under hotel blankets, Mexico City was rocked by a severe earthquake. Jack had another death flash, like the one he had had on the boat to Tangier, but this time no benevolent God appeared to enfold him. Shaken, he headed north as soon as he had recovered—riding the bus through "nightmare" New Orleans for the fourth time in as many months.

PART FIVE
FAME

．　　．　　．

KEROUAC went to New York to help promote *On the Road*. There, as he soon wrote to Cassady, "everything exploded."[1] The novel appeared in stores on September 5, 1957. The following night, at Joyce Glassman's apartment, Jack dreamed he was first being chased by police in Lowell, then rescued by "a parade of children chanting [his] name," who allowed him to escape by hiding in their "endless ranks."[2] But from the publicity generated from his book there was to be no refuge, especially among those who followed and "chanted" Jack's name, both in worship and derision.

That fall marked the launching of the great media beachhead of the "united front" that Ginsberg had been putting together for two years. Within months articles on the Beats were to be found in *Harper's Bazaar*, *Mademoiselle*, *Evergreen Review*, *New Directions*, the *New York Times*, the *Nation*, the *New Republic*, *New World Writing*, *Dissent*, the *Chicago Review*. But Allen himself was away in Europe, safely out of reach of the "explosion." Jack was left to bear the brunt alone. Never having intended the Beat Generation as a campaign, merely as a description, he now had no

This is a copy of the first edition of

ON THE ROAD

by

Jack Kerouac

It will be published in September 1957 by The Viking Press and is certain to cause violently conflicting reactions among readers and critics. We believe that readers will find truth in the book; to some this truth may be beautiful, to others it may be ugly, but no one can fail to be impressed by what this book says and the way it says it.

After World War I a certain group of restless, searching Americans came to be called "The Lost Generation." This group found its truest voice in the writings of the young Hemingway. For a good many of the same reasons after World War II another group, roaming America in a wild, desperate search for identity and purpose, became known as "The Beat Generation." Jack Kerouac is the voice of this group and this is his novel.

continued...

"The novel appeared in the stores on September 5, 1957 . . . 'everything exploded.' "

"The hot pursuit of pleasure

enables Mr. Kerouac to serve up the great, raw slices of America that give his book a descriptive excitement unmatched since the days of Thomas Wolfe . . . As a portrait of a disjointed segment of society acting out of its own neurotic necessity, *On the Road* is a stunning achievement."
—DAVID DEMPSEY, *N. Y. Times Book Review*

"The most beautifully executed, the clearest and the most important utterance yet made by the generation Kerouac himself named years ago as 'beat'. . . There are sections of *On the Road* in which the writing is of a beauty almost breathtaking. There is a description of a cross-country automobile ride fully the equal, for example, of the train ride told by Thomas Wolfe in *Of Time and the River*. There are the details of a trip to Mexico (and an interlude in a Mexican bordello) that are, by turns, awesome, tender and funny. And, finally, there is some writing on jazz that has never been equaled in American fiction, either for insight, style or technical virtuosity. *On the Road* is a major novel."
—GILBERT MILLSTEIN, *N. Y. Times*

a novel by Jack Kerouac

ON THE ROAD

by JACK KEROUAC

At all bookstores $3.95

THE VIKING PRESS · New York 22

First American and English editions
of On the Road

program to present in its support. Nonetheless, critics immediately took him as proponent of a hundred social evils supposedly advocated in his book.

The confusion, excitement, drinking, and total disordering of Kerouac's private life that accompanied the publication of *On the Road* was no dream. Within two weeks of the book's publication, Jack was seen several times on television. The most notable appearance came on John Wingate's "Nightbeat." Jack showed up at the studio well-oiled but nonetheless was "plenty scared."[3] In front of "40 million viewers," he "sprung God" on Wingate—and then Wingate "sprung dope"[4] on him. Kerouac felt like "a kid dragged in by a cop" and refused to say anything he thought might get him in "trouble."[5]

Jack was now "drunk all the time," as he told Cassady in a letter—"no more wine, just whiskey." There were cocktail parties for the book, thrown by Viking, with "screaming interviewers" and "drunk" publishers unrolling the original 1951 scroll on carpets of expensive hotel suites. There were also "Broadway producers," who—claimed Kerouac—brought "beautiful models"[6] to sit on the edge of Joyce Glassman's bed and feed him drinks. They asked Jack to write a play, which he promptly did, dashing off a three-act quickie that was memorable only because its third act—about "the night of the bishop" in San Jose—later turned into *Pull My Daisy*.

On the Road briefly rose to the best-seller lists, its ascent impelled by a very positive review that appeared in the daily *New York Times* on September 5. A young *Times* reviewer, Gilbert Millstein, called *Road* a "major novel" and said its publication was a "historic occasion in so far as the exposure of an authentic work of art is of any great moment."[7] Later reviewers, however, were less kind. What was to become a long, slow execution of Kerouac's work at the hands of establishment critics began with attacks on *Road* like those by Carlos Baker in the *Saturday Review* ("dizzy travelog . . . what is really sad and blank is Kerouac's American landscape"),[8] David Dempsey in the *New York Times Book Review* ("throws his characters away . . . plotless . . . a road . . . that leads nowhere"),[9] and Herbert Gold in the *Nation* ("Kerouac has appointed himself prose celebrant to a pack of unleashed zazous . . . a blend of nihilism and mush . . . a proof of illness rather than a creation of art").[10] Even more painful to Kerouac, considering the source, was Kenneth Rexroth's review in the *San Francisco Chronicle*. Rexroth, one of the few critics armed to appreciate it, paid only cursory homage to "the power and beauty of the writing" before ironically dismissing the book as the work of a "furious square" (". . . these characters have the time sense of May flies and little children . . . Their values are those of the most conformist members of the middle class they despise").[11]

In spite of the negative reviews, Sterling Lord had a whole armload of sudden business propositions. Foremost was the sale of *On the Road* to the movies. Kerouac was told there had been an offer of $110,000 for the movie rights from Warner Brothers but that Lord had "turned it down because it wasnt enuf money or something." The details made Kerouac's mind whirl —"Marl Brando definitely interested," he soon reported to Cassady. He assumed it was merely a matter of waiting for Hollywood to up the ante. Then, as he told Neal in an October letter, he would be relaxing on a sizable trust fund for life, and they would be taking "Mercedes Benz rides . . . to Mexico City." Coasting along on the daydream, Jack even "promised Buddha" that if his book sold to the movies for $150,000 he would meditate in solitude for a month, eat no meat, and spend the whole time "praying for all living creatures."[12] (When *Road* slipped from the best-seller lists almost as fast as it had climbed, however, the movie deal failed to materialize; it was not finally consummated until well after Kerouac's death, when it brought his estate a sum higher than the total of his entire literary earnings while he lived.)

Lord also set up sales of foreign translation rights of *Road*, as well as several deals with magazines that yielded instant cash—$500 from *Esquire*, $300 from *Pageant*, $500 from *Playboy*—in return for article-length slices of prose on "beat" subjects. Coming after such a long dry spell, even these small windfalls gave Kerouac visions of a sky raining dollars, like Ste. Thérèse's shower of roses. He spent his last two weekends in the city frantically celebrating the success that he was sure would soon follow, no matter what the critics said. All around him there were new friends—and also, now, "girls girls girls."[13]

Jack was barely able to maneuver through the final publicity appointments. Two weeks after *Road* came out, the reviewer Gilbert Millstein threw a soirée for the author, inviting some prominent literary people. Unable to face such a crowd, the guest of honor holed up in Joyce Glassman's apartment and did not attend his own party. The storm of attention had flattened him; he was, in the words of John Clellon Holmes, who was among those waiting for him at Millstein's apartment, "temporarily discombobulated by the image of himself . . . He no longer knew who the hell he was supposed to be."[14]

Shortly after Millstein's party, Kerouac canceled his remaining dates and returned to Florida ("always go back to my mother,"[15] he had told a *Village Voice* reporter who had asked about his plans). In Orlando he spent ten weeks getting over his publication month in New York. He went back to work—now aiming at the "big" novel that publishers and agent told him should follow *Road*. He picked up where he had left off two years earlier on a "Proustian" evocation of Lowell, now called *Memory Babe*, but the results soon proved too lyrical, too personal—neither topical nor straightforward enough to satisfy publishers whose eyes were on the emerging drugstore mass-paperback audience *Road* had tapped.

Kerouac's orders from his Viking contact, Malcolm Cowley, were to write an easy-to-read, marketable book. After his sudden success with a novel he now considered a "potboiler," he would have preferred at this time to publish a book that would show his intention to be "a serious artist, like James Joyce"[16]—either his 1952 "modern prose" masterpiece, *Visions of Cody* or something "Proustian" like *Maggie Cassidy* or *Memory Babe* (never to be completed). Instead he sat down and dutifully produced the book Cowley wanted. This was *The Dharma Bums*. Composed on a long roll of paper like the 1951 *Road*, this full-length novel was completed in ten mammoth November typing sessions, each one producing 15,000–20,000 words. In terms of sheer athleticism, it was easily Kerouac's "greatest" work.

The book comprised Kerouac's "Vision of Gary" as modern Deerslayer, and was executed in a *faux-naif* "good-boy" style that betrayed the author's powerful aim to please. The sustained up-tempo feeling, shorter sentences, and generally passive tone of *Bums*, after the momentum and hyperactivism of *Road*, made it immediately more "accessible"—and thus assured its quick acceptance by Viking.

A week before Christmas 1957, Jack was back in New York for the opening of what was scheduled as a three-week reading engagement at a high-class jazz club, the Village Vanguard. It turned out to be a one-week flop. The crowds were small and contained a high ratio of poets and friends of Kerouac—for whom the Vanguard's dollar-and-a-quarter beers were out of range. On stage Kerouac appeared flustered, showing the effects of all the booze, benzedrine, and coffee it took to get him to stand up in front of an audience. He "read his heart out," nonetheless, and when saxophonist Lee Konitz—one of his jazz heroes—told him he was really "singing"[17] when he read, Jack was thrilled. Still, the cancellation of the gig came as a relief.

Kerouac returned with the predictable hangover to Florida. He expected to go back to writing, as usual. But this time exhaustion and distraction seemed to follow him home. He told Creeley in a January 1958 letter that he had had to cancel all publicity appointments to save his energy for writing. A state of "beatitude," he explained to a national magazine audience, was a necessary condition of artistic creation, and could be attained only by "practicing a little solitude, going off by yourself once in a while to store up the most precious of golds, the vibrations of sincerity."[18] This was the technique that had always worked for Jack in the past: travel, experience, rest up, clear your mind, and write. Now, it seemed, the balanced rhythm of storage and expenditure cycles had slipped out of kilter. After *The Dharma Bums*, four years were to go by before he wrote another book.

Kerouac's correspondence from his rented back porch in Orlando hinted of the inner turmoil brought on by fame. "What has all this done to you," he asked Cassady, "are people bugging you & chasing you in Frisco?"[19] Neal did not reply. Another letter enquired of Robert Creeley— then surviving on little money in New Mexico—whether Jack's success bothered *him*. To Kenneth Rexroth, Kerouac wrote at length, complaining about Rexroth's dismissal of *On the Road* as politically naive. In the letter Jack insisted he wanted nothing to do with politics. (Kerouac had told Creeley that the idea of himself and Cassady as protesters was ridiculous, when all they wanted to do was get high.)

Rexroth didn't reply to Kerouac's letter. But he continued to deride Jack in print. Passing through New York, he stopped in at the *Village Voice* office and told the editors that this "Beat" fad—solely the product of Kerouac's "naiveté"—would soon be "as dead as Davy Crockett caps."[20] And when *The Subterraneans* appeared from Grove Press in February 1958, Rexroth appropriated space in the *San Francisco Chronicle* to lash Jack again with a prejudicial, patronizing put down, calling the book a story of "jazz and Negroes . . . two things Jack knows nothing about."[21] A few months later he struck again, this time in the *New Yorker*—questioning Kerouac's authenticity as a writer and bragging that he himself had *"lived* in the kind of world that Jack Kerouac *imagines* he has lived in."[22]

The Subterraneans was caught in the critical switches. Sniped at by its most likely prospective supporter, the supposedly broad-minded Rexroth, the book was simply cut to ribbons in more conservative quarters. To David Dempsey (*New York Times Book Review*) it seemed "a boy meets girl story of the lower depths" that seeped out "like sludge from a leaky drainpipe. . . . The best way to read Kerouac is with an oxygen mask,"[23] Dempsey warned the book-buying public.

Following hard on the disturbance caused by *Road*, the publication of Kerouac's "confessional" story of an interracial love affair triggered an epidemic of hand wringing in the literary quarterlies. Critics like Robert Brustein (in *Horizon*) and Norman Podhoretz (in *Partisan Review*) suggested that such works could only be seen as promoting "instinct," "primitivism," and even "violence."[24] Kerouac attempted to defend himself against such charges in several lectures and articles, reminding his audiences that to him "beat" meant "beatific" ("to be in a state of beatitude like St. Francis, trying to love all life")[25] and pointing out that the sociological problems of the day—juvenile delinquency and the like—were not his fault. The original "beat characters" he had portrayed—and most of them had by now "vanished into jails and madhouses" or been "shamed into silent conformity"—were "hot" and shouldn't, Kerouac insisted, be mixed up with the new late-fifties "cool" beatness, as symbolized by the " 'twisted' slouchy look"[26] of James Dean.

As the critics blew his work up past recognition, Kerouac squirmed in Florida, where his only recourse was to sweat it out. He combed *The Decline of the West* for clues to understanding the hysteria his work had induced and discovered evidence that the whole "beat" phenomenon was a historical fulfillment of Spengler's prophecy that in the "sunset of our culture" there would arise a "late-day glow" revealing "a beatific indifference to things that are Caesar's . . . and a yearning for . . . Heaven."[27] On a trip to the city in early 1958, he tried to explain all this to Mike Wallace on CBS television :

Q. You mean beat people are mystics?
A. Yeah, it's a revival prophesied by Spengler. He said that in the late movements of Western civilization there would be a great revival of religious mysticism. It's happening.
Q. What do the mystics believe in?

A. Oh, they believe in love . . . and . . . all is well . . . we're in heaven now, really.

Q. You don't sound happy.

A. Oh, I'm tremendously sad, I'm in great despair.

Q. Why?

A. Oh, it's a great burden to be alive.[28]

The TV interview was printed in the *New York Post*, appeared in syndication all over America, and was even excerpted by *Time*. Kerouac, who had formerly suffered at length from the obscurity of nonpublication, now was finding out there were also perils in the opposite condition. Without asking him, the national media had appointed him the spokesman for an entire generation, and his slightest thoughts made the wires hum from coast to coast. Socially, the only way Jack could deal with this was to screw the cap off another bottle of cheap wine, pass it around, and hope everybody else had forgotten who he was—even if he no longer could.

I N the spring of 1958, Kerouac made another trip north from Orlando, this time to make a sound recording of a reading from his work—backed by Steve Allen on piano—for Dot Records. Jack showed up for the date with his "huge suitcase full of untyped manuscripts of prose and poetry"; without rehearsal he reached into his suitcase "as if blindfolded," pulled out a text, and began to read to Allen's improvised accompaniment. An engineer rolled the tape. Between cuts Jack shared his pint of Thunderbird with the famous piano player. After an hour of reading, the engineers told Jack it had been "a great first take." "It's the only take,"[29] he replied, packing up his suitcase.

The result was Kerouac's finest recorded reading performance, a gentle, reflective session to which Allen Ginsberg later accurately attributed "a kind of mellow Frank Sinatra beauty."[30] The project's only real problem was the president of Dot Records, who decided the album was in "bad taste" and backed off releasing it; after some contractual haggling, it finally came out a year later on the Hanover label as *Poetry for the Beat Generation*. Kerouac recorded two other albums of readings in 1958—*Blues and Haikus* (Hanover), with a couple of Jack's favorite tenor sax players, Zoot Sims and Al Cohn, playing "like pretty babies"[31] behind him, and *Readings on the Beat Generation* (Verve), a solo effort featuring Kerouac's memorable rendering of the "Three Stooges" passage from *Visions of Cody*.

In addition to the recordings, there were more television and radio appearances; after a while they all swam together in a sea of booze as far as Jack was concerned. One night in April 1958, not long after the session with Steve Allen, he got noisily drunk in the Kettle of Fish bar on McDougal Street, then stepped outside into the fists of three punks eager for the secondhand fame of beating up a celebrity. Bleeding heavily, he crawled and staggered to the Village apartment of Joyce Glassman, who brought him to a hospital.

This incident caused him to fear that he was going to pieces. He had to find a way out of the desperate commute between the spotlight in New York and the steaming back porch in Orlando. After the Kettle of Fish episode, he revived an old fantasy of getting a nice, quiet "house for ma" on Long Island. The big movie money was just around the corner, Lord kept telling him; it was just a matter of time before money would no longer matter. Kerouac counted his savings, went to Northport, Long Island (a quiet north shore village suggested by Joyce Glassman), and for $14,000 bought a large, oldish wooden frame house with a yard and a grape arbor.

IN June 1958 Sterling Lord sold *The Subterraneans* to an independent film company for $15,000—less than Kerouac had hoped for but still the largest lump sum he had ever earned. Jack put his typewriter on a table under the grape arbor at 34 Gilbert Street in Northport and went to work again on *Memory Babe*. There was money to live on now, and time to work. But he found his concentration had degenerated badly. The only thing he could pay undivided attention to was late-night television, and then only after he had drunk himself into a stupor.

July brought a major struggle with Viking over Malcolm Cowley's editing of *The Dharma Bums*. Cowley, Jack complained, had "made endless revisions, . . . inserted thousands of needless commas,"[32] and "deleted [the] Catholicism"[33] from his novel. The restoration of all these changes finally cost Kerouac $500. "That's my last potboiler!"[34] he vowed angrily.

While laboriously restoring the line-by-line "spontaneity" of his book, Jack was interrupted by a first trickle of curiosity seekers. They were eventually to appear in waves. Before it was over, this flood of unwanted guests in Northport was to include a front yard full of high school kids in "Dharma Bums" jackets; a reporter who invaded Jack's bedroom (while Kerouac sat in pyjamas, trying to transcribe a dream); several teenagers

In the neon spotlight: Kerouac in front of the Kettle of Fish Bar, McDougal Street, New York, 1958 (photo by Jerome Yulsman)

who climbed over the six-foot-high back-yard "privacy fence"; and a woman who came to the door asking for "a real beatnik" for her "annual shindig party." There also came uncounted "drunken visitors," not only wasting Kerouac's time but also stealing his books and "puking in [his] study." Jack found himself incapable of resisting. Before long he was getting "drunk practically all the time to put on a jovial cap to keep up with all this."[35]

Also suffering from the fallout of the Beat explosion was Neal Cassady. Cassady had been set up by undercover police and busted for dealing marijuana. In the spring of 1958, he was sentenced to five years to life at San Quentin. He had already begun serving his sentence before word of it reached the Kerouac household. Jack, of course, would never have told his mother such news. But Gabrielle habitually inspected his mail, sometimes before he did. Allen Ginsberg wrote to Jack from Paris in July. She distrusted Ginsberg and opened the letter. It contained not only news of the Cassady bust but also several references Gabrielle regarded as "insults" to "Catholic priests" ("He was telling Franciscan monks to take their clothes off,"[36] she complained to her son). A stormy argument ensued, in which Gabrielle bitterly reiterated to Jack her disapproval of his "beat" pals. After the quarrel she took matters into her own hands and wrote a letter to Ginsberg in Paris, informing him that she would turn him over to the FBI as a homosexual if he ever came near her son again. Ginsberg, who returned to New York from Europe shortly afterward, took her seriously enough to steer clear of Northport.

Jack didn't see Allen again until he stopped off at Ginsberg's East 2nd Street apartment on the day of the publication party for *The Dharma Bums* (October 15, 1958). Ginsberg offered a careful list of suggestions about how Kerouac could save both his sanity and his publishing career— no more tourist potboilers for Viking, ignore Sterling Lord, publish *Sax* with Grove Press, avoid Madison Avenue—and then announced that he had already succeeded in interesting James Laughlin of New Directions in *Visions of Cody* and Don Allen of Grove in *Mexico City Blues*.

The Dharma Bums was a more conventional work than anything Jack had published since *The Town and the City*. It was, indeed, the first book he had allowed his mother to read since her bad experience with *On the Road*, which she had abandoned in distaste on page 34 (he had advised her not even to look at *The Subterraneans*). She evidently liked it. In this respect her tastes resembled those of press critics, who gave it relatively kind treatment. *Newsweek* approved; even *Time* had to admit that "if [Kerouac's] style irritates, it seldom bores."[37] The most informative review was the one by Ginsberg in the *Village Voice*. Though he had privately encouraged Jack to stop writing such "travelogues," Allen loyally touted *Bums* in the review and also coined a catchy nickname for his friend's style of writing—"spontaneous bop prosody."[38]

Ginsberg's review implied, however, that Kerouac's recent life was not quite as triumphant as his prose. "I begin to see why Pound went paranoiac, if he did,"[39] Allen hinted darkly. In truth, the paranoid streak Jack had inherited from Leo was showing under the stress of sudden fame. Three weeks after *Bums* came out, Kerouac appeared in a "symposium" at Hunter College on the question, "Is There a Beat Generation?" The event was sponsored by Brandeis University. Unaware that the symposium was meant to be a debate, Jack had come ready to give a lecture. He read a prepared text, later published as "The Origins of the Beat Generation." It was a thoughtful, articulate, and impassioned statement, but Kerouac, who had been drinking, had difficulty reading it—especially after another panelist, *New York Post* editor James Wechsler, walked in late and "spoiled" one of Jack's favorite long sentences. During the ensuing debate, Jack grabbed Wechsler's hat and pranced across the stage in it, while the unamused editor delivered an acid, ironic analysis of the Kerouac oeuvre. When it was his turn to respond, Jack swayed over to the podium, glared at the veteran journalist, and slurred, "Admit it, Wechsler, you came here tonight determined to hate me."[40]

"TOO much adulation is worse than non-recognition, I see now," Kerouac wrote to Carolyn Cassady early in 1959. "Too much adulation means also the disgusting abuse from critics, which has caused my family in Lowell to announce, for instance, that I have disgraced the name of Kerouac, when all the time the disgrace emanates from critics and press."[41]

The "abuse" of critics, Jack felt, came in part from misguided envy. By 1959 *Road* had sold 20,000 hard-cover and 500,000 paperback copies. But in an interview he gave in February of that year, he insisted that he had made only $20,000 in total from his work. He complained that columnist Dorothy Kilgallen was saying he lived in "a $30,000 mansion in Long Island," whereas, in fact, the old house in Northport badly needed a coat of paint and both porches were rotting. Kerouac wrote to Carolyn Cassady after income tax day, 1959, that he had only "a $30 deficit" in the bank, as proof that he was "not rich at all." He did, however, manage to send Carolyn a check to buy a portable typewriter Neal needed in jail. The latter gesture only partially assuaged Jack's sense of guilt over his friend's fate. To Carolyn he exonerated himself by saying that his book (*Road*) hadn't had "anything to do with [Neal's] arrest, after all he was too reckless."[42]

The "disgusting abuse" didn't let up. In February gossip columnists picked up a remark dropped on the David Susskind "Open End" TV show by Truman Capote. In response to Norman Mailer's defense of Jack's "rapid" writing, Capote had scoffed, "Writing! That's not writing, it's just . . . typing!"[43] This became a standard thumbnail description of Jack's work, even, or perhaps especially, in circles where it wasn't read.

Similarly snobbish motives seemed to lie behind the nasty John Updike parody of *On the Road* that appeared in the *New Yorker* in February 1959. The ingenuousness of Kerouac's work made it a perfect target for lampooning; Updike reduced the epic cross-country scale of *On the Road* to the ridiculous dimension of a five-year-old wheeling a scooter around a "sad backyard" in the "American noon." Kerouac considered the Updike parody a low blow because it played on the semipublic joke about his being hung up on his mother. (Updike's five-year-old is "not allowed to cross the street.")[44] Gabrielle was, indeed, the Achilles heel of Jack's image as a gypsy writer. He understandably became very defensive about their relationship and tried to keep her out of most newspaper interviews.

In early 1959 Jack had a new city girlfriend, a "Bohemian painter" named Dodie Muller. He hung around her Greenwich Village studio, talking to her as she worked—and, using her materials, even did some painting of his own, including a large oil of Pope Paul II done from a charcoal sketch and based on a *Life* magazine photograph. Finally, he invited her home to meet his mother. The visit was a disaster; midway through it Gabrielle took her son aside and told him his new girlfriend was a "witch." Once Dodie had gone, Gabrielle listed her deficiencies: she "has long, long hair . . . doesn't tie it up . . . likes to go barefoot . . . she's an Indian . . . *la sauvage*."[45]

Gabrielle hadn't liked Joyce Glassman, either, because of the way Joyce did dishes. Beneath all her criticisms, of course, lay a more powerful motive—her fierce possessiveness toward her son. Jack sometimes felt suffocated by it but was powerless to resist it. As he had written in a poem a few years earlier, "I keep falling in love/with my mother."[46]

PETER ORLOVSKY, who during this period saw Jack only in New York, wrote to Carolyn Cassady that he suspected Jack's Northport life, however suffocating, must be pleasant in comparison with the city trips—when "too much comotion flies around and he gets drunk to fast & argues."[47]

"Kerouac would come in to New York, he was sort of like 'Momma let me out to play,'" recalls Ted Joans, a black painter-poet who became one of Jack's steady party companions around this time. "Jack came in to have fun."[48] There were occasions, however, when Kerouac's "good-timing" (as Joans calls it) backfired and turned into bad alcoholic scenes. At a large poetry benefit held at the Living Theatre in 1959, Jack put on an embarrassing public show of bad manners. Not scheduled to read himself, he sat on stage drinking from a bottle and heckling readers who made him impatient. Allen Ginsberg recalls that attempts were made to control Jack's behavior—even by such physically imposing presences as painters Franz Kline and Willem de Kooning—but to no avail. While Frank O'Hara read, Jack grumbled audibly that he was hearing "all yatter and no poetry." When he shouted "You're ruining American poetry, O'Hara,"[49] the poet finally reacted in annoyance, "That's more than you could ever do."

There was more to such bull-in-the-china-shop shows than mere drunken rudeness. Jack was starting to crack under the strain of fame.

ALTHOUGH Kerouac's increased drinking was beginning to mar his social relations, it didn't prevent his participation in the 1959 underground film *Pull My Daisy*. This project came about after Robert Frank, the photographer with whom Kerouac had worked on an assignment for *Life* magazine, suggested that painter Al Leslie make a movie from Kerouac's work. Leslie visited Northport, considered various Kerouac manuscripts, and eventually chose to stage the third act of Jack's play "The Beat Generation." With cash backing from a financier named Walter Guttman, Robert Frank as cameraman, and Ginsberg, Orlovsky, Corso, Amram, painters Alice Neel and Larry Rivers, and Delphine Seyrig (the lone professional) as actors, the movie was shot in January and February at Leslie's studio on 4th Avenue.

Although the production was almost totally free-form, there was enough discipline for Leslie to eventually bar Kerouac from the set on grounds that his frequent arrivals from bars, with liquor and miscellaneous companions, were disruptive. When the film was complete, Jack was picked up in Central Park, taken to a sound studio, and shown *Daisy* twice; as he watched he recited two variant impromptu narratives, which were spliced together and taped as the movie's sound track. "Jack's narration," recalls David Amram, who wrote the film's score, "was almost like a great jazzman . . . he played around the [musical] chords or played around the situation, improvising on certain things, and made a beautiful tapestry out of nothing."[50] The movie came out possessing a gnomic, childlike quality that both reflected the spirit of the lyrics Jack had composed under the same title exactly ten years earlier and foreshadowed a whole movement toward low-key experimental cinema in the decade to come. When it opened in June, *Daisy* became one of the rare *critical* successes with which Jack was ever associated—even Dwight Macdonald, a critic whose liberal humanist aesthetics had nothing in common with Kerouac's, liked it.

Dr. Sax and *Mexico City Blues*, which Grove Press published in 1959, certainly didn't get as warm a reception. Editor Don Allen this time left Kerouac's texts unaltered, which pleased Jack but made no difference to the critics. David Dempsey, by now a familiar nemesis, blared in the *New York Times Book Review* that the poetic, revelatory *Sax* (arguably Jack's finest novel) was "not only bad Kerouac, but a bad book."[51] Other reviewers in most major and polite publications followed suit. Even Ralph J. Gleason, who had liked both *Road* and *Bums*, briskly dismissed *Sax* in the *San Francisco Chronicle* as "the work of a novelist practicing to be a novelist," in which Kerouac "attempts to go all Joycean on us . . . and fails."[52]

If the negative views of a relatively "hip" critic like Gleason were damaging to Jack, so much the more so was the continuing onslaught of Kenneth Rexroth. In the *New York Times Book Review* of November 29, 1959, Rexroth attacked again—this time to the jugular. In what was ostensibly a review of *Mexico City Blues*, he put down the entirety of Kerouac's published work (it consisted, said Rexroth, in a great deal of writing on subjects about which the author knew "less than nothing") and then narrowed in on the "naive effrontery" of Jack's attempts at poetry, which were "more pitiful than ridiculous." After quoting, with a righteous sneer, some references to "dope" in Jack's spontaneous verse (actually the words of Bill Garver, transcribed by Kerouac), Rexroth concluded, "I've always wondered what ever happened to those wax work figures in the old rubber-neck dives in Chinatown. Now we know; one of them at least writes books."[53] It was less a review than an intellectual's voodoo curse on Kerouac's career.

Apart from *Holiday*, for which he wrote travel pieces, *Playboy, Swank, Escapade*, and the other girlie magazines were just about the only publications that held no prejudice against Kerouac. Accordingly, much of his writing of this period went into them. His columns in *Escapade*—the first of which appeared in April 1959—are of particular interest, since they document Kerouac's preoccupation with "real life" (everything from baseball to bop) at a time when "fiction" had come to seem to him, as he told Alfred Aronowitz, "nothing but idle daydreams."[54] The *Escapade* columns adhered strictly to "real things and real people."

In his June 1959 column—the first to fall under his regular "commentator's" byline, "The Last Word"—Kerouac explained his "position in the current American literary scene": that of someone who had "got sick and tired of the conventional English sentence which seemed so ironbound in its rules, so inadmissible with reference to the actual format of [his] mind." His most inventive experimental prose, he claimed, had "yet to be published"; it was contained, he said, in his *"Visions* and *Dreams* and *Dharmas."*[55]

Visions of Cody was the book that Jack hoped to be remembered by above all others. In a November appearance on the Steve Allen show, he smuggled passages from *Cody* inside the covers of the published *Road* and read those instead of the earlier book, clearly indicating his personal preference between the two texts. Yet no one would publish *Cody*; the book was too *big*—both in size and as an aesthetic proposition—for the publishing world of its time. Realizing this, Kerouac finally allowed James Laughlin of New Directions to bring out an eviscerated version—a 120-page slice, about a fifth of the whole text—which appeared in December 1959 in an edition of only 750 copies. The publication went practically unnoticed by the general reader and the 750 copies quickly disappeared into the hands of collectors. Though Jack continued to push it on Don Allen and other editors, the complete *Cody* remained unpublished in Kerouac's lifetime.

Kerouac had one other book out in 1959, the 1953 tale of young love, *Maggie Cassidy*, published as a paperback original by Avon. Since *Maggie* offered neither dope nor sex nor footloose rambling, it sold poorly and went largely without comment in the critical press, which had by this time pretty much ceased to consider Kerouac as a serious writer. John Ciardi put it most bluntly when he wrote off the book in the *Saturday Review*: "My guess is that Avon is banking on whatever mileage may be left in the legend of the beatniks to sell a badly mothy bit of juvenilia . . . it is mistaken seriousness to treat this stuff as if it could be asked to respond to the criteria of serious writing. There is no interest here in the art of writing."[56]

REGARDLESS of what the academic critics decreed, *Life* and other popular periodicals were still banging the Beat gong. By the summer of 1959, the sociological heat had grown intense; Jack jumped around like a bug on a griddle. To escape the hordes of reporters and curiosity seekers, he sold the Gilbert Street house and fled with Gabrielle back to Florida. But Florida was "a flooded swamp all summer," and the Kerouacs made a quick, sweaty U-turn. "My Ma prefers Northport after all," Jack wrote to Don Allen in October. By that time they had moved into a "new little cottage"[57] back in Northport—a small white house with a picket fence at 49 Earl Avenue.

Kerouac was now hitting the bottle harder than ever; on a visit to Northport, poet Phil Whalen walked in on a tranquil scene of both Kerouacs, *mère et fils*, out cold from drinking. Yet in mid-November Jack pulled himself together to make it to the West Coast for a TV appearance with Steve Allen, a tour of the set of *The Subterraneans*, then in production, and a visit to a film festival where *Pull My Daisy* was being shown.

The television appearance paid for Kerouac's trip (and also for an attic workroom in the Earl Street house, where he was getting rheumatism from typing in a damp bedroom). After two rehearsals under the hot studio lights of Burbank, however, he wished he had stayed home. The producer wanted one more run-through. Jack refused. Steve Allen pleaded. Jack walked out in the direction of the nearest bar. He was back in time for the show and afterward found himself in a Hollywood restaurant with Mamie Van Doren, who turned out "to be a big bore trying to read me her poetry and won't talk love because in Hollywood man love is for sale."[58]

After an alcoholic stop at *The Subterraneans* set, Kerouac was driven north by *Daisy* director Al Leslie. At the San Francisco Film Festival, Jack tried to rub elbows with cinema people, who only snubbed him. He fell back on the bards of the town, spending several days boozing with and riding around in the jeep of a new volunteer chauffeur, poet Lew Welch. Albert Saijo, with Welch a fellow resident of a communal house at Post and Buchanan where Jack slept during this stay, later recalled that Kerouac had hit town looking "tired" and "drinking heavy, but . . . determined to party on." The mornings after, Saijo says, Jack arose "with a look in his eyes verging on the dead eye look of metabolic extremity . . . You understood then that his drinking was some kind of penance."⁵⁹

On November 20 Kerouac was scheduled to address a convicts' study group on comparative religions organized by Cassady at San Quentin. Neal had been looking forward to Jack's visit for weeks. Welch was appointed to drive Kerouac to the prison. But the morning of the twentieth passed like the other mornings of Jack's stay; both he and Welch lay unconscious on the floor until past noon. Jack's well-laid plans swirled down the bottomless sink of guilt. Without attempting to contact Cassady, he persuaded Welch to drive him to New York so that he could be home with his mother for Thanksgiving. Saijo accompanied them in the jeep. Jack paid for motels en route, bought bottles of expensive Scotch, and traded haikus with his fellow travelers. Passing through Las Vegas, he paused from his boozy rendition of a Sinatra standard, looked off past the casinos to the silent, dry mountains beyond, and told Lew and Albert that "back in those hills" the "fellaheen [were] waiting to come down."⁶⁰

Kerouac, however, no longer had visions of joining them.

I N a January attempt at drying out, Jack stayed away from the city for weeks, took hikes around Northport, and holed up for hours in his new attic workroom with his new electric typewriter, attempting to piece together the story of the past few years of his life. It was like stitching together clouds; no substance remained of all those drunken adventures, and the writing failed to cohere. Even a heavy dose of benzedrine—Jack's first in years—didn't help. With trembling hands he finally ran from his attic to the city and the bottle.

Kerouac's state of mind at this time leaks out between the lines of his *Escapade* columns for February and April 1960. In these he addressed himself—by way of "the Berlin question"—to the meaninglessness of history. Recent experience had convinced him that the universe was a black comedy, acted out in the "confusion of the world of living beings." The arbitrary connections between human intentions and actual events made "no sense." And "history" was "based on confusion, like when in football the T-Quarterback flips the ball to the right half back who ain't there."⁶¹ In June he suggested how history's confusion was affecting him through

First editions of The Dharma Bums (courtesy Bradford Morrow)

DOCTOR SAX
BY
JACK KEROUAC

■ Now, the leading (and bestselling) voice of the Beat Generation proves that he is as unpredictable and versatile as he is controversial. His remarkable new novel is about a fantasy-ridden New England youth. National advertising. Free, pre-pack counter displays available. An Evergreen Original. Ready in April. E 160, $1.75 (cloth $3.50).

GROVE PRESS INC., 795 BROADWAY, N. Y. 3

A new novel by
JACK KEROUAC
author of *"The Subterraneans"* and *"On the Road"*

MAGGIE
CASSIDY
A Love Story

The Bard of the Beat Generation reveals a startling new dimension to his personality in this brilliant and profoundly moving novel of adolescence and first love

An Avon Original—50c—Not available in any other edition —G-1038

ABOVE: Dr. Sax *published by Grove Press,*
1959

Maggie Cassidy, *Avon first edition, 1959*

Larry Rivers, Kerouac, David Amran, Ginsberg (Corso in stocking cap) during Pull My Daisy: "The production was . . . free-form." (photo courtesy *the unspeakable visions of the individual)*

ABOVE: *Carolyn Cassady: "To Carolyn he exonerated himself."* (courtesy Carolyn Cassady)

LEFT: *Kerouac, 1960: "It was like stitching together clouds."* (courtesy *the unspeakable visions of the individual*)

the distortion of his work by the media—"*Time, Life*, TV and the paper reviewers."[62]

In February 1960 John Ciardi published a funereal "Epitaph for the Dead Beats" in *Saturday Review*.[63] Two months later, however, Kerouac was still alive and kicking rubberneckers from the media out of his front yard. Reporters surrounded the picket fence in Northport, waiting for him to come out so they could ask him whether he thought Lawrence Ferlinghetti's new poem about Christ was anti-Christian, un-American—or what. Jack refused to answer the door. "All I could possibly say is that I have written about Jesus in my own way," he told Carolyn Cassady in a letter, "but you can guess how it would emerge all twisted in the papers."[64] Ferlinghetti was now planning Kerouac's *Book of Dreams* as a City Lights publication, but that didn't mean Kerouac agreed with Ferlinghetti's radical views on religion and politics. Jack was, in fact, adamantly antileft; around this time he refused to sign an antinuclear petition circulated by Kenneth Tynan because he considered Tynan a "Communist."[65] But he was by now much too wary to say any such thing to the newspapermen who held vigils at his gate.

Tristessa came out from Avon and was largely ignored (it received four American reviews, all unfriendly). In June *The Subterraneans* premiered in New York, starring Leslie Caron in the role of Mardou and George Peppard as Jack. The movie turned Kerouac's book, his life, and his friends into cartoon mutations. After it came out, his party pal Ted Joans "didn't see Jack any more. . . . The rumor around the Village," recalls Joans, "was that he was embarrassed about what Hollywood had done to the thing."[66]

Indeed, the movie culminated a season of shame and disgrace for Kerouac. He felt "surrounded and outnumbered," and that he "had to get away to solitude again or die." In the midst of editorial correspondence, Lawrence Ferlinghetti had dropped the suggestion that Jack take a work vacation at his cabin near Big Sur. Kerouac could come out in July, Ferlinghetti proposed, and work on editing the *Book of Dreams* at the Bixby Canyon hideaway. Jack accepted the offer. He "neatly packed" his "hopeful rucksack . . . with everything necessary to live in the woods"[67] and rode the California Zephyr west in the last week of July 1960.

THE problem with living in Big Sur, poet William Everson has said, is that "the spectacular beauty of the place has a way of searching out the flaw in man. Too often he breaks up on the rocks." To live in the Sur, Everson suggests, "you had better be ready to cope with the negative capability within yourself because you are going to be put to the test."[68]

Kerouac's "book of interior chaos,"[69] as Everson calls *Big Sur*, is the story of a nervous breakdown, provoked in part by the awesome extremity of nature at Bixby Canyon. The place itself is a principal character in the drama of Jack's frightening descent to the "terrifying night of Sept. 3"—when (as he later put it in a letter to Carolyn) he "went mad for the first time."[70]

Throughout his stay at Bixby Canyon, Kerouac would register only negative readings on nature's wavelength. After just a few peaceful days, he felt himself turning—like the character in the Robert Louis Stevenson novel he found and read at the cabin—from "serene Jekyll to hysterical Hyde," gradually losing "absolute control of the peace mechanisms of [his] mind." When he donned his rain gear and went to the beach at night to sit "in the dark writing down the sound of the waves" in a notebook (a carefully planned attempt to pick up where James Joyce had left off), he felt not like an artist but like "an idiot" committing "fantastic inanities" and was terrified by the unresponding "blackness" of the night sea. Returning to the beach in the afternoon sunshine, he tried to gulp in the "good sea air" and consolatory vibrations; instead he got a dizzying whiff "of iodine, or of evil," which he was sure was some kind of "overdose."[71]

Before the end of his third week, Jack tried to flee to the city. Sticking out his thumb on the coast highway, he got an unnerving surprise: no one would pick him up. He finally had to walk miles on bloody feet to a bus. The whole ordeal took seven hours, during which time he decided that things had "changed in America,"[72] and that he would never hitchhike again in his life. In San Francisco he called up Lew Welch, and on a brief wave of euphoria created by Jack's purchase of a fifth of Scotch, they rolled down to Los Gatos in the jeep, arriving about eleven at night.

Jack hadn't seen either of the Cassadys since before Neal's San Quentin term. Neal was now out on parole after pulling two years of "good" time. Carolyn Cassady remembers that a badly rumpled Kerouac unexpectedly banged on their patio door, then stumbled in "drunk and disorderly" with Welch and another passenger. Jack's "tormented eyes foretold the future," recalls Carolyn, "his face was like a character from Poe."[73]

Seeing Neal again was a moment of powerful—and mixed—emotion for Jack. Through the booze he felt both sadness—"the circle's closed in on the old heroes of the night"—and, as always in recent years, a certain amount of guilt. He blurted to Cassady that he had missed the San Quentin appearance because he had felt that "visiting inside a prison" was "SIGNIFYING." Without looking up from the chess problem he was studying, Cassady merely remarked, "Drinkin again, hey?"[74]

Kerouac and friends drove to San Jose to watch Cassady recap tires on' the midnight shift ("a martyr of the American Night in goggles"), then returned the next afternoon to the city. There Jack wailed away the days on his "old fatal double bourbons and gingerale"[75] until Neal called with an emergency: he had been laid off, was short on a house payment, and needed a loan. Eager to be able to compensate in cash for the soul generosity he was too weak to muster, Jack rode to San Jose again, this time at the head of a large caravan of poets, and proudly gave Cassady $100. Then the whole group continued on to Big Sur for a weekend party.

That weekend and the weeks that followed were full of "horror" for Jack. A "sinister" August wind had begun to blow at the Sur, just one of the many natural "signs" he now started detecting. The poets went to bathe in the hot water pools at Tassajara, but Jack (like Neal) refused to enter the water unclothed; Jack picked out a "gang of fairies" also using the baths and "with horror" even spied "spermatozoa floating in the hot water." Afterward, at the Nepenthe cafe, he shot his mouth off drunkenly about war strategy to a military man at an adjoining table; then pivoted, decided suspiciously that the "general" was taking a "sinister"[76] interest in his remarks, and felt a flash of paranoia that went all the way to the bottoms of his hiking boots.

When the weekend company left, Kerouac stayed behind, twisting in the depths of alcohol sickness and delirium tremens. As the slow days passed, he applied himself to basic tasks like chopping wood, trying to dispel his suspicions that poet friends like Welch and Michael McClure were "witching [him] to madness." On the following weekend, the arrival of the Cassady family was a welcome relief—"a strange apocalyptic burst of gold." Jack walked up a trail with Neal, smoked a joint, and for a few moments believed again that his friend was really an "archangel."[77] Then the present clicked back in. At the cabin a new party swirled. Kerouac slipped into a paranoid frenzy of jealousy: he thought a handsome young friend of Welch's was trying to seduce Carolyn, whom he really wanted for himself. The next day he rode to San Jose with the Cassadys, got drunk

Kerouac in Northport, 1960: "Reporters surrounded the picket fence." (photo by Jerry Bauer)

Northport, 1960 (photo by Jerry Bauer)

"*In June,* The Subterraneans *premiered in New York. . . . The movie turned Kerouac's . . . life and . . . friends into cartoon mutations.*" (courtesy Bradford Morrow)

TOP RIGHT: *Hiding out in Northport after* The Subterraneans *premiered, summer 1960* (courtesy John Clellon Holmes)

BOTTOM RIGHT: *Kerouac and Lawrence Ferlinghetti:* "*Ferlinghetti proposed . . . Jack accepted . . . 'neatly packed' his 'hopeful rucksack' and rode West.*" (courtesy Lawrence Ferlinghetti)

"Tristessa *came out from Avon.*" (1960)

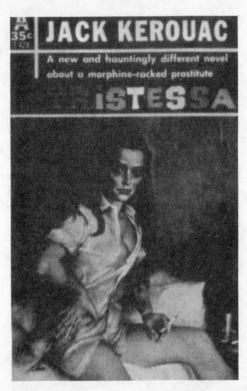

TOP RIGHT: *Ferlinghetti's cabin at Bixby Canyon, near Big Sur: "Negative readings on nature's wavelengths."* (courtesy Lawrence Ferlinghetti)

TOP LEFT and BOTTOM RIGHT: *Kerouac on the corner of Columbus and Broadway, North Beach, San Francisco, 1960: "Jack wailed away the days on his 'old fatal double bourbons and gingerale.' "* (courtesy James Mitchell)

again, and offended the owner of a theater where Carolyn was designing sets for a play.

Bouncing from disaster to disaster, he then went with Neal to the city and there allowed himself to be pushed into a nightmarish one-week relationship with an art student named Jacqueline Gibson, a sometime mistress of Cassady's. It was "just another of a long line of occasions when [Neal] gets me to be a sub-beau for his beauties so that everything can tie in together," Kerouac wrote in *Big Sur*. But this time, principally because of the woman's uncanny physical resemblance to Lucien Carr—which both fascinated and repelled Jack—he got in over his head. For one drunken week he moved slowly back and forth between an armchair in her apartment, where he sat all day and drank port wine, and her bed, where every night they pitched "into love again like monsters."[78]

Jacky Gibson was soon convinced Kerouac intended to marry her. She mentioned this to a few people, and within hours it made the newspaper gossip column of the man who had coined the term "beatnik," Herb Caen. Ironically, by this time Jack had developed a certain paranoid aversion to her—and an even more powerful one to her small son, who came with the package. Unable to break away, he brought them along on his final spasmodic weekend cabin party at Big Sur.

It was the black climax of Kerouac's whole trip. On the way out of the city, he insisted that his driver, Welch, stop at the Cassadys' in Los Gatos; drinking again, he "secretly wanted" Carolyn and Jacky to meet. By this time even his own motives had become too turbid for him to make out. When he got his wish, he instantly knew it was a mistake from the "look of absolute fright"[79] on Neal's face, as well as from Carolyn's reaction of controlled rage, which caused Jack to cringe in guilt for years. (He never saw her again.)

The Kerouac–Welch jeep gang plowed on to the "poor haunted canyon" to play out a final two days of bad drunkenness. Feeling heavily depressed, Jack tried making love with Jacky, but the act only brought out "an awful paranoiac element"—an orgasm of "token venom" and "great ghastly hatred of myself and everything." In revulsion he went off to drink from a creek whose clear water he had sampled earlier, but found this time it tasted "different," as though contaminated by "gasoline or kerosene." Back at the cabin Welch served a fish he had cooked—but Jack now decided Welch was "jealous" of his *own* "ten novels" and conspiring to poison him. His mind skidded off the track; the "expert poisoning society" of his imagination suddenly expanded to include not only Welch but also Jacky, her son, and Welch's girlfriend, poet Lenore Kandel. Kerouac's paranoiac reasoning leaped insanely from premise to premise: they wanted to poison him because he was Catholic; it was "a big anti-Catholic scheme"[80]; Communists had plotted it.

Through the night he tossed in a cold sweat in his sleeping bag, seeing apparitions of the cross, hearing flying saucers, and experiencing the unspeakable visions of madness. A year later, when he had partially recovered, he tried to tell Carolyn about it in a letter. "It was the night of the end of Nirvana, in fact," he wrote. "I realized all my Buddhism had been words—comforting words, indeed, but when I saw those masses of devils racing for me. . . ."[81]

He escaped from the gulfs of Sur to San Francisco, hid out for two days with Ferlinghetti, then, with his horror of the world still crouching like a demon on his shoulder, wobbled aboard a plane back to New York.

THERE he was able at first to resume only a mechanical simulacrum of his former life as a writer. Though his introduction to *Lonesome Traveler*, a collection of work and travel pieces published by McGraw-Hill on September 27, stated that he had always considered "writing his duty on earth,"[82] there were several months after his return from California when Kerouac was able to produce little more than an occasional letter or scattered notes on ideas for books. His agent, Sterling Lord, later told an interviewer that he "assumed" Jack had had a "breakdown"—but that they "never discussed it."[83]

Several weeks after his return to Northport, Kerouac wrote to Cassady saying that though he supposed he would soon write a new book—out of sheer boredom, if for no other reason—he had come in the meantime to an impasse in style, which left him unable to write at all. For Kerouac this was a new experience. It frightened him. He undertook to change his life and vowed to follow a monastic discipline, with Gabrielle acting as a kind of mother superior.

On weekends, however, he often renounced asceticism, as in former times, and went to New York. There he had a new girlfriend, Lois Sorrels. In *Escapade*, Al Aronowitz broke the news that Kerouac had formally "left Buddhism," because—Jack had told Aronowitz—it "preaches against entanglement with women" and to him "the most important thing in life is love."[84]

In the city Jack also hung out again with Ginsberg, who suddenly had access to all kinds of new and interesting drugs. Though Kerouac didn't yet recognize it (and later, when he did, he didn't like it), the "psychedelic" movement was at this time just starting to roll—in places like Cambridge, Palo Alto, and the Lower East Side of New York. Ginsberg was already riding the leading edge of this experiment in mass cultural hallucination.

In January 1961, grasping at a possible cure for his alcoholism, Kerouac joined Ginsberg as a subject in Timothy Leary's drug experiments, taking a dose of psychedelics in Ginsberg's New York apartment. During his trip he regressed unhappily to his pivotal failure in the U.S. Navy in 1943. Afterward, it took him some time to get over his dose of the hallucinogen; he later suggested that, contrary to Leary's claims for such drugs, LSD actually "stupefies the mind and hand for weeks on end."[85] Six years after his experience Kerouac was still telling friends he "hadn't been right since";[86] and by the mid-sixties he was commonly announcing in bars that LSD and other psychedelic drugs had been introduced into America by Russians to destroy the country.

T H E same month Kerouac wrote to his Italian editor and translator Nanda Pivano, that he had to "protect himself from 3 types of jackals here [in America]—the polizia, the hoodlums, the critics."[87] The "hoodlums" were the punks and lion hunters who clung to him in bars, followed him on the streets, and even tried to sneak in his front door (during his 1960 trip to California, Gabrielle had actually barricaded it with furniture). "The critics," to Jack, were a persecuting agency sent by the Devil to suck his blood. But when his *Book of Dreams* came out at the end of 1960, they were apparently busy with other victims; the book got no reviews at all in New York and only two in the entire country. So much for his precious book of "immense sagas all night long," so carefully assembled over a decade of nights in strange beds and sleeping bags, river bottoms, and cheap flops. The heroism of the *Book of Dreams*, Kerouac stubbornly insisted on believing, was over the heads of the "Marxist critics" of New York, who still had (as he bitterly told Ginsberg in January 1961) "their cocks covered with the blood of Mayakovsky & Yesenin."[88]

That third class of "jackals," the "polizia," closed in on Kerouac (at least in his imagination) early in 1961, when he was sued for child support by Joan Haverty. His second wife had come to New York intent on getting a piece of the fantastic income he was rumored to be enjoying. She told reporters Jack was making $50,000 a year. Seeing such figures printed in the daily papers made Kerouac furious, particularly because, as he told Cassady in a letter, he didn't have a fifth that much in the bank—and what he did have he considered untouchably Gabrielle's. Joan Haverty, Jack complained to Neal, was trying to take his mother's life away. He advised his old friend that to avoid further such trouble he now thought it was "Best to cut it off, brother."[89]

In March 1961 Joan Haverty had Kerouac served with another warrant. Jack again retained Ginsberg's brother, attorney Eugene Brooks, for his defense. Brooks's legal maneuvering stalled Joan's case. But the strain and apprehension of the lawsuit made Jack step up his solitary drinking in Northport to a point that seemed dangerous even to his mother, with whom he now alternately conspired, to keep the royalty income away from Joan Haverty, and quarreled—often violently, using obscenities both French and English. Beyond the Kerouacs' locked front door, old ladies of the town were organizing to get Jack's books removed from the shelves of local stores. In May he threw in the towel, surrendered to Gabrielle's desire to be close to the rest of the family, and moved south to a house two doors from Nin's home in Orlando.

The subdivision house had "big fences," wall ovens, air conditioning, shower stalls, terrazo floors—everything, Kerouac told Don Allen in a letter, "real fawncy and comfortable."[90] But he and Gabrielle had been in it only a little over a month when Jack fled again, this time to Mexico City.

He told Carolyn Cassady in a letter from Florida that even there, life was made impossible by "thousands of interrupting maniacs from here to Sweden," in consequence of which he was going to Mexico "to think alone" until his New York court call. Though he also told Carolyn that she remained "the only woman in the world" that he could "love with" or "really talk to without having subject changed,"[91] Jack now—partly out of deference to Neal but also in acknowledgment of his own general hopelessness—held back all talk of their ever getting together.

IN July 1961 Jack rented "a dismal dusty streetdoor apartment" in Mexico City, and before some "old friends" moved in to sponge off and divert him, completed the hasty 50,000 words of autobiographical inventory that became the second part of *Desolation Angels*. This was his first extended burst of writing in four years; it was done in the old ritual pencil-and-candlelight method, and though it was far off the standard of his best work, it at least showed Jack that the writer in him was still alive. But even that pleasure was taken from him with the theft of his packed suitcase from his room, which caused him to revolt in "disgust"[92] against both Mexico and the writing he had done there.

Back in Florida his anger took weeks to subside, during which interval he drank a daily fifth of Johnny Walker Red; read Joan Haverty's *Confidential* piece, "My Ex-Husband, Jack Kerouac, Is an Ingrate;"[93] and mourned the meaninglessness of life, love, and literature. His drinking reached a physical danger point; one bad episode ended in a minor abdominal hemorrhage that foreshadowed his fatal attack of eight years later. But by October he had tapered off to sips of Martell cognac chased by readings in Balzac and Dostoevsky, and he finally settled down to write about his 1960 California breakdown.

Although he had "thought for years and months" of it, *Big Sur* "rolled along" once begun and "only took ten days"[94] to write—on a continuous teletype scroll, with benzedrine to keep him going.

"If I were a big Russian novelist writing fiction it would be so easy," Kerouac wrote to Carolyn Cassady just after finishing *Big Sur*. Indeed, the book contained little "fiction," other than the light veiling of real names under pseudonyms. The stricter discipline of truth, as he saw it through his "eye keyhole," had given Jack little chance to protect tender feelings. "I hope you appreciate the fact I feel, well, shamed? awful? shitty? for writing about everybody as they are."[95] But this rhetorical disclaimer to Carolyn came after the fact; the truth was already out. Kerouac had no choice left, he felt, except to be honest—"because if I don't write what actually I see happening in this unhappy globe which is rounded by the contours of my deathskull I think I'll have been sent on earth by poor God for nothing."[96]

A week or so after writing those words, he rolled up the typescript of *Big Sur*, put it away in a drawer, and headed north. The ostensible purpose of the trip was to buy land in Vermont to begin a solitary life in the woods. But after a cursory look along the Connecticut River, where all the "idiots" were "cutting down trees before they sell you any land," Kerouac returned to New York "disgusted" and (as he told Carolyn in January 1962) went on a "30 day drunk, awful."[97]

During the "30 day drunk" he slept by turns at the lofts of two painters. (One of them, Hugo Weber, allowed him to tack up a big canvas and paint a "vast Pieta.")[98] Kerouac made the rounds of Village bars and saw several girls—including Lois Sorrels, whom he still considered "his" girl—but was so constantly drunk that he was able to make love to nobody.

He also met with Joan Haverty, whom he hadn't seen for six years, and with his nine-year-old daughter, Janet Michele—whom he had never laid eyes on and whose paternity he had been steadily denying. They got together, along with lawyer Eugene Brooks, in Brooklyn. Jack dragged the group to a bar for a liquid "lunch." Her father's "deep blue eyes"[99] and nonstop jokes immediately captivated Jan. After lunch Jack accompanied Joan and Jan to their Village apartment, where, refueling on a bottle of Harvey's Bristol Cream sherry, he continued to play the entertainer.

In March 1962 he returned to New York for a blood test and the much-dreaded court hearing. At the hearing his fears of losing his savings were allayed. The judge let him off with a $52-a-week child support tab to be paid until Jan's twenty-first birthday.

IN Florida Kerouac retyped the single-spaced *Big Sur* scroll onto double-spaced carbons and sent it off to Sterling Lord, who dangled it between Viking and Farrar, Straus. Finally, Robert Giroux grabbed it—along with the 1956 *Visions of Gerard*—for Farrar, Straus.

Once his book was taken care of and the paternity suit was resolved, Jack lapsed back into his cognac and the long, slow blues of his life in Orlando. To Carolyn he admitted the emptiness of his existence there: he had "no girl friends, no men friends, nobody to talk to, nothing"; he was just alone with his books and bottles all the time. He felt his mind was getting "dotty"; he forgot small things, stumbled through daily hangovers, talked only to his mother and three cats—the life was "not enuf for a grown man." But, at forty, he could imagine no other. He joked to Carolyn that because of "excessive drinking" his "cells had changed so often" that he was looking younger and younger. "Like Dorian Gray," he added more ominously, "underneath I may start cropping a corpse."[100]

That summer, in the broiling sun of suburban Florida, Kerouac worked out with iron bars and sweated behind a lawn mower because he was forty pounds overweight. He planned a trip to France but instead lurched onto a plane to New England, where he went house hunting "among the Canucks." Descending from Maine to Hyannis to Cape Cod, he ended up "crying in a rainy field," bruised from a beating by a black bouncer in a jazz joint.[101]

By the end of this hellish Florida summer, even Gabrielle was des-

Book of Dreams, *published 1960: "No reviews at all in New York . . . over the heads of the 'Marxist critics.'"*

New York, 1962: " 'Cells had changed.' " (courtesy David Markson)

perate to move. In September 1962 Jack went north again, ostensibly to look for a home in John Holmes's Connecticut neighborhood. But at Holmes's place, instead of looking at houses, he sat in a chair for a week without shaving, barely eating, drinking cognac by the quart, and reading Balzac. At the end of the week, he got into a big literary argument with his host. Against Holmes's claims for fiction, Kerouac ranted about writing only from personal experience.

From Holmes's place he took a $60 taxi ride to Lowell. There he encountered a Lowell con man who hit him with a "blood-relative" pitch. Kerouac fell for it, convinced he had found a long-lost "Iroquois cousin." Paul Bourgeois, the thirty-four-year-old self-proclaimed "Chief of the Four Nations of the Iroquois," told Jack that after serving seven years in a state prison on "false suspicion of robbery," he had recently returned to Prince of Wales Isle in the Arctic archipelago to assume leadership of a tribe of 3,000 surviving half-French "Canuck Iroquois." The "chief" explained that the "tribe" had been "pushed"[102] further and further north and was now threatened with the contamination of their fish by Polaris nuclear submarines cruising under the polar ice cap; he was, he said, on his way to discuss the matter with Secretary of State Dean Rusk in Washington.

Kerouac met Bourgeois in a bar. Drink often brought out Jack's native ingenuousness. He considered the chief's tale "the saddest story and the most personal-to-me story of all time"—especially after the chief confided that two of the "Four Nations" represented his paternal and maternal ancestors, "Kirouac" and "L'Evesque." As a "cousin" of the tribe, Jack was informed by the chief that after a quarantine period of two years, he would be entitled to move north with his mother and join the semisavage blood-drinking Iroquois. ("Of course the young chief knows I ain't about to start skinning hot blooded animals," Jack wrote to Ferlinghetti a few weeks later, "so I will simply earn my keep chopping wood, nothing else, and gets to drink my Caribou blood in a cup.")[103]

Jack towed the chief off to New York, where they celebrated the publication of *Big Sur* and got drunk with Lucien Carr; then Kerouac bought two plane tickets and they flew to Florida. Jack proudly introduced his mother to their "new cousin." Gabrielle fed the visitor and sang "Indian songs" for him, but after a day or two she concluded that Bourgeois was neither chief nor cousin, only "a juvenile delinquent from Lowell." Sister Nin agreed. Soon Bourgeois was on a train back to Lowell, whisked out of the house by Gabrielle while Jack was dozing. (Kerouac continued to hold credence in Bourgeois' tale until June 1963, when—as Jack wrote Ginsberg —"the Indian fessed up" and told Jack "that his story was shit.")[104]

By October Gabrielle was "desperate to leave," and Jack decided that he would have to change his drinking habits if he really wanted to get them out of Orlando. Accordingly, he shifted from cognac (which he now decided had "depressed [him] more than anything except Irish whiskey") to "Canadian Club whiskey with Sodie."[105] It was like changing colors of fog. Though he wrote to Holmes that alcoholism was "the only *joyous* disease, at least!"[106] there was now little joy in Orlando. He needed to do no more than glance at the review clippings sent on by Farrar, Straus. *Big Sur* had been described as "ridiculous" and "pathetic" by *Time*. "What can a beat do when he is too old to go on the road?" sneered the *Time* reviewer. "He can go on the sauce."[107]

To Carolyn Cassady Jack wrote after looking through the reviews that he was "so sick and tired of being insulted" by the "Jew talk" of "critics" that he had "just about decided not to publish any more, except for the already-written VISIONS OF GERARD and DESOLATION ANGELS." While the critics vaunted "their Philip Roths and Herbert Golds and Bernard Malamuds and J.D. Salingers and Saul Bellowses," Kerouac's only clientele was "kids who steal my books in bookstores."[108]

KEROUAC flew north again around November 1, 1962, found a modern ranch-style house with full finished basement and a big yard in Northport, plunked down an advance on it, and then went back south to arrange the details of transferring his mortgage from the house he had been buying at 1309 Alfred Drive in Orlando to the one he now wanted to buy at 7 Judy Ann Court in Northport. He and Gabrielle moved north in December.

That winter Jack laid plans for a book about the downfall of his family, as reflected in and consummated by his own personal disasters. He described the projected novel—to be titled "Vanity of Duluoz"—in letters to friends. But for this entire stay in Northport, the "family tragedy" lingered unrealized in a stack of notes and yellowed news clips and old letters from Leo, piled on Kerouac's desk at Judy Ann Court. The plight of the Kerouacs proved easy to ponder, hard to write.

One December night as Jack slowly sipped highballs in front of his living room television, his daughter phoned from the Lower East Side. (She had got the unlisted number from a 10th Street neighbor, Allen Ginsberg.) Though he hadn't spoken with her in more than a year, the only subject Jack wanted to talk about was the Kerouac family crest, to which he devoted "a long fascinating tirade." "You're a Canuck, not a *Breton*," he told Jan in a tone so emphatic that she felt "it was some kind of arcane secret of utmost importance," which she "had to keep in mind or perish."[109]

But instead of writing his Canuck "family tragedy" story at Judy Ann Court, Jack found himself brooding day after day over the faded letters from 1940 and losing track of Leo's handwritten words, which melted after a few drinks into a meaningless verbal haze through which all he could see or remember was his father's face. He prayed, said his rosary, lit candles to St. Mary in church every Saturday night, and sent poems to *Jubilee* magazine. When Carolyn wrote in February 1963 to announce she would divorce Neal as soon as his parole was over, Jack wrote admonishing her to reconsider the whole matter in light of the Sermon on the Mount. "Have faith in St. Mary," he told both Cassadys in his new role as "the Old Counsellor," "because she's human like us, and intercedes in Christ her Son for us."[110]

In July 1963 Neal's parole ended and the Cassadys divorced. Neal drove east with two friends. Inevitably, he showed up at Northport. It was a sad visit. Jack had the hangover shakes, and the behavior of Neal's friends made him feel even worse: they helped themselves to the contents of Gabrielle's pantry and icebox without invitation and put their feet on her spotless kitchen table. Kerouac feared the guests were driving a hot car and that the police would roll up any minute. He spent only brief moments alone with Neal.

For a month after the Cassady visit, Jack made one of his few sustained efforts to stop drinking. It lasted until the end of the summer, when he was again stung by the media. First, there was Joyce Glassman's remark about him that had been printed in *Esquire*—Kerouac had "settled down on Long Island with his mother." The innuendo bothered Jack. He couldn't understand why anybody should make jokes about something as innocent as his love for Gabrielle. "I've always been 'settled with my mother' who supported me by working in shoe factories while I wrote most of my books," he wrote in a Farrar, Straus press release. "She's my friend as well as my mother."[111] ("I'm not about to throw my mother to the dogs of eternity,"[112] Kerouac told Allen Ginsberg.)

Even more distressing were the reviews of *Visions of Gerard*, Jack's elegy for his "sainted brother" published by Farrar, Straus on September 6, 1963. Bad reviews were by now no surprise, but in this instance,

Kerouac felt not only his writing but also his feeling for his brother was being dismissed. Saul Maloff, in the *New York Times Book Review*, said the figure of Gerard was not "visible or audible" in the "clangor" of Jack's "garrulous hipster yawping."[113] *Newsweek* called Kerouac a "tin-eared Canuck."[114]

IN the summer of 1964, a cranked-up, full-tilt Neal Cassady roared into New York again, this time at the wheel of Ken Kesey's psychedelic bus, "Further." Neal picked up the gloomy, reluctant Kerouac in Northport and drove him back into New York to meet Kesey and the Merry Pranksters at a big party on Park Avenue. At the party Jack acted "unwilling" and "surprised," says Allen Ginsberg—an "old red face W. C. Fields Toad Guru trembling shy hungover sick pot bellied Master . . . afraid to drink himself to death." One of Kesey's Merry Pranksters had draped an American flag over a couch. Jack quietly removed it and folded it up. Watching, Ginsberg "marveled sadly: . . . History was . . . out of Jack's hands now."[115]

An ironic full circle had been reached; Ginsberg, who had once worshipped Jack physically, now had occasion to reject him. Kerouac, says Ginsberg, was by then complaining to him, "I'm old, ugly, red-faced, beer-bellied and I'm drunk and nobody loves me any more. I can't get girls, come on and give me a blow job." "There are times he'd get drunk and really insistent on it," Ginsberg recalls, "[but] by that time I no longer saw him as the handsome, young glamor-beau of post-war, dark, doomed, maddened Spengler hippie-dom."[116]

IN August 1964, about a month after the Kesey party, the Kerouacs moved again, this time to a St. Petersburg, Florida, house that Jack considered too fancy—but Gabrielle thought just right. She wanted to be near the family; Jack just wanted to be left alone to write his "family tragedy," which had eluded him during the last twenty-one months in Northport. Within a month of their arrival in Florida, however, real-life tragedy struck the Kerouacs again, upsetting both Jack and Gabrielle badly. After Caroline's husband announced he wanted a divorce, she suffered a fatal coronary occlusion. Now Jack and his mother were truly alone.

To get away from the morguelike silence of his house, he went to bars in St. Petersburg and Tampa and gamely drank beer and shot pool with the locals, but in the words of one acquaintance of the time, "was so sad he could hardly look anyone in the eye without bursting into tears."[117]

Kerouac was befriended around this time by a young man named Cliff Anderson, from whom he bummed a quarter for a pool game in the Tic-Toc bar. Anderson became Jack's main bar pal and protector in fights and later introduced him to the "Tampa hippie crowd" that came to congregate around the Wild Boar Tavern on the Hillsborough River. Several anecdotes of Kerouac's drunken exploits in Tampa survive, some funny, like the one involving a brouhaha at a New Year's Eve beach party (caused by Jack's disparagement of the French spoken by a Parisian visitor), others much more serious, including an overnight jailing for urinating in a public place while drunk and later a beating at a very low-down local bar. To the locals Jack was a walking "Beat" monument, "dancing bop" and hollering "Go!" in all-night hamburger joints in the Florida boondocks.

BY late 1964 most of Jack's work was out of print and unavailable. As editor Ellis Amburn has said, "Kerouac fans must have been out to lunch in the 1960s."[118] Amburn bought Kerouac's 1956 *Desolation Angels* for Coward-McCann. When he then suggested that Jack conjoin it in one book with the 50,000 words written in 1961 in Mexico City ("An American Passed Here"), Kerouac agreed. In the scope of his autobiographical "legend," this material made up a single unit, the bridge between the "purity" of 1956 and the "crack-up" of 1960.

The book, titled *Desolation Angels*, was published in May 1965, generally dismissed by reviewers (except Dan Wakefield in *Atlantic Monthly*, who suggested that no other recent novel had been so "representative of American life"),[119] and sold poorly (between 5,000 and 6,000 copies, recalls Amburn). But Bantam Books, which felt it could promote the book as a testament of "drugs, perversion . . . and promiscuous sex,"[120] paid $50,000 for paperback reprint rights; Jack's share represented his first major earnings in several years. The windfall allowed him to discharge several outstanding debts and even take a trip to France in the summer of 1965.

After *Desolation Angels* came out, Jack presented Ellis Amburn with an outline of his "family tragedy" novel, still unwritten. Kerouac told the editor he wanted to "make a lot of money like your author John Le Carré," who had just brought out *The Spy Who Came In from the Cold* with Coward-McCann. When Amburn asked Kerouac what kind of a story he had that would match "spy stuff" at grabbing readers, Jack replied, "How about a murder?" Amburn said "Now you're talking"[121] and commissioned

Vanity of Duluoz, Kerouac's "family tragedy-turned-murder" novel. Jack presented an outline of the book and received an advance of $7,500.

AFTER long and careful preparation—he had been studying French literature, maps, and genealogical guidebooks for months and had even packed a special set of writing tools for transcribing the sounds of the sea at Finistère ("notebook and pencil . . . with large plastic bag to write inside of") [122]—Kerouac's July 1965 trip to Paris was an alcoholic disaster. Jack had intended to stay six months, study his family genealogy, visit the ancestral landscapes of Brittany, and hopefully even get started on the "family tragedy-murder" novel. Instead he reeled drunkenly through a swirl of embarrassing and distressing incidents that took him from Paris to Brest and back in ten days. He then stumbled in shame and distraction onto a return flight to the United States.

Once he had recuperated, he spent ten days writing a story about the "illumination of some kind" that he had received somewhere on the voyage and which "seemed" to have "changed" [123] him in some way—none of the details of his satori were clear, even to Jack. The trip had gone by in a blur, and that word is the best description of *Satori in Paris*, a disturbing, unintentional "confession" of how badly Jack had deteriorated. The story appeared serially in *Evergreen*—an event that did little to improve Kerouac's fallen reputation but did contribute greatly to the public impression that he was a hopeless lush. Later in 1965 it appeared in book form from Grove.

IN May 1966 Jack finally found a new place to live, a resort home at Hyannis, Massachusetts. The town had quieted down—and lost a president —since Kerouac's last visit. But he had barely begun to work on his "family tragedy" novel there when disaster struck again in his own family. In September Gabrielle suffered a stroke. It left her paralyzed, except, Jack bitterly told Dodie Muller shortly afterward, "for her asshole and her mouth." [124]

His mother's medical expenses forced Jack to accept a public appearance trip to Italy, arranged by Nanda Pivano. He arrived in Milan drunk, had to be talked out of flying straight home, and made it through his itinerary only by staying close to a bottle all the way. On his return, however, he summoned whatever Canuck practicality and shrewdness he had left and did something that exhibited rare good sense. On November

19, 1966, he remarried. The ceremony occurred at his home in Hyannis; the legal paper was signed by a judge in tennis shorts. The bride was Stella Sampas of Lowell, an older sister of Sammy Sampas, Jack's childhood poetry pal. This was a marriage not of convenience but of necessity; without someone to look after his mother, Kerouac simply could not go on with his own writing life.

In January 1967, after two arrests for public drunkenness on Cape Cod, Kerouac moved his bride and paralytic mother to a brick ranch-style house on Sanders Avenue in the most expensive section of Lowell. It was a strange homecoming. Jack's boyhood pals largely avoided him, as did many members of the French Canadian community in which his family had lived for thirty years. But he now had a whole new family, consisting of Stella's numerous Greek relatives. In his lumberjack shirt and fatigue pants, Jack was a fixture at his brother-in-law Nicky's bar on Gorham Street, which became his unofficial second home; when he traveled he was often accompanied by one or more of the accommodating Sampas brothers.

In the bar Kerouac made new friends, the closest being Joe Chaput, a local college graduate to whom Jack preached night after night about everything from religion to philosophy (he was reading Pascal) to race and politics (he raved endlessly against "Jews" and also against "Communists"—among whose ranks he now numbered his old friend Ginsberg).

The "grandeur" of America, Jack pronounced over his endless beers and shots, had been lost in a flood of "broken convictions," replaced only by the hypnotic, empty, "mosaic mesh of television." But the menacing technological future he had foreseen in a letter two years earlier— "computers, machine-tooled minds, mechanistic cops, robots, antennae, beeps, and creeps"[125]—was now closing in not only on the rest of America but also on Kerouac himself. He sat at home for hour after hour in front of the television, his eyes fixed on "Beverly Hillbillies" and the like, his mind nobody could say where. He stored Johnny Walker Red by the case in his basement for those emergencies when Stella hid his shoes to prevent him from making bar visits.

In March 1967 Kerouac finally began the actual composition of *Vanity of Duluoz*, the "family tragedy." Retarded by the demands of his deteriorating physical condition, the work went slowly—in isolated sessions of 8,000 words (less than half of what Kerouac had been able to produce in his athletic writing prime). The prose came out straightforward and unadorned. "Now there's no time for poetry anyway,"[126] he admitted sadly.

Jack had sometimes said that the 1951 *On the Road* had been written to amuse his first wife; much more obviously, *Vanity of Duluoz* was directed to Stella. Not only is the book dedicated to her but also Kerouac uses the second-person address ("wifey") as a formal device—one perhaps suggested, as Ginsberg has pointed out, by Jack's early reading of Melville's *John Marr and Other Sailors.* Kerouac's generally jocular tone allowed him to introduce "tragic" material into his story without putting himself through the emotional rigors of his trademark "confessional" style. That kind of pain was something he could no longer bear. With week-long periods of "resting and sighing" in between, he completed the book in approximately ten bursts, the last one in May 1967.

ALLEN GINSBERG attempted to visit Kerouac in Lowell that summer. The last time they had seen each other, Jack had conclusively termed Ginsberg, whose full black beard now made him internationally recognizable, "a hairy loss." But Allen did not give up easily. He journeyed to Lowell and knocked on Jack's front door. Kerouac "just hid out and didn't answer the door," Ginsberg recalls; "he sort of lurked in the shadows."[127] Allen went around to the back but still couldn't find a way in, and Jack wouldn't open the door to him.

Not long afterward, Kerouac's teenage daughter, Jan, stopped in Lowell on her way to Mexico with a hippie boyfriend. She found her father cradled in a rocking chair in a blue plaid shirt, "about one foot from the TV, upending a fifth of whiskey." Throughout the visit he continued to nurse the fifth, "like a giant baby bottle," while regarding his daughter wordlessly from behind his liquid suit of armor. Stella stood by watchfully; finally, hearing Jan's voice, the semiconscious Gabrielle stirred in partial recognition from the twilight zone of her wheelchair, inquiring if "Caroline was there." When Jan left, Jack suggested by way of farewell that she write a book in Mexico and added magnanimously, "You can use my name."[128] Other than the often-begrudged $52 a week, the wacky-sounding family moniker—which he had made famous—was all he had to give his daughter.

Even that was a halfhearted present from Jack the Indian giver. A month or two later he tried to tell an interviewer—poet Ted Berrigan of the *Paris Review*—that he had no daughter. "I said, 'I know your daughter, I saw her last week in Tompkins Square Park,' " Berrigan recalls. "He made this little set speech—'she's not my daughter.' I was shocked. I said,

'Jack, she looks just *like* you.' " At that, says Berrigan, Kerouac's "face fell. . . . He *knew* it was his daughter, but he thought it was not his fate to make and have a family."[129]

APPEARING as a subject in the *Paris Review*'s "Art of Fiction" interview series was an important occasion for Jack, one that he naively hoped might somehow at long last legitimize him in uptown literary circles. When Berrigan first contacted him with the avant-gardish proposal that they stage the interview as a "one-act Noh play," Kerouac replied cautiously by mail —"I'd like to be in the series [of interviews], please don't spoil my chances."[130]

Interviewer Berrigan, accompanied by poet friends Duncan Mc-Naughton and Aram Saroyan (son of one of Kerouac's first "favorite writers"), arrived unannounced one day in October 1967. Seeing her husband open the door to the visitors, Stella Kerouac rushed forward "in fury"—as Berrigan recalls—"threw her arms around Jack, and started dragging him off, while telling us to go away." The interviewer persisted, carefully explaining his identity and purpose. Finally, Jack extorted from him the promise of a $100 payment, and Stella "very explicitly" spelled out the ground rules of the visit: "no drinks."[131]

The interview was conducted in the Kerouac living room. Stella stood guard and Gabrielle—"Mémêre"—lurked "behind this curtain, in this curtained-off alcove, incredibly groaning every once in a while," Berrigan remembers. Though the visitors weren't drinking, Jack sipped from a bottle throughout the interview. Berrigan also supplied him with amphetamine pills. Jack, who rarely used stimulants any more, then took over the floor, "prowling up and down and making these long speeches using all his incredible voice stops and changes."[132]

Stella gave Berrigan a tour of Jack's "little upstairs office room," where his books and manuscripts were impeccably arranged in shelves and filing cabinets. Noting that "the place was shining," Berrigan asked Stella if she kept the room in order. "He wouldn't let me touch a thing in it," Mrs. Kerouac replied. "He does it all."[133]

At the conclusion of the interview, Kerouac signed a printed broadside for each of the guests and then they were ready to leave. "At that point the whole thing had been terrific," Berrigan recalls. "But as we were leaving, Jack wanted to go with us, and go to a bar. Stella didn't want him to go. It was a very poignant moment: she said to him, 'Jacky, we have a date, remember?' And Jack said, 'Ah, what fun is that?' It was very touching, and very sad, because we were obviously taking the energy out of the room—there were three of us, you know, and we were *young*."[134]

WHILE Kerouac accepted the entropic embrace of alcohol, Neal Cassady had tried to hold off old age at the pass; but the chemical weapons had backfired and were burning out his brain in stages. The strain of being "Keroassady"—as Neal had sometimes sarcastically called the figure he played in public, which was half himself and half Jack's literary creation—proved too much even for Cassady's constitution; he was human, after all. On February 3, 1968, he imbibed heavily of various substances (Seconals and pulque allegedly heading the list) at a wedding party in San Miguel de Allende, Mexico, then took off on a twenty-mile walk down some railroad tracks toward the next town, counting the ties as he went. But the rails turned out to be endless for Neal; after a mile and a half, he collapsed into a coma. A few hours after being discovered the next morning, he died of congestive heart failure.

On receiving the news in a phone call from Carolyn, Jack expressed disbelief—or perhaps mere *refusal* to believe. He insisted to her that Neal must still be alive, hiding out somewhere—maybe Africa. Two and a half months after the event, still unable to accept Neal's death, he wrote to Ed White in Denver, reiterating his doubts that Cassady had really died—then half-conceding it and confiding also that there were some people who were "even hinting that it was all [Jack's] fault."[135]

Kerouac's last published statements on his friend—in the *Paris Review* interview—were as respectful and reverential as any of his earlier encomiums. There he called Neal a "Jesuit" (Jack himself was now a "General of the Jesuit Army," he claimed) who had taught him "everything that [he] now believed about anything that there may be to be believed about divinity." Cassady was a "beautiful" writer, Jack said, and "the most intelligent man" he had ever met in his life; together, they had had "more fun than 5000 Socony Gasoline Station attendants can have."[136]

TWO days after Cassady's death, *Vanity of Duluoz* came out in New York. *Time* called it Kerouac's "best book," then quickly devalued the compliment by suggesting that Jack was "far less talented" than Norman Mailer and that his prose suffered from a "dreadful indiscipline."[137] Other reviewers took a similar tack; Kerouac was told by the book critics to grow up and

Jack Kerouac is the author of the most famous novel of his generation, *On the Road*, as well as many other books of fiction, comment, and poetry. Prior to the present volume, his most recent work was *Desolation Angels*, which appeared last year. Grove Press has just published a new paperbound edition of Kerouac's earlier novel, *The Subterraneans*. He currently lives and works in Florida.

GROVE PRESS, INC., 80 University Place, New York, N.Y. 10003

TOP: Satori in Paris, *published in 1965*

BOTTOM: *During a visit to John Holmes in Old Saybrook, Connecticut, November 1965* (courtesy John Clellon Holmes)

Kerouac, summer 1967: " *'He sort of lurked in the shadows.'* " (courtesy Stanley Twardowicz)

Kerouac in Milan with Nanda Pivano (courtesy *the unspeakable visions of the individual*)

Kerouac with his third wife, Stella, in Lowell: "Vanity of Duluoz *was directed . . . to* Stella." (courtesy James F. Coyne)

TOP RIGHT: *Jan Kerouac:* " 'He thought it was not his fate to make and have a family.' "

BOTTOM RIGHT: *February 1968:* "Two days after Cassady's death, Vanity of Duluoz came out in New York."

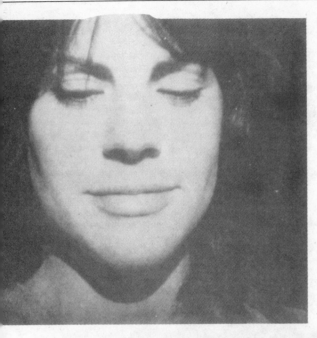

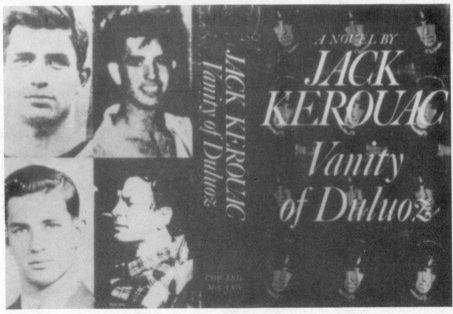

Kerouac in Lowell with Manny Bello: "Jack was now almost beyond injury." (courtesy Manuel Bello)

Kerouac with John Sampas, Lowell, 1968: "The ever-protective Sampas brothers" (courtesy *the unspeakable visions of the individual*)

get serious or else stop wasting their time. "Be Your Age,"[138] snapped the London *Times Literary Supplement*. "Hit the space bar and GO!"[139] mocked the *Christian Science Monitor*.

But Jack was now almost beyond injury. A month after the anti-climactic publication of his "family tragedy," he put away his disappointment over its commercial failure in a quick liquid tour of Europe (Spain, Portugal, Germany) with four Lowell friends, including Joe Chaput and two of the ever-protective Sampas brothers. Back in Lowell for the summer, he found himself in need of money, getting no writing done, and restive as ever. His mother had been complaining for some time that she needed a warmer winter climate for her health. Jack sold some old letters to Columbia (a deal handled by a New York book dealer, with Ginsberg also participating) to finance yet another move to Florida.

In the fall of 1968, Kerouac rode to New York with Joe Chaput and Paul Bourgeois (the would-be "chief") to appear on the television show "Firing Line," hosted by one of Jack's heroes, William F. Buckley. When they arrived in the city, Jack had several drinks and then took a room at the Delmonico Hotel, where Bill Burroughs was being put up by *Esquire* while writing a piece on the 1968 Democratic National Convention. "He was really hittin' it heavy," Burroughs recalls, "ordering up bottles of whiskey. I told him, 'No, Jack, don't go [on the show], you're not in any condition to go.'"[140] Seeing that he would get little support from Burroughs, Jack called Ginsberg, who arrived shortly. Through the afternoon Kerouac continued to drink heavily and get high on pot, which he hadn't smoked for some time.

He was to appear as Buckley's guest along with progressive sociologist Lewis Yablonsky and underground poet Ed Sanders. "Jack was really nervous being with those kids," says Joe Chaput; "I guess he was paranoid or something. By the time [he] made it to the studio, he was smashed to the gills."[141] On the show Kerouac acted loud, drunk, and belligerent. Sanders, who had long admired Jack's work, was appalled by the decline of his hero but refused to respond to Kerouac's drunken needling. "I had vowed not to confront Jack, even when he was mildly hostile," Sanders recalls. "He was drinking and his chain slipped off the riser." After the taping of the first segment of the show, says Sanders, "the producer wanted to substitute Allen for Jack, but we all refused." Kerouac staggered through the remainder of the program; when Ginsberg's name was brought up by Sanders on camera, Jack blurted, "I'm not connected with Allen

Ginsberg, and don't you put my name next to his."[142] At the show's conclusion, Kerouac was taken back to the Delmonico to pass out. After this
evening he never again saw any of his former "beat" associates.

In the wake of the Buckley show, Jack spoke to no one for a week.
When he recovered he loaded his possessions. ¯vife, and mother into Joe
Chaput's station wagon and rode south to Florida once again. "He talked
and drank all the way down,"[143] recalls Chaput with awe.

By mid-November 1968, the Kerouacs had settled uneasily in their
new concrete bungalow in St. Petersburg. Gabrielle's wheelchair was late
arriving; Jack cracked his shinbone but couldn't get a doctor to come. Still,
he fixed up a new "cozy" office bedroom; read Pascal and sat in the winter
sunshine nodding over his afternoon wines; and collected a December
translation royalty check from Italy and used it to build a five-foot
"privacy fence" enclosing the pine- and banyan tree-shaded backyard. But
his efforts at writing were confined to gnomic jottings and poetic non-
sequiturs, mostly composed with bottle in hand and one eye on the sound-
less television, his principal link with outside "reality." Not only were there
now no outlines for books sketched in his letters, there were very few
letters. Past and present swam together in his alcohol-saturated mind.
Owners of the shops in between the Kerouacs' house and the local discount
liquor store soon became familiar with the unshaven, jowly drunk in the
lumberjack shirt and unpressed pants who shuffled past at least once daily.
"To be frank," one merchant later recalled, "he looked like a bum. He was
always red-eyed and his hands shook."[144]

By midsummer the Kerouac household was out of money. Jack's literary earnings for the first half of that year totaled $1,770. Stella had to take
a menial garment-work job that paid less than $2 an hour. Demand for
Kerouac titles (on the part of both buyers and publishers) had hit its
lowest point in twelve years. Knowing no other way of making a dollar,
Jack now made a token effort to brew up a book called *Beat Spotlight*,
about "the last ten years of his life," but it never got beyond the talking
stage. In desperation he finally pulled out of his drawer the hoary "Pictorial Review Jackson" version of *On the Road*, slapped a quick ending on
it, and sent it off to Lord—but though it eventually sold to Grove (and
came out as *Pic*), the money arrived too late to relieve Jack's present
penury.

Ironically, Kerouac was temporarily rescued at this point by his very
obsolescence. Played out as a force on the contemporary writing scene,

he had been made a nostalgia item by the simple process of passing time.

In late summer 1969, Clarus Backes, then articles editor of the *Chicago Tribune* Sunday magazine, was putting together an end-of-decade issue, "devoted to the Fifties—a sort of nostalgia issue, on Fifties lifestyle, fashions, etc. Somebody suggested, 'we gotta get Jack Kerouac in there.' " The editor contacted Sterling Lord, who at that time was attempting "to form a syndicate, circulating articles by his clients to several papers, each of which would pay a part of the writer's fee." Through Lord, Backes obtained a phone number for Kerouac. He reached first the "protective" Stella, then Jack, sober for once. Backes offered $1,500—"a price considerably above the magazine's rate"—and not long afterward received a "long rambling thing"[145] in the mail from Kerouac, which the editor cut by about two-thirds.

This was "After Me, the Deluge," an eloquent, agonizing essay on the condition of the stranded writer. "I'm trying to figure out where I am," Kerouac honestly admitted, "between the establishment politicians and the radicals, between cops and hoods, tax collectors and vandals." In the article he objected to being identified as the "intellectual forebear," spawning "a deluge of alienated radicals, war protestors, dropouts, hippies and even 'beats.' " ("How could I possibly spawn Jerry Rubin, Mitchell Goodman, Abbie Hoffman, Allen Ginsberg?") He felt lost in contemporary America, caught between, on the one hand, "shiny hypocrisy . . . political lust and concupiscence, a ninny's bray of melody backed by a ghastly neurological drone of money-grub;" and on the other the "retardate happenings inside of giant plastic balloons" promoted by Merry Prankster chieftain Ken Kesey and the "guiding proselytization" of acid guru Tim Leary, under which "no one in America could address a simple envelope or keep a household budget or a checkbook balanced or for that matter legible." Mourning the death of the "written word which is the only way to keep the record straight," Kerouac implied that he was disappearing with it: an "inconsolable orphan . . . yelling and screaming . . . to make arrangements for making a living yet all bespattered and gloomed-up in the nightsoil of poor body and soul . . . and all so *lonered*."[146]

He received payment on acceptance by the *Tribune* and also picked up several other syndication fees for the article (which appeared under its original title in the *Chicago Tribune* on September 28, in the *Miami Tropic* on October 12—and eventually, variously retitled after Kerouac's death, in numerous other papers like the *Boston Globe, Washington Post,* and *Los*

Angeles Times). By late September it had also earned him a badly needed $3,000.

For Jack McClintock, a reporter from a local paper who visited him at that time, he pulled out his draft of "After Me"—typed on yellow legal paper—and performed a full-blown dramatic recitation "with broad, wild gestures, grinning and mugging and assuming various foreign accents." Neither he nor the reporter was conscious of it, but when Kerouac went on to rave about his pet phobias ("Ginsberg's anti-American . . . I don't like Ken Kesey, he ruined Cassady . . . the Communist is the main enemy—the Jew"),[147] he was actually performing another dramatic representation: an imitation of Leo Kerouac in his angry final days.

JACK was not well in October. To visitors he appeared ashen and un-kempt. He had lost at least twenty pounds in recent months, yet was boozing as much as ever (Falstaff and Johnny Walker). After yet another beating in a local bar, he stopped going out of the house at all. He was also now suffering from a navel hernia ("my goddam belly-button is popping out,"[148] he complained). To Stella Jack seemed distracted, sad, but nonetheless—as always—"busy in thought and dreams."[149]

On October 20, a Monday, St. Petersburg was still and overcast as Hurricane Laurie moved in from the gulf. The night before Jack had stayed up late, reading to Stella from his father's old letters; afterward he slept poorly, rose at four, and talked with his mother till the heat of morning set in, when he went to sit in front of the television with an open can of tuna, his two-ounce medical vial of whiskey, and his notebook. Internal pain struck suddenly and drove him into the bathroom, where he began vomiting up the products of a massive internal hemorrhage. His liver had collapsed and was bleeding up into the throat and chest arteries. Stella hurried him by ambulance to a hospital, St. Anthony's, where, eighteen hours later, after surgery from which he never regained consciousness, he died alone, drowning in his own blood.

"He was a very lonely guy," the distraught Stella Kerouac told the first reporters at the hospital. "He was drinking heavily the past few days."[150] Kerouac's physician, Dr. Kenneth Baker, rendered a telephone postmortem to the New York papers. "The hemorrhaging was caused by cirrhosis of the liver," Dr. Baker reported. "He had been told many times to stop drinking but Jack was a peculiar type person. He knew he was overdrinking but he went ahead anyway."[151]

Of all Kerouac's friends, the most long suffering had been Allen Ginsberg. Allen told Al Aronowitz of the *New York Post* that after hearing the news he had walked in the woods at his Cherry Valley, New York, farm with Gregory Corso and carved Jack's name into a tree. "He was very sweet," Ginsberg told the reporter. "He was just unhappy." Allen then began to quote a Blake verse—"The days of my youth rise fresh in my mind"[152]—but was too choked up to finish.

J A C K pondered in writing the moment and meaning of death too many times to count; death was the ground bass of his understanding of life, the undertow that moved the deep currents in his work and gave it what Kerouac himself called, in a 1962 article on "genius" in writing, "that inescapable sorrowful depth that shines through."[153]

No one but his wife and agent knows what he was writing in his lap notebook just before he was fatally stricken, and not even *they* know whether in the ensuing moments—that swoon toward the abyss—Jack remembered some of his earlier visions of the final culmination of life's pain, like the one in Chorus 184 of *Mexico City Blues*: "Wow . . . when I start falling/in that inhuman pit/of dizzy death/I'll know (if/smart enough t'remember)/that all the black/tunnels of hate/or love I'm falling/through, are/really radiant/right eternities/for me . . ."[154]

T H E R E was a wake in St. Petersburg to which, noted one observer, "nobody much came." A local reporter remembers Gabrielle "wailing over [Jack's] grey face in its casket: 'O my little boy . . . Isn't he pretty? . . . What will I do now?'"[155] while Stella stood by in a black dress, silently gripping the handles of the wheelchair.

A second wake for local friends and family (and a few guests who turned up from out of town, like Ginsberg, Orlovsky, and a black-head-banded, movie-camera-toting Corso) was held in Lowell at the Archambault Funeral Home on Pawtucket Street. Jack lay in the casket decked out in a white shirt, a small bow tie, and a houndstooth check jacket. "His black hair was cut short and neatly combed aside," reported Vivian Gornick in her *Village Voice* account. "His face was a waxen cosmetic mask that bore no resemblance whatever to the appearance of a human face. . . . He had been stripped of all his ravaging joy. They had turned him into what they probably thought he should have been all along: a decent, properly dead Lowell businessman."[156] To Ginsberg Jack simply wore the

Jack Kerouac's grave (photo by Robert B. Perreault, courtesy Joy Walsh, first published by *Moody Street Irregulars*, #11, spring – summer 1982)

BOTTOM LEFT and ABOVE: *1949 – 1950* (photo by Elliott Erwitt)

"mid-aged heavy" mask of Leo, handed down from "earlier dream decades."[157]

The funeral took place at St. Jean Baptiste Church—the "ponderous Chartres cathedral of the slums" where Jack had studied to become an altar boy. In the service his old spiritual tutor, Father "Spike" Morissette, read from the Book of the Apocalypse: "They shall rest from their labors for they shall take their works with them."[158] No mention was made of the reference in Kerouac's work (*Dr. Sax*) to his dread of a church funeral under the "Stone" of "St. Jean de Baptiste": "I prefer rivers in my death, or seas, and other continents, but no satin death in Satin Massachusetts Lowell . . ."[159]

On a clear, cold fall day, Jack's body was driven across Lowell to Edson Cemetery and planted in the Sampas family plot. This was at least in keeping with his aversion—stated in *Visions of Gerard*—to having his bones lie among "bleak gray jowled pale eyed sneaky fearful French Canadians," but still fell short of the disposition he had requested: "Lay me down in sweet India or old Tahiti, I don't want to be buried in *their* cemetery—In fact, cremate me and deliver me to les Indes . . ."[160]

CODA: JAZZ FOR JACK (*April 5, 1949*)

Clarence 'Cootie' Williams was a
big shoulder man from Mobile
blew hot trumpet for the Duke
many years, had his own group too
w|Bud Powell during wartime
recorded 'House of Joy' 'Gator Tail'
wildly swinging sides for Capitol
c. 1943–1944   (w|Willis Jackson
on tenor)
                braying woman-mad
all night balls
                        that gassed
Jack Kerouac at 25
                        and led
that boy down
                muddy alleys

Fame

of the mind
            cross creaking beds
in shacks of honk
            while Memphis Trains
blast thru world nights
            to pour out that hot come
and joy and tears
                        in pools
on starlit banks
                        and brews
of Saturday Night
                'I'm pulled
out of my shoes
                        by wild
stuff like that—
                pure whiskey'
scribbling these notes
on a Saturday night
in the last chance saloon
of life
            where it's
'really our last chance
to be honest'

            Kerouac
hits the city
again, cuts down
to that neon-lit
crazy jazz shack
of the night
                        little notebook
in shirt pocket
                'I like
Saturday night in the shack
to be crazy
            I like things to GO
and rock and be flipped

I want to be stoned
if I'm going to be stoned at all'

Life is combustion
everybody's a small blue flame
that doesn't mean it doesn't hurt,

a small bunsen burner flame
jewel point
like a gas jet
of dry lunacy
with an orange halo
like a fuzzy crysanthemum,
   yay,

and this is the night
in America
and what it does to you

the night does things like that
it makes you burn too fast
you lose all that heat, you crash
on the floor of Clellon Holmes' pad
wake up bugged, like in a blue
zone, w|sullen yet curious 'pout
eyes down however—*out*—nothing happening
later shambling w|serious thoughtful frown
handspockets under sunday trees like in Proust
tho only on gray alien US street, you stroll
to the subway
and fly home to Long Island like a quiet ghost
just before the Birth of the Cool
and preparing the arrival of the long and coruscating line.

—Tom Clark

NOTES

(NB. Frequently cited sources have been listed in full the first time they appear, along with an abbreviation, for example, Jack Kerouac, *Book of Dreams* [BD]. Subsequent listings give the abbreviation. The most accessible editions have been used here; for the first editions see the bibliography.)

EPIGRAPH
1. William Burroughs, "Kerouac," *High Times* (March 1979), p. 53.

PART ONE
1. Jack Kerouac, *Book of Dreams* [BD] (San Francisco: City Lights Books, 1967), p. 30.
2. *BD*, p. 32.
3. Jack Kerouac, "The Origins of the Beat Generation," *Playboy* (June 1959), p. 32; also Kerouac to Raman Singh, May 24, 1965, in Joy Walsh, "Jack Kerouac: The American Alien in America," *Street Magazine* 2, No. 4 (1978), p. 49.
4. Ted Berrigan, "Jack Kerouac: The Art of Fiction," *Paris Review*, [PR] No. 43 (Summer 1968), p. 105.

5. Jack Kerouac, *Lonesome Traveler* [*LT*] (New York: Grove Press, 1960), p. vii.
6. Ibid.
7. Kerouac to Raman Singh, May 24, 1965, *Street Magazine*, p. 50.
8. *PR*, p. 70.
9. Jack Kerouac, *Satori in Paris* [*SP*] (New York: Grove Press, 1966), p. 104.
10. Jack Kerouac, *Vanity of Duluoz* [*VD*] (New York: Putnam's, 1979), p. 66.
11. Allen Ginsberg, conversation with author, 1982.
12. Jack Kerouac, "The Origins of the Beat Generation," *Playboy* (June 1959), p. 32.
13. Jack Kerouac, *Visions of Gerard* [*VG*] (New York: McGraw-Hill, 1976), p. 94.
14. Ibid., p. 95.
15. Jack Kerouac, *Desolation Angels* [*DA*] (New York: Putnam's, 1979), p. 283.
16. *VG*, p. 61.
17. Jack Kerouac, *Dr. Sax* [*SAX*] (New York: Ballantine Books, 1973), p. 15.
18. Jack Kerouac, "Not Long Ago Joy Abounded at Christmas," *New York World Telegram and Sun* (December 5, 1957), pt. II, p. 31.
19. Jack Kerouac, *The Scripture of the Golden Eternity* (New York: Totem Press, 1960), p. 34.
20. *VG*, p. 13.
21. Ibid., p. 96.
22. *BD*, p. 72.
23. *SAX*, p. 30.
24. *VG*, p. 26.
25. Ibid., p. 7.
26. Ibid., p. 10.
27. Ibid., p. 151.
28. Ibid., p. 24.
29. Ibid., p. 96.
30. Ibid., p. 97.
31. Ibid., p. 103.
32. *BD*, p. 40.
33. Jack Kerouac, *Heaven & Other Poems* [*H*] (Bolinas, Calif.: Grey Fox Press, 1977), p. 40.
34. Ibid., p. 57.
35. Ibid., p. 40.
36. Jack Kerouac, *Visions of Cody* [*VC*] (New York: McGraw-Hill, 1972), p. 270.
37. *SAX*, p. 31.
38. Ibid., pp. 4, 39.

39. Jack Kerouac, *Mexico City Blues* [*MCB*] (New York: Grove Press, 1959), p. 93.
40. Ibid., p. 92.
41. *BD*, p. 89.
42. *LT*, p. vii.
43. *H*, p. 39.
44. *SAX*, p. 30.
45. *BD*, p. 160.
46. *SAX*, pp. 57, 30.
47. Ibid., p. 3.
48. Jack Kerouac, *Maggie Cassidy* [*MC*] (New York: McGraw-Hill, 1959), p. 43.
49. *BD*, p. 38.
50. Ibid., p. 98.
51. Ibid., p. 126.
52. *H*, p. 51.
53. Jack Kerouac, "In the Ring," *Atlantic* (March 1968), p. 110.
54. *SAX*, p. 37.
55. Ibid.
56. Ibid.
57. Ibid., p. 40.
58. Ibid., p. 43.
59. Ibid., p. 64.
60. Jack Kerouac, *Uncollected Writings* (New York: "C" Press, 1971), p. 122.
61. *PR*, p. 85.
62. *MC*, p. 41.
63. *SAX*, p. 112.
64. Ibid., p. 105.
65. Ibid., p. 106.
66. Ibid., p. 114.
67. Ibid., p. 133.
68. *BD*, pp. 117–118.
69. Charles Jarvis, *Visions of Kerouac* (Lowell, Mass.: Ithaca Press, 1974), p. 41.
70. Jack Kerouac, *The Town and the City* [*TC*] (New York: Grosset & Dunlap, 1950), p. 120.
71. *H*, p. 39.
72. *TC*, p. 120.
73. *VC*, p. 267.
74. *SAX*, p. 79.
75. Ibid., p. 35.
76. Ibid., p. 47.

77. Ibid., p. 91.
78. *VC*, p. 255.
79. *SAX*, pp. 178, 82; also Jarvis, *Visions of Kerouac*, p. 29.
80. *VC*, p. 256.
81. *SAX*, p. 88.
82. *VD*, p. 11.
83. Ibid., p. 14.
84. *SAX*, p. 160.
85. Ibid., p. 153.
86. Ibid., p. 145.
87. Ibid., p. 163.
88. *MC*, p. 20.
89. *SAX*, p. 34.
90. *VD*, p. 17.
91. Ibid.
92. Father Armand Morissette, "A Catholic's View of Kerouac," *Moody Street Irregulars* [*MSI*] No. 5 (Summer–Fall 1979), p. 7.
93. *VD*, p. 27.
94. *SAX*, p. 11.
95. *MC*, p. 21.
96. *BD*, p. 134.
97. *SAX*, p. 11.
98. *VD*, p. 17.
99. *VG*, p. 13.
100. Jarvis, *Visions of Kerouac*, p. 28.
101. Morissette, *MSI*, No. 5, p. 7.
102. *VD*, p. 20.
103. Ibid., p. 27.
104. Ibid., p. 75.
105. *MC*, p. 79.
106. Ibid., pp. 37, 35.
107. Ibid., pp. 55–56.
108. Ibid., p. 74.
109. Ibid., p. 156.
110. Ibid., pp. 158, 160.
111. *VD*, p. 27.
112. Ibid., p. 28.
113. *MC*, pp. 165, 168.
114. *VD*, p. 53.
115. Ibid., pp. 32–33.

116. *PR*, p. 84.
117. *H*, p. 51.
118. Jack Kerouac, "The Brothers," *Horace Mann Quarterly* (Fall 1939), p. 13.
119. *VD*, p. 45.
120. *MC*, p. 176.
121. Ibid., pp. 179–180.
122. Ibid., p. 184.
123. *VD*, p. 35.
124. Jack Kerouac, "Count Basie's Band Best in Land," *Horace Mann Record* (February 16, 1940), p. 3.
125. Jack Kerouac, "Real Solid Drop Beat Riffs," *Horace Mann Record* (March 23, 1940), p. 4.
126. *PR*, p. 84.
127. Jarvis, *Visions of Kerouac*, p. 28.

PART TWO

1. *VD*, p. 65.
2. Ibid., p. 74.
3. *H*, p. 51.
4. *VD*, p. 78.
5. *VC*, p. 391.
6. *LT*, p. vii.
7. *BD*, p. 118.
8. *VD*, p. 80.
9. Ibid., p. 93.
10. Ibid., p. 95.
11. Ibid., p. 94.
12. Ibid., p. 95.
13. Ibid., p. 97.
14. Ibid., p. 98.
15. *TC*, p. 274.
16. *VD*, p. 99.
17. Ibid., p. 106.
18. Ibid., p. 109.
19. Ibid., p. 112.
20. *VC*, p. 264; also *TC*, p. 290.
21. *VD*, p. 121.
22. Jarvis, *Visions of Kerouac*, pp. 86–87.
23. *BD*, p. 47.
24. Jarvis, *Visions of Kerouac*, p. 91.

25. *VD*, p. 123.
26. Ibid., p. 134.
27. Ibid., p. 136.
28. Ibid., p. 135.
29. *DA*, p. 11.
30. *PR*, p. 72.
31. *VD*, p. 150.
32. *VC*, p. 187.
33. *BD*, pp. 47–48.
34. Edie Kerouac Parker, "Addenda and Annotations," *MSI*, No. 10 (Fall 1981), p. 18.
35. *VD*, p. 151.
36. *BD*, p. 48.
37. *VD*, p. 153.
38. *MC*, p. 194.
39. *VD*, p. 157.
40. Ibid., p. 163.
41. Ibid., p. 158.
42. Ibid., pp. 166–167.
43. *TC*, p. 329.
44. *VD*, p. 169.
45. *VC*, pp. 97, 186.
46. *VD*, p. 173.
47. Ibid., pp. 174–175.
48. *VC*, p. 188.
49. *VD*, p. 182.
50. Ibid., p. 181.
51. Ibid., p. 196.
52. Edie Parker Kerouac, *MSI*, No. 10, pp. 19–20.
53. *VD*, p. 198.
54. Ibid., p. 199.
55. Ibid.
56. *VC*, p. 182.
57. Ibid., p. 183.
58. *VD*, p. 204.
59. Allen Ginsberg, in Dennis McNally, *Desolate Angel* (New York: Random House, 1979), p. 67.
60. *PR*, p. 97.
61. *VD*, p. 218.
62. Ibid.

63. Allen Ginsberg, *Allen Verbatim* (New York: McGraw-Hill, 1974), pp. 111, 103.

64. *VD*, p. 206.

65. Ibid., p. 207.

66. Ibid., pp. 207–208.

67. Ibid., p. 211.

68. Ibid., p. 220.

69. Ibid., p. 239.

70. Ibid., p. 243.

71. Ibid., pp. 259–260.

72. Ibid., p. 264.

73. Ibid., p. 267.

74. Ibid.

75. Ibid., p. 272.

76. Herbert Huncke, "Guilty of Everything," *The unspeakable visions of the individual [TUVOTI]* 10 (1980), p. 39.

77. Herbert Huncke, in Barry Gifford and Lawrence Lee, *Jack's Book* (New York: St. Martin's Press, 1978), p. 57.

78. *VD*, p. 257.

79. John Montgomery, *Kerouac West Coast* (Palo Alto, Calif.: Fels & Firn, 1976), unnumbered.

80. Jack Kerouac, in Al Aronowitz, "The Beat Generation," *New York Post* (March 10, 1959), p. 9.

81. Allen Ginsberg, *Gay Sunshine Interview* (Bolinas, Calif.: Grey Fox Press, 1974), p. 4.

82. Ibid.

83. *VD*, p. 211.

84. Jack Kerouac to Carl Solomon, April 7, 1952, in *TUVOTI*, 10, p. 152.

85. *VD*, p. 270.

86. Ibid.

87. Jack Kerouac, "The Beginning of Bop," *Escapade* (May 1959), p. 104.

88. Jack Kerouac, "The Origins of the Beat Generation," *Playboy* (June 1959), p. 32.

89. *VD*, p. 269.

90. Ibid., p. 278.

91. *BD*, p. 106.

92. *VD*, p. 278.

93. Ibid., p. 279.

94. Ibid., p. 338.

95. Ibid.

96. Jack Kerouac, *On the Road* [*OR*] (New York: Signet Books, 1957), p. 8.
97. *VC*, p. 343.
98. Ibid.
99. Neal Cassady, *The First Third* (San Francisco: City Lights Books, 1974), p. 121.
100. *VC*, p. 344.
101. Ibid., p. 343.
102. *OR*, p. 14.
103. Ibid., pp. 16, 22.
104. Ibid., p. 34.
105. *VC*, p. 345.
106. *OR*, p. 41.
107. Ibid., p. 53.
108. Ibid., p. 88.
109. Kerouac journal, in John Holmes to Jack Kerouac, November 30, 1948, in *The Beat Diary*, *TUVOTI* 5 (1977), p. 117.
110. Ibid.
111. John Clellon Holmes, *Nothing More To Declare* (New York: Dutton, 1967), p. 48.
112. Kerouac journal, in Holmes to Kerouac, November 30, 1948, in *The Beat Diary*, p. 117.
113. Jack Kerouac, "Journal During First Stages of 'On the Road' (note for November 29, 1948)," *A Creative Century* (Austin, Texas: Humanities Research Center, 1964), p. 36.
114. Jack Kerouac, in Holmes to Kerouac, December 27, 1950, in *The Beat Diary*, p. 154.
115. John Clellon Holmes, *Go* (New York: Paul P. Appel, 1972), p. 120.
116. *VC*, p. 346.
117. *OR*, p. 96.
118. *VC*, p. 347.
119. *OR*, p. 103.
120. Ibid., p. 107.
121. *OR*, p. 108.
122. Ibid., p. 121.
123. Ibid., p. 131.
124. Ibid., p. 117.
125. *OR*, p. 142.
126. Ibid., pp. 141–142.
127. Ibid., p. 145.
128. Jack Kerouac, "The Great Western Bus Ride," *Esquire* (March 1970), p. 137.
129. Allen Ginsberg to Neal Cassady, May 1949, in *As Ever: The Collected Cor-*

respondence of Allen Ginsberg & Neal Cassady (Berkeley, Calif.: Creative Arts, 1977), p. 60.

130. Tim Hunt, *Kerouac's Crooked Road* (Hamden, Conn.: The Shoe String Press, 1981), p. 89.

131. Jack Kerouac, journal entry for March 29, 1949, in Allen Ginsberg and Jack Kerouac, *Take Care of My Ghost, Ghost* (New York: Ghost Press, 1977), unnumbered.

132. Jack Kerouac to Ed White, March 29, 1949, in *Street Magazine*, p. 47.

133. *H*, p. 39.

134. Herbert Huncke, in *Jack's Book*, p. 59.

135. Allen Ginsberg to John Clellon Holmes, June 16, 1949, in *TUVOTI*, 10, p. 104.

136. *OR*, p. 148.

137. Ed White, in Ivan Goldman, "Kerouac's Friend," *Denver Post* (January 1, 1965), p. 49.

138. Jack Kerouac to John Clellon Holmes, June 24, 1949, in *The Beat Diary*, p. 128.

139. *VC*, p. 293.

140. Ibid.

141. *OR*, p. 150.

142. Ibid., p. 160.

143. Ibid., p. 170.

144. *VC*, p. 358.

145. *OR*, p. 176.

146. *VC*, p. 304.

147. Ibid., p. 370; also *OR*, pp. 193–194.

148. *OR*, pp. 196–197.

149. *VC*, pp. 373–374.

150. *OR*, p. 203.

151. *VC*, p. 374; also *OR*, p. 203.

152. Jack Kerouac, *The Subterraneans* [*SUBS*] (New York: Ballantine Books, 1973), p. 100.

153. *VC*, p. 375; also *OR*, p. 226.

154. *OR*, p. 226; also *VC*, pp. 375, 297.

155. *VC*, p. 389.

156. Ibid., p. 88.

157. Jack Kerouac to John Clellon Holmes, July 11–12, 1950, in McNally, *Desolate Angel*, p. 129.

158. John Clellon Holmes to Jack Kerouac, December 27, 1950, in *The Beat Diary*, p. 122.

159. Ibid., pp. 122–123.

160. *OR*, p. 250.

161. Montgomery, *Kerouac West Coast*, unnumbered.
162. *VC*, p. 93.
163. *OR*, p. 251.
164. Cassady, *The First Third*, p. 131.
165. Neal Cassady to Jack Kerouac, December 30, 1950, in Hunt, *Kerouac's Crooked Road*, p. 109; also in Charters, *Kerouac*, p. 123.
166. *PR*, p. 65.
167. Hunt, *Kerouac's Crooked Road*, p. 5.
168. *OR*, p. 9.
169. *PR*, p. 65.
170. Allen Ginsberg to Neal Cassady, May 7, 1951, in *As Ever*, pp. 106–107.
171. Robert Giroux, in Charters, *Kerouac*, p. 134.
172. John Clellon Holmes, in *The Beat Book*, p. 40.
173. Allen Ginsberg to Jack Kerouac, 1951, in Hunt, *Kerouac's Crooked Road*, p. 115.
174. *VC*, p. 49.
175. Jack Kerouac to John Clellon Holmes, July 14, 1951, in Holmes, *Nothing More to Declare*, pp. 80–81.
176. *VC*, p. 42.
177. Ibid., p. 92.

PART THREE

1. *VC*, pp. 8, 43.
2. Ibid., p. 33.
3. Jack Kerouac, "The Last Word," *Escapade* (December 1960), p. 104.
4. *BD*, p. 101.
5. Jack Kerouac to Neal Cassady, quoted by Cassady in conversation with the author, 1967.
6. *VC*, 93.
7. Jack Kerouac to Allen Ginsberg, May 18, 1952, in *The Beat Journey*, *TUVOTI*, 8 (1978), p. 142.
8. Ibid., p. 143.
9. *H*, p. 47.
10. *VC*, p. 103.
11. Ibid., p. 21.
12. Ibid., p. 92.
13. Ibid., pp. 115–116; also *DA*, p. 118.
14. *LT*, p. 3.
15. *VC*, p. 115.
16. Ibid., p. 116.

17. Carl Solomon to Jack Kerouac, February 6, 1952, in McNally, *Desolate Angel*, p. 162; also Solomon, in *The Beat Book*, p. 170; also Allen Ginsberg, in Jane Kramer, *Allen Ginsberg in America* (New York: Random House, 1969), p. 140.
18. Jack Kerouac to Raman Singh, May 13, 1965, in *Street Magazine*, p. 52.
19. *VC*, p. 260.
20. Jack Kerouac to John Clellon Holmes, March 12, 1952, in Hunt, *Kerouac's Crooked Road*, p. 137.
21. *VC*, p. 335.
22. Carolyn Cassady, *Heart Beat* (Berkeley: Creative Arts, 1976), p. 18.
23. *VC*, p. 331.
24. Cassady, *Heart Beat*, p. 24.
25. Allen Ginsberg to Carolyn Cassady, late 1952, in *As Ever*, p. 135.
26. Carolyn Cassady to the author, January 26, 1982.
27. Jack Kerouac to Carl Solomon, April 7, 1952, in *TUVOTI*, 10, p. 153.
28. William S. Burroughs to Jack Kerouac, April 3, 1952, in McNally, *Desolate Angel*, p. 158.
29. William S. Burroughs to Allen Ginsberg, May 15, 1952, in McNally, *Desolate Angel*, p. 159.
30. Ginsberg, journal note, April 15, 1952, in McNally, *Desolate Angel*, p. 152.
31. Carolyn Cassady to the author, January 26, 1982.
32. Jack Kerouac to Allen Ginsberg, May 10, 1952, in *TUVOTI*, 10, p. 162.
33. Cassady, *Heart Beat*, p. 50.
34. Jack Kerouac to Allen Ginsberg, May 10, 1952, in *TUVOTI*, 10, p. 162.
35. *LT*, p. 21.
36. *PR*, p. 84.
37. Jack Kerouac to Allen Ginsberg, May 18, 1952, in *The Beat Journey*, p. 142.
38. *SAX*, pp. 188–189.
39. Jack Kerouac, "The Origins of the Beat Generation," *Playboy* (June 1959), p. 42.
40. *H*, p. 47.
41. *SAX*, p. 3.
42. Ibid., p. 108.
43. Jack Kerouac to Carolyn Cassady, June 3, 1952, in *Dear Carolyn*, *TUVOTI*, 13 (1983), pp. 6–7.
44. Jack Kerouac to Allen Ginsberg, May 18, 1952, in *The Beat Journey*, p. 141.
45. Jack Kerouac to John Clellon Holmes, June 3, 1952, in Holmes, *Nothing More To Declare*, p. 81.
46. Allen Ginsberg to Jack Kerouac and William S. Burroughs, June 12, 1952, in McNally, *Desolate Angel*, p. 161.

47. Jack Kerouac to John Clellon Holmes, June 15, 17, 21, 1952, in *The Beat Diary*, pp. 137–138.

48. William S. Burroughs to Allen Ginsberg, July 13, 1952, in McNally, *Desolate Angel*, p. 163.

49. Jack Kerouac to Neal and Carolyn Cassady, July 3, 1952, in *Heart Beat*, p. 63.

50. Cassady, *Heart Beat*, p. 74.

51. Neal Cassady to Allen Ginsberg, October 4, 1952, in *As Ever*, p. 133.

52. Jack Kerouac to Allen Ginsberg, November 8, 1952, in *Bombay Gin* (Boulder, Colo.: Poetics Department, Naropa Institute, 1982), p. 4.

53. Jack Kerouac to Allen Ginsberg, October 8, 1952, in *Bombay Gin*, pp. 2–3.

54. Ibid., p. 3.

55. *LT*, p. 57.

56. *PR*, p. 65.

57. Cassady, *Heart Beat*, p. 78.

58. Jack Kerouac to Carolyn Cassady, February 1953, in *Dear Carolyn*, p. 9.

59. Allen Ginsberg to Carolyn Cassady, late 1952, in *As Ever*, p. 135.

60. Jack Kerouac to Carolyn Cassady, December 9, 1952, in *Heart Beat*, pp. 82–83.

61. Cassady, *Heart Beat*, p. 81.

62. Jack Kerouac to Carolyn Cassady, December 1952, in *Heart Beat*, p. 84.

63. Allen Ginsberg to Neal Cassady, January 1953, in *As Ever*, pp. 137–138.

64. *BD*, pp. 142, 76, 118.

65. Ibid., p. 54.

66. *MCB*, p. 146.

67. Allen Ginsberg to Neal Cassady, June 23, 1953, in *As Ever*, p. 146.

68. *LT*, pp. 95, 90.

69. Neal Cassady to Allen Ginsberg, June 29, 1953, in *As Ever*, p. 151.

70. *LT*, pp. 95, 101, 103.

71. Ibid., p. 104.

72. Allen Ginsberg, *Journals: Early Fifties Early Sixties* (New York: Grove Press, 1977), p. 18.

73. *SUBS*, pp. 27, 10.

74. Ibid., pp. 108–109.

75. Malcolm Cowley to Allen Ginsberg, July 14, 1953, in McNally, *Desolate Angel*, p. 171.

76. *SUBS*, p. 135.

77. Ibid., p. 113.

78. Allen Ginsberg to Neal Cassady, September 4, 1953, in *As Ever*, p. 154.

79. Gore Vidal, "All Our Lives," *Partisan Review*, 37, No. 1 (1970), p. 35.

80. *SUBS*, p. 22.

81. Jack Kerouac to Carolyn Cassady, August 10, 1953, in *Dear Carolyn*, pp. 12–13.

82. *SUBS*, pp. 98, 9, 64.
83. Ibid., p. 125.
84. Ibid., p. 148.
85. Ibid., p. 156.
86. Al Aronowitz, "The Yen for Zen," *Escapade* (October 1960), p. 70.
87. Ann Charters, *A Bibliography of the Works of Jack Kerouac* (New York: Phoenix Book Shop, 1975), p. 23.
88. *SUBS*, p. 1.
89. Charters, *Bibliography*, p. 23.
90. Jack Kerouac, "Essentials of Spontaneous Prose," *Black Mountain Review*, No. 7 (Autumn 1957), p. 228.
91. *BD*, pp. 20, 19, 11.
92. Jack Kerouac to Carolyn Cassady, December 3, 1953, in *Dear Carolyn*, pp. 13–14.
93. Neal Cassady to Jack Kerouac, December 4, 1953, letter provided by Carolyn Cassady.

PART FOUR
1. Jack Kerouac, "The Last Word," *Escapade* (October 1959), p. 72.
2. Ibid.
3. Ibid.
4. Carolyn Cassady to the author, May 13, 1982.
5. Jack Kerouac, *Big Sur* [*SUR*] (New York: Bantam Books, 1963), p. 111.
6. Jack Kerouac to Allen Ginsberg, May 1954, in *Beat Angels*, *TUVOTI*, 12 (1982), p. 40.
7. Neal Cassady to Allen Ginsberg, April 23, 1954, in *As Ever*, p. 178.
8. Jack Kerouac to Allen Ginsberg, May 1954, in *Beat Angels*, p. 50.
9. Malcolm Cowley, "Invitation to Innovators," *Saturday Review* (August 21, 1954), p. 39.
10. Jack Kerouac to Allen Ginsberg, May 1954, in *Beat Angels*, p. 57.
11. Ibid., pp. 56, 39.
12. Jack Kerouac to Allen Ginsberg, July 14, 1955, in *Bombay Gin*, p. 7.
13. *DA*, p. 47.
14. Al Aronowitz, "The Beat Generation," *New York Post* (March 10, 1959), p. 9.
15. Jack Kerouac journal, December 19, 1954, in *Robert Lowry's Book U.S.A.*, No. 1 (Fall 1958), unnumbered.
16. Ibid.
17. Jack Kerouac to Allen Ginsberg, January 18, 1955, in *TUVOTI*, 10, p. 171.
18. Ibid., p. 172.
19. "230th Chorus," *MCB*, p. 232.
20. Jack Kerouac, *Tristessa* (New York: McGraw-Hill, 1960), p. 32.

21. Charters, *Bibliography*, p. 36.
22. Jack Kerouac, *The Dharma Bums* [*DB*] (New York: Signet Books, 1959), p. 6.
23. Tom Clark, "Allen Ginsberg: The Art of Poetry," *Paris Review*, 37 (Spring 1966), p. 17.
24. Allen Ginsberg, in Kramer, *Allen Ginsberg in America*, p. 47.
25. Allen Ginsberg, in *The Beat Journey*, p. 5.
26. *DB*, p. 10.
27. *OR*, p. 9.
28. Kenneth Rexroth, in Bruce Cook, *The Beat Generation* (New York: Scribner's, 1971), pp. 65, 63.
29. Allen Ginsberg, in Gifford and Lee, *Jack's Book*, p. 198.
30. *DB*, p. 44.
31. Montgomery, *Kerouac West Coast*, unnumbered.
32. *DB*, p. 85.
33. Ibid., pp. 87–88.
34. Ibid., pp. 92–94.
35. *BD*, p. 167.
36. "211th Chorus," *MCB*, p. 211.
37. Jack Kerouac to Carolyn Cassady, February 11, 1956, in *Dear Carolyn*, p. 17.
38. Ibid.
39. *DB*, pp. 116, 117.
40. William S. Burroughs to Allen Ginsberg, December 28, 1954, in Burroughs, *Letters to Allen Ginsberg* (New York: Full Court, 1982), unnumbered.
41. Jack Kerouac, "Old Angel Midnight," *Big Table*, 1, No. 1 (Spring 1959), p. 7.
42. Jack Kerouac, *Uncollected Writings* (New York: "C" Press, 1971), p. 42.
43. Montgomery, *Kerouac West Coast*, unnumbered.
44. Jack Kerouac to John Clellon Holmes, May 21, 1956, in *TUVOTI*, 10, pp. 11–12.
45. *DB*, pp. 140, 151.
46. Ibid., p. 133.
47. Robert Creeley to author, 1982.
48. Ibid.
49. Jack Kerouac to John Clellon Holmes, May 21, 1956, *TUVOTI*, 10, p. 9.
50. Creeley to author (1982).
51. Kenneth Rexroth, "San Francisco's Mature Bohemians," *Nation* (February 23, 1957), p. 161.
52. *LT*, pp. 122, 125, 128.
53. *DA*, pp. 61, 67.
54. Ibid., p. 173.
55. Ibid., p. 220.

56. Ibid., p. 229.
57. *PR*, p. 67.
58. Ibid., p. 91.
59. *DA*, pp. 237, 252–253.
60. Ibid., pp. 252–255, 262.
61. Ibid., p. 277.
62. Ibid., p. 286.
63. Ibid., pp. 286, 228.
64. Jack Kerouac to Edie Parker Kerouac, January 28, 1957, *Detroit News* (August 19, 1979), p. 19A.
65. *DA*, p. 293.
66. *LT*, p. 136.
67. Jack Kerouac to John Clellon Holmes, June 23, 1957, in *The Beat Journey*, p. 47.
68. *DA*, p. 300.
69. Jack Kerouac to John Clellon Holmes, June 23, 1957, in *The Beat Journey*, p. 48.
70. *DA*, p. 311.
71. Ibid., p. 315.
72. Jack Kerouac to John Clellon Holmes, June 23, 1957, in *The Beat Journey*, p. 50.
73. *DA*, pp. 317, 321.
74. Jack Kerouac to John Clellon Holmes, June 23, 1957, in *The Beat Journey*, p. 51.
75. *LT*, p. 170.
76. Jack Kerouac to John Clellon Holmes, June 23, 1957, in *The Beat Journey*, pp. 50, 52.
77. Ibid.
78. *DA*, pp. 352–353.
79. Ibid.

PART FIVE
1. Jack Kerouac to Neal Cassady, October 29, 1957, in *Beat Angels*, p. 59.
2. *BD*, p. 173.
3. Jerry Tallmer, "Jack Kerouac: Back to the Village," *Village Voice* (September 18, 1957), pp. 1, 4.
4. Jack Kerouac to Neal Cassady, October 29, 1957, in *Beat Angels*, p. 60.
5. Tallmer, *Village Voice*, p. 4.
6. Jack Kerouac to Neal Cassady, October 29, 1957, in *Beat Angels*, p. 60.
7. Gilbert Millstein, "Books of the Times," *New York Times* (September 5, 1957), p. 27.

8. Carlos Baker, "Itching Feet," *Saturday Review* (September 7, 1957), p. 19.
9. David Dempsey, "In Pursuit of Kicks," *New York Times Book Review* (September 8, 1957), p. 4.
10. Herbert Gold, "Hip, Cool, Beat—and Frantic," *Nation* (November 16, 1957), p. 349.
11. Kenneth Rexroth, "It's an Anywhere Road," *San Francisco Chronicle* (September 1, 1957), p. 18.
12. Jack Kerouac to Neal Cassady, October 29, 1957, in *Beat Angels*, pp. 59–60.
13. Ibid., p. 60.
14. John Clellon Holmes, in *The Beat Book*, p. 38.
15. Tallmer, *Village Voice*, p. 4.
16. Ibid.
17. *H*, pp. 39–40.
18. Jack Kerouac, "Lamb No Lion," *Pageant* (February 1958), p. 160.
19. Jack Kerouac to Neal Cassady, October 29, 1957, in *Beat Angels*, p. 60.
20. Kenneth Rexroth, letter to *Village Voice*, 1957, in *Village Voice Reader* (New York: Doubleday, 1962), p. 339.
21. Kenneth Rexroth, "The Voice of the Beat Generation Has Some Square Delusions," *San Francisco Chronicle* (February 16, 1958), p. 23.
22. "The Talk of the Town," *New Yorker* (May 3, 1958), p. 29.
23. David Dempsey, "Diary of a Bohemian," *New York Times Book Review* (February 23, 1958), p. 5.
24. Robert Brustein, "The Cult of Unthink," *Horizon*, 1 (Spring 1958), p. 41; also Norman Podhoretz, "The Know-Nothing Bohemians," *Partisan Review*, 25 (Spring/Summer 1958), p. 37.
25. Jack Kerouac, "Aftermath: The Philosophy of the Beat Generation," *Esquire* (March 1958), pp. 24–26.
26. Ibid.
27. Ibid.
28. "Mike Wallace Asks Jack Kerouac What Is the Beat Generation," *New York Post* (December 1, 1958), p. 3.
29. Jack Kerouac, album notes, *Jazz for the Beat Generation*, Hanover Records, 1959.
30. "The Kerouac and Allen Record," *New York Post* (June 31, 1959), p. 75.
31. Jack Kerouac, album notes, *Blues and Haikus*, Hanover Records, 1959.
32. *PR*, p. 64.
33. Jack Kerouac, publicity release for *Visions of Gerard*, Farrar, Strauss, 1963.
34. Montgomery, *Kerouac West Coast*, unnumbered.
35. *SUR*, p. 2.
36. Jack Kerouac to Al Aronowitz, "The Beat Generation," *New York Post* (March 10, 1959), p. 9.

37. "The Yab-Yum Kid," *Time* (October 6, 1958), p. 95.
38. Allen Ginsberg, "The Dharma Bums," *Village Voice* (November 12, 1958), p. 3.
39. Ibid.
40. Kingsley Amis, "The Delights of Literary Lecturing," *Harper's* (October 1959), p. 189.
41. Jack Kerouac to Carolyn Cassady, April 17, 1959, in *Dear Carolyn*, p. 22.
42. Ibid.
43. Norman Mailer, in Bruce Cook, *The Beat Generation*, p. 96.
44. John Updike, "On the Sidewalk," *New Yorker* (February 21, 1959), p. 32.
45. Aronowitz, "The Beat Generation," *New York Post* (March 10, 1959), p. 9.
46. "149th Chorus," *MCB*, p. 149.
47. Peter Orlovsky to Carolyn Cassady, January 10, 1959, in *As Ever*, p. 193.
48. Ted Joans, in *Beat Angels*, pp. 133, 138.
49. Allen Ginsberg to author, 1982; also Charters, *Kerouac*, p. 310.
50. David Amram, in *MSI*, No. 8 (Summer–Fall 1980), p. 6.
51. David Dempsey, "Beatnik Bogeyman on the Prowl," *New York Times Book Review* (May 3, 1959), pp. 28–29.
52. Ralph Gleason, "New Kerouac Effort Has Its Moments," *San Francisco Chronicle* (May 15, 1959), p. 37.
53. Kenneth Rexroth, "Discordant and Cool," *New York Times Book Review* (November 29, 1959), p. 14.
54. Jack Kerouac, in Aronowitz, "The Beat Generation," *New York Post* (March 10, 1959), p. 9.
55. Jack Kerouac, "The Last Word," *Escapade* (June 1959), p. 105.
56. John Ciardi, "In Loving Memory of Myself," *Saturday Review* (July 25, 1959), pp. 22–23.
57. Jack Kerouac to Don Allen, October 1, 1959, in *H*, p. 50.
58. *SUR*, p. 19.
59. Jack Kerouac, Albert Saijo, and Lew Welch, *Trip Trap* (Bolinas, Calif.: Grey Fox Press, 1973), pp. 3–4.
60. Ibid.
61. Jack Kerouac, "The Last Word," *Escapade* (April 1960), p. 72.
62. Jack Kerouac, "The Last Word," *Escapade* (June 1960), p. 72.
63. John Ciardi, "Epitaph for the Dead Beats," *Saturday Review* (February 6, 1960), p. 6.
64. Jack Kerouac to Carolyn Cassady, April 20, 1960, in *The Beat Book*, p. 19.
65. Jack Kerouac to Peter Orlovsky, March 23, 1960, in McNally, *Desolate Angel*, p. 276.
66. Ted Joans, in *Beat Angels*, p. 140.
67. *SUR*, pp. 2, 4.

68. William Everson, *Birth of a Poet* (Santa Barbara, Calif.: Black Sparrow Press, 1982), pp. 164–165.
69. Ibid.
70. Jack Kerouac to Carolyn Cassady, October 17, 1961, in *The Beat Journey*, p. 90.
71. *SUR*, pp. 13, 24–26, 32.
72. Ibid., p. 36.
73. Carolyn Cassady, "The Third Word," in *The Beat Journey*, p. 69.
74. *SUR*, p. 56.
75. Ibid., pp. 57, 60.
76. Ibid, pp. 83, 85, 87.
77. Ibid, pp. 94, 101.
78. Ibid., pp. 110, 128.
79. Ibid., p. 145.
80. Ibid., pp. 157, 163, 166.
81. Jack Kerouac to Carolyn Cassady, October 17, 1961, in *The Beat Journey*, p. 90.
82. *LT*, p. vii.
83. Sterling Lord, in Bruce Cook, *The Beat Generation*, p. 83.
84. Al Aronowitz, "The Yen for Zen," *Escapade* (October 1960), p. 70.
85. Jack Kerouac, "After Me, the Deluge," *Chicago Tribune* (September 28, 1969), Sunday magazine section, p. 3.
86. Jack Kerouac to Joe Chaput, in McNally, *Desolate Angel*, p. 328.
87. Jack Kerouac to Nanda Pivano, January 5, 1961, in *The Beat Book*, p. 56.
88. Allen Ginsberg, *Journals: Early Fifties Early Sixties*, p. 178.
89. Jack Kerouac to Neal Cassady, April 3, 1961, in *The Beat Book*, p. 9.
90. Jack Kerouac to Don Allen, June 10, 1961, in *H*, p. 55.
91. Jack Kerouac to Carolyn Cassady, June 23, 1961, in *The Beat Book*, p. 22; also in *Dear Carolyn*, p. 24.
92. Jack Kerouac to Carolyn Cassady, October 17, 1961, in *Dear Carolyn*, p. 25.
93. Joan Haverty, "My Ex-Husband Is An Ingrate," *Confidential* (August 1961), pp. 18–19, 53–54.
94. Jack Kerouac to Nanda Pivano, October 24, 1961, in *The Beat Book*, p. 56.
95. Jack Kerouac to Carolyn Cassady, October 17, 1961, in *Dear Carolyn*, p. 25.
96. *SUR*, p. 135.
97. Jack Kerouac to Carolyn Cassady, January 7, 1962, in *Dear Carolyn*, p 26.
98. Ibid.
99. Jan Kerouac, *Baby Driver*, pp. 63–64.
100. Jack Kerouac to Carolyn Cassady, January 7, 1962, in *Dear Carolyn*, p. 28.
101. Jack Kerouac to Carolyn Cassady, October 21, 1962, in *Dear Carolyn*, p. 30.
102. Jack Kerouac to Allen Ginsberg, October 4, 1962, in *Street Magazine*, p. 51.

103. Jack Kerouac to Lawrence Ferlinghetti, 1962, "Among the Iroquois," *City Lights Journal* No. 1 (1963), p. 45.
104. Jack Kerouac to Allen Ginsberg, October 4, 1962, in *Street Magazine*, p. 51.
105. Jack Kerouac to Carolyn Cassady, October 21, 1962, in *The Beat Book*, p. 12; also in *Dear Carolyn*, p. 30.
106. Jack Kerouac to John Clellon Holmes, October 9, 1962, in *TUVOTI*, 10, pp. 12–13.
107. "Lions & Cubs," *Time* (September 14, 1962), p. 106.
108. Jack Kerouac to Carolyn Cassady, October 21, 1962, in *The Beat Book*, p. 13; also in *Dear Carolyn*, p. 31.
109. Jan Kerouac, *Baby Driver*, pp. 85–86.
110. Jack Kerouac to Neal and Carolyn Cassady, February 21, 1963, in *The Beat Book*, p. 17.
111. Farrar, Straus publicity release for *Visions of Gerard*, 1963.
112. Allen Ginsberg to author, 1982.
113. Saul Maloff, "A Yawping at the Grave," *New York Times Book Review* (September 8, 1963), pp. 4–5.
114. "Children Should Be . . ." *Newsweek* (September 9, 1963), p. 93.
115. Allen Ginsberg, *The Visions of the Great Rememberer* (Amherst, Mass.: Mulch Press, 1974), p. 40.
116. Allen Ginsberg, *Gay Sunshine Interview*, p. 8.
117. Carl Adkins, "Jack Kerouac, Off the Road for Good," in *Story: The Yearbook of Discovery/1971* (New York: Four Winds, 1971), p. 27.
118. Ellis Amburn, in *MSI*, No. 9 (Winter–Spring 1981), p. 11.
119. Dan Wakefield, "Jack Kerouac Comes Home," *Atlantic* (July 1965), p. 69.
120. Ellis Amburn, in *MSI*, No. 9, p. 10.
121. Ibid., p. 11.
122. *SP*, p. 42.
123. Ibid., p. 7.
124. McNally, *Desolate Angel*, p. 322.
125. *VD*, pp. 105–106.
126. Jack Kerouac, "In the Ring," *Atlantic* (March 1968), p. 110.
127. Gerald Clarke, "Checking in with Allen Ginsberg," *Esquire* (April 1973), p. 95.
128. Jan Kerouac, *Baby Driver*, pp. 183–185.
129. Ted Berrigan to author, 1982.
130. Ibid.
131. Ibid.
132. Ibid.
133. Ibid.
134. Ibid.

135. Jack Kerouac to Ed White, April 21, 1969, in *Denver Post* (January 1, 1975), p. 49.
136. *PR*, p. 77.
137. "Sanity of Kerouac," *Time* (February 23, 1968), p. 96.
138. "Be Your Age," [London] *Times Literary Supplement* (March 27, 1969), p. 317.
139. Melvin Maddocks, "Hit the Space Bar and GO!" *Christian Science Monitor* (March 21, 1968), p. 13.
140. William Burroughs, in *High Times* (February 1979), p. 49.
141. Joe Chaput, in *MSI*, No. 3 (Winter 1979), p. 8.
142. Ed Sanders to author, February 18, 1982.
143. Joe Chaput, in Vivian Gornick, "Jack Kerouac: The Night and What It Does to You," *Village Voice* (October 30, 1969), p. 27.
144. Gloria Jahoda, *River of the Golden Ibis* (New York: Holt, Rinehart & Winston, 1973), p. 378.
145. Clarus Backes to author, 1982.
146. Jack Kerouac, "After Me, the Deluge," *Chicago Tribune* (September 28, 1969), Sunday magazine sec., p. 3.
147. Jack McClintock, "This Is How the Ride Ends," *Esquire* (March 1970), pp. 138–139.
148. Ibid.
149. Al Aronowitz, "Jack Kerouac: Beyond the Road," *New York Post* (October 22, 1969), p. 100.
150. Jahoda, *River of the Golden Ibis*, p. 380.
151. Aronowitz, "Jack Kerouac: Beyond the Road," *New York Post* (October 22, 1969), p. 100.
152. Ibid.
153. Jack Kerouac, "Are Writers Made or Born," *Writers Digest* (January 1962), p. 13.
154. "184th Chorus," *MCB*, p. 184.
155. McClintock, "This Is How the Ride Ends," *Esquire* (March 1970), pp. 138–139.
156. Gornick, "Jack Kerouac: The Night and What It Does to You," *Village Voice* (October 30, 1969), p. 30.
157. Allen Ginsberg to Carolyn Cassady, February 19, 1970, in *As Ever*, p. 217.
158. Gornick, "Jack Kerouac: The Night and What It Does to You," *Village Voice* (October 30, 1969), p. 30.
159. *SAX*, p. 58.
160. *VG*, p. 17.

BIBLIOGRAPHY

FIRST AMERICAN AND ENGLISH EDITIONS OF
KEROUAC'S MAJOR PUBLISHED WORKS AND A
SELECTION OF KEROUAC'S ARTICLES:
A CHRONOLOGICAL LISTING

The Town and the City. New York: Harcourt, Brace, 1950. London: Eyre &
    Spottiswoode, 1951.
On the Road. New York: Viking Press, 1957. London: Andre Deutsch, 1958.
"Essentials of Spontaneous Prose"; "October in the Railroad Earth" (excerpt)
    The Black Mountain Review (Autumn 1957), pp. 226–228; 30–37.
The Subterraneans. New York: Grove Press, 1958. London: Andre Deutsch, 1960.
The Dharma Bums. New York: Viking Press, 1958. London: Andre Deutsch, 1959.
"Aftermath: The Philosophy of the Beat Generation." *Esquire* (March 1958),
    pp. 24, 26.
"Lamb, No Lion." *Pageant* (February 1958), pp. 160–161.
"The Beginning of Bop." *Escapade* (April 1959), pp. 4–5, 52.

"The Last Word" ("My position in the current American literary scene"). *Escapade* (June 1959), p. 72.

"Belief and Technique for Modern Prose." *Evergreen Review* 2, No. 8 (Spring 1959), p. 57.

"The Electrocution of Block 38383939383 . . ." *Nugget* (August 1959), pp. 12–14, 57–60. (Later appeared under the title "CITYCitycity.")

Doctor Sax. New York: Grove Press, 1959. London: Andre Deutsch, 1974.

Maggie Cassidy. New York: Avon Books, 1959. London: Panther Books, 1960.

Mexico City Blues. New York: Grove Press, 1959.

Visions of Cody (excerpts). New York: New Directions, 1959.

"The Origins of the Beat Generation." *Playboy* (June 1959), pp. 31–32, 42, 79.

"Old Angel Midnight." *Big Table* (Spring 1959), pp. 7–42.

Rimbaud. San Francisco: City Lights Books, 1960.

Tristessa. New York: Avon Books, 1960. London: World Distributors, 1963.

The Scripture of the Golden Eternity. New York: Totem Press, 1960.

Lonesome Traveler. New York: McGraw-Hill, 1960. London: Pan Books, 1964.

"Home at Christmas." *Glamour* (December 1961), pp. 72–73, 145.

Book of Dreams. San Francisco: City Lights Books, 1961.

Pull My Daisy. New York: Grove Press, 1961.

"He Went on the Road." *Life,* June 29, 1962, p. 22.

Big Sur. New York: Farrar, Straus & Cudahy, 1962. London: Andre Deutsch, 1963.

Visions of Gerard. New York: Farrar, Straus, 1963. London: Andre Deutsch, 1964.

"Among the Iroquois." *City Lights Journal,* No. 1 (1963), pp. 43–45.

"Written Address to the Italian Judge." *Evergreen Review,* 7, No. 31 (October/November 1963), pp. 108–110.

"Good Blonde." *Playboy* (January 1965), pp. 139–140, 192–194.

Desolation Angels. New York: Coward-McCann, 1965. London: Andre Deutsch, 1966.

Satori in Paris. New York: Grove Press, 1966.

"The Art of Fiction" (interview with Kerouac). *Paris Review,* 43 (Summer 1968), pp. 61–103.

"In the Ring." *The Atlantic* (March 1968), pp. 110–111.

Vanity of Duluoz: An Adventurous Education, 1935–46. New York: Coward-McCann, 1968. London: Andre Deutsch, 1969.

"After Me, the Deluge." *Chicago Tribune,* September 28, 1969, Sunday magazine section, p. 3.

"The Great Western Bus Ride." *Esquire* (March 1970), pp. 136–137, 158.

Pic. New York: Grove Press, 1971.

Scattered Poems. San Francisco: City Lights Books, 1971.

Visions of Cody. New York: McGraw-Hill, 1972. London: Andre Deutsch, 1973.

Two Early Stories. New York: Aloe Editions, 1973.

Old Angel Midnight. London: Booklegger/Albion, 1973.

Trip Trap. (Jack Kerouac, Albert Saijo, and Lew Welch.) Bolinas, Calif.: Grey Fox Press, 1973.

Heaven & Other Poems. Bolinas, Calif.: Grey Fox Press, 1977.

Take Care of My Ghost, Ghost. (Jack Kerouac and Allen Ginsberg.) New York: Ghost Press, 1977.

SELECTED ARTICLES AND BOOKS ON KEROUAC AND
HIS WORK: AN ALPHABETICAL LISTING BY AUTHOR

Adkins, Carl. "Jack Kerouac: Off the Road for Good." In *Story, the Yearbook of Discovery/1971.* Edited by Whit and Hallie Burnett. New York: Four Winds Press, 1971. Pp. 27–35.

Amis, Kingsley. "The Delights of Literary Lecturing." *Harper's* (October 1959), pp. 181–182.

Amram, David. *Vibrations: The Adventures and Musical Times of David Amram.* New York: Macmillan, 1968.

Anastas, Peter. "Reflections of a Kerouac Lover; Of the Time the Author of 'On the Road' Came to Gloucester." *Gloucester Daily Times* (Massachusetts), October 5, 1974, North Shore '74 sec., pp. 3–4.

Aronowitz, Alfred G. "The Beat Generation." *New York Post*, March 9, 10, 11, 16, 19, 1959.

———. "The Yen for Zen." *Escapade* (October 1960), pp. 50–52, 70.

———. "Jack Kerouac: Beyond the Road." *New York Post*, October 22, 1969, p. 100.

Beaulieu, Victor-Lévy. *Jack Kerouac: A Chicken-Essay.* Translated by Sheila Fischman. Toronto: Coach House Press, 1976.

Burroughs, William. "Kerouac." *High Times: The Magazine of High Society* (March 1979), pp. 52–55.

Cassady, Carolyn. *Heart Beat: My Life with Jack & Neal.* Berkeley: Creative Arts, 1976.

Charters, Ann. *Scenes Along the Road: Photographs of the Desolation Angels/1944–1960.* New York: Portents/Gotham Book Mart, 1970.

———. *Kerouac: A Biography.* San Francisco: Straight Arrow Press, 1973.

———. *A Bibliography of Works by Jack Kerouac (Jean Louis Lebris De Kerouac), 1939–1975.* Revised edition. New York: Phoenix Bookshop, 1975.

Cook, Bruce. *The Beat Generation.* New York: Scribner's, 1971.

Creeley, Robert. "Ways of Looking." *Poetry*, 98 (June 1961), pp. 195–196.

DiPrima, Diane. *Memoirs of a Beatnik.* New York: Traveller's Companion, 1969.

Everson, William. *The Birth of a Poet: The Santa Cruz Meditations.* Santa Barbara: Black Sparrow Press, 1982.

Fagin, Larry, ed. *Bombay Gin.* Boulder, Colo.: Poetics Department, Naropo Institute, 1982.

Feied, Frederick. *No Pie in the Sky: The Hobo as American Cultural Hero in the Works of Jack London, John Dos Passos, and Jack Kerouac.* New York: Citadel, 1964.

Fiedler, Leslie. "Death of the Novel." *Ramparts* (Winter 1964), pp. 2–14.

Gifford, Barry. *Kerouac's Town: On the Second Anniversary of His Death.* Santa Barbara: Capra, 1973.

————, and Lawrence Lee. *Jack's Book: An Oral Biography of Jack Kerouac.* New York: St. Martin's Press, 1978.

Ginsberg, Allen. "The Dharma Bums." *Village Voice,* November 12, 1958, pp. 3–5.

————. *The Gates of Wrath.* Bolinas, Calif.: Grey Fox Press, 1972.

————. *Improvised Poetics.* San Francisco: Anonym, 1972.

————. *Allen Verbatim: Lectures on Poetry, Politics, Consciousness.* Edited by Gordon Ball. New York: McGraw-Hill, 1974.

————. *The Visions of the Great Rememberer: With Letters by Neal Cassady & Drawings by Basil King.* Amherst, Mass.: Mulch Press, 1974.

————. *Journals: Early Fifties Early Sixties.* Edited by Gordon Ball. New York: Grove Press, 1977.

————, and Neal Cassady. *As Ever: The Collected Correspondence of Allen Ginsberg and Neal Cassady.* Edited by Barry Gifford. Berkeley: Creative Arts, 1977.

————, and Allen Young. *Gay Sunshine Interview.* Bolinas, Calif.: Grey Fox Press, 1974.

Gold, Herbert. "Hip, Cool, Beat—and Frantic." *Nation,* November 16, 1957, pp. 349–355.

Goldman, Ivan. "Visit in Summer of 1947." *Denver Post,* December 29, 1974, p. 34.

————. "Cassady 'A Bum,'" *Denver Post,* December 30, 1974, p. 12.

————. "Babe on 'On The Road.'" *Denver Post,* December 31, 1974, p. 21.

————. "Architect Ed White Jr." *Denver Post,* January 1, 1975, p. 49.

Gornick, Vivian. "Jack Kerouac: 'The Night and What It Does to You.'" *Village Voice,* October 30, 1969, pp. 1, 27, 30.

Hipkiss, Robert A. *Jack Kerouac: Prophet of the New Romanticism.* Lawrence, Kansas: Regents Press, 1976.

Holmes, John Clellon. "The Philosophy of the Beat Generation." *Esquire* (February 1958), pp. 35–38.

————. *Nothing More to Declare.* New York: Dutton, 1967.

Huncke, Herbert. *And the Evening Sun Turned Crimson.* Cherry Valley, N.Y.: Cherry Valley Editions, 1980.

Hunt, Timothy A. *Kerouac's Crooked Road.* Hamden, Conn.: Shoe String Press, 1981.

Jahoda, Gloria. "Strangers in a Strange Land." In *River of the Golden Ibis*. New York: Holt, Rinehart & Winston, 1973. Pp. 370–382.

Jarvis, Charles E. *Visions of Kerouac*. Lowell, Mass.: Ithaca Press, 1974.

Jones, LeRoi. "Correspondence." *Evergreen Review* (1959), pp. 253–256.

————, ed. *The Moderns: An Anthology of New Writing in America*. New York: Corinth Press, 1963.

Kerouac, Jan. *Baby Driver*. New York: St. Martin's, 1981.

Knight, Arthur and Glee, eds. *the unspeakable visions of the individual*, 3, Nos. 1 & 2 (1973). California, Pennsylvania, 1973.

————. *The Beat Book: Volume 4, the unspeakable visions of the individual*. California, Pennsylvania, 1974.

Knight, Arthur and Kit, eds. *The Beat Diary: Volume 5, the unspeakable visions of the individual*. California, Pennsylvania, 1977.

————. *The Beat Journey: Volume 8, the unspeakable visions of the individual*. California, Pennsylvania, 1978.

————. *the unspeakable visions of the individual*, Volume 10 (1980). California, Pennsylvania, 1980.

————. *Beat Angels: Volume 12, the unspeakable visions of the individual*. California, Pennsylvania, 1982.

————. *Dear Carolyn: Volume 13, the unspeakable visions of the individual*. California, Pennsylvania, 1983.

Kramer, Jane. *Allen Ginsberg in America*. New York: Random House, 1969.

Krim, Seymour. "King of the Beats." *Commonweal*, January 2, 1959, pp. 359–360.

Latham, Aaron. "The Columbia Murder That Gave Birth to the Beats." *New York Magazine*, April 19, 1976, pp. 41–53.

McClintock, Jack. "This Is How the Ride Ends: Not with a Bang, with a Damn Hernia." *Esquire* (March 1970), pp. 138–139, 188–189.

McClure, Michael. *Scratching the Beat Surface*. Berkeley, Calif.: North Point Press, 1982.

McNally, Dennis. *Desolate Angel: Jack Kerouac, the Beats and America*. New York: Random House, 1979.

Milewski, Robert J. *Jack Kerouac: An Annotated Bibliography of Secondary Sources, 1944–1979*. Metuchen, N.J.: Scarecrow Press, 1981.

Miller, Henry. Preface to *The Subterraneans*. New York: Avon Books, 1958.

Montgomery, John. *Kerouac West Coast: A Bohemian Pilot, Detailed Navagational Instructions*. Palo Alto, Calif.: Fels & Firn, 1976.

Morrow, Bradford. Catalogue Five: Walter Reuben Collection of Jack Kerouac. Santa Barbara, Calif.: Bradford Morrow, Bookseller, n.d.

Podhoretz, Norman. "The Know-Nothing Bohemians." *Partisan Review*, 25 (Spring/Summer 1958), pp. 305–318.

Rexroth, Kenneth. "San Francisco's Mature Bohemians." *Nation*, February 23, 1957, pp. 159–162.

———. "It's an Anywhere Road for Anybody Anyhow." *San Francisco Chronicle*, September 1, 1957, p. 18.

———. "The Voice of the Beat Generation Has Some Square Delusions." *San Francisco Chronicle*, February 16, 1958, This World magazine sec., p. 23.

———. "Discordant and Cool." *New York Times Book Review*, November 29, 1959, p. 14.

Smith, Howard. "Jack Kerouac: Off the Road, Into the Vanguard, and Out." *Village Voice*, December 25, 1957, pp. 1–2.

Tallmer, Jerry. "Jack Kerouac: Back to the Village—But Still on the Road." *Village Voice*, September 18, 1957, pp. 1, 4.

Tytell, John. *Naked Angels: The Lives & Literature of the Beat Generation*. New York: McGraw-Hill, 1976.

Updike, John. "On the Sidewalk: (After Reading, At Long Last, 'On The Road' by Jack Kerouac)." *New Yorker*, February 21, 1959, p. 32.

Wakefield, Dan. "Night Clubs." *Nation*, January 4, 1958, pp. 19–20.

———. "Jack Kerouac Comes Home." *Atlantic Monthly* (July 1965), pp. 69–72.

Walsh, Joy. "Jack Kerouac: The American Alien in America." *Street Magazine*, 2, No. 4 (1978), pp. 45–52.

———, ed. *Moody Street Irregulars: A Jack Kerouac Newsletter*, 1, Nos. 1–11 (1978–1982).

Wilentz, Elias, ed. *The Beat Scene*. New York: Corinth, 1960.

INDEX